# Excel

Get the Results You Want!

# SmartStudy 10

# English

Catherine Minett

Reprinted 2019, 2023, 2024

ISBN 978 1 74125 605 5

Pascal Press
PO Box 250
Glebe NSW 2037
(02) 9198 1748
www.pascalpress.com.au

Publisher: Vivienne Joannou
Project editors: Mark Dixon and Rosemary Peers
Edited by Michael Wyatt
Answers checked by Justine Hodgson
Proofread by Barbara Bessant
Cover and typesetting by Kim Webber
Printed by Vivar Printing/Green Giant Press

The author and publisher wish to thank the following for their permission to use their work:
Patrick Boyle for 'Deadly Australians' (pages 9 and 130) and 'Responsible pet ownership' (pages 49 and 132)
Sally Llewellyn for 'Tanzania journal' (page 89).

# TABLE OF CONTENTS

Study steps to success! ........ v
How to use this book ........ vii
Types of reading questions ........ viii

**Unit 1: Informative Text—Online information report**

Reading Work ........ 2
Comprehension Work ........ 3
Spelling Work ........ 4
Vocabulary Work ........ 5
Grammar Work ........ 6
Punctuation Work ........ 7
Writing Work 1 ........ 8
Writing Work 2 ........ 9
Writing Sample ........ 10
Writing Your Own Sample ........ 11

**Unit 2: Informative Text—Review**

Reading Work ........ 12
Comprehension Work ........ 13
Spelling Work ........ 14
Vocabulary Work ........ 15
Grammar Work ........ 16
Punctuation Work ........ 17
Writing Work 1 ........ 18
Writing Work 2 ........ 19
Writing Sample ........ 20
Writing Your Own Sample ........ 21

**Unit 3: Informative Text—Biographical article**

Reading Work ........ 22
Comprehension Work ........ 23
Spelling Work ........ 24
Vocabulary Work ........ 25
Grammar Work ........ 26
Punctuation Work ........ 27
Writing Work 1 ........ 28
Writing Work 2 ........ 29
Writing Sample ........ 30
Writing Your Own Sample ........ 31

**Unit 4: Informative Text—Procedure**

Reading Work ........ 32
Comprehension Work ........ 33
Spelling Work ........ 34
Vocabulary Work ........ 35
Grammar Work ........ 36
Punctuation Work ........ 37
Writing Work 1 ........ 38
Writing Work 2 ........ 39
Writing Sample ........ 40
Writing Your Own Sample ........ 41

**Unit 5: Persuasive Text—Speech**

Reading Work ........ 42
Comprehension Work ........ 43
Spelling Work ........ 44
Vocabulary Work ........ 45
Grammar Work ........ 46
Punctuation Work ........ 47
Writing Work 1 ........ 48
Writing Work 2 ........ 49
Writing Sample ........ 50
Writing Your Own Sample ........ 51

**Unit 6: Persuasive Text—Advertising script**

Reading Work ........ 52
Comprehension Work ........ 53
Spelling Work ........ 54
Vocabulary Work ........ 55
Grammar Work ........ 56
Punctuation Work ........ 57
Writing Work 1 ........ 58
Writing Work 2 ........ 59
Writing Sample ........ 60
Writing Your Own Sample ........ 61

# TABLE OF CONTENTS

## Unit 7: Persuasive Text—Playbill


Reading Work.......... 62
Comprehension Work.......... 63
Spelling Work.......... 64
Vocabulary Work.......... 65
Grammar Work.......... 66
Punctuation Work.......... 67
Writing Work 1.......... 68
Writing Work 2.......... 69
Writing Sample.......... 70
Writing Your Own Sample.......... 71


## Unit 8: Persuasive Text—Open letter


Reading Work.......... 72
Comprehension Work.......... 73
Spelling Work.......... 74
Vocabulary Work.......... 75
Grammar Work.......... 76
Punctuation Work.......... 77
Writing Work 1.......... 78
Writing Work 2.......... 79
Writing Sample.......... 80
Writing Your Own Sample.......... 81


## Unit 9: Narrative Text—Journal


Reading Work.......... 82
Comprehension Work.......... 83
Spelling Work.......... 84
Vocabulary Work.......... 85
Grammar Work.......... 86
Punctuation Work.......... 87
Writing Work 1.......... 88
Writing Work 2.......... 89
Writing Sample.......... 90
Writing Your Own Sample.......... 91


## Unit 10: Narrative Text—Allegory


Reading Work.......... 92
Comprehension Work.......... 93
Spelling Work.......... 94
Vocabulary Work.......... 95
Grammar Work.......... 96
Punctuation Work.......... 97
Writing Work 1.......... 98
Writing Work 2.......... 99
Writing Sample.......... 100
Writing Your Own Sample.......... 101


## Unit 11: Narrative Text—Satirical script


Reading Work.......... 102
Comprehension Work.......... 103
Spelling Work.......... 104
Vocabulary Work.......... 105
Grammar Work.......... 106
Punctuation Work.......... 107
Writing Work 1.......... 108
Writing Work 2.......... 109
Writing Sample.......... 110
Writing Your Own Sample.......... 111


## Unit 12: Narrative Text—Short story


Reading Work.......... 112
Comprehension Work.......... 115
Spelling Work.......... 116
Vocabulary Work.......... 117
Grammar Work.......... 118
Punctuation Work.......... 119
Writing Work 1.......... 120
Writing Work 2.......... 121
Writing Sample.......... 122
Writing Your Own Sample.......... 123

**Tips for the Sample Tests.......... 124**

**Sample Test 1.......... 125**

**Sample Test 2.......... 131**

**Answers.......... 137**

# STUDY STEPS TO SUCCESS!

## Step 1 Reading Work

- In each chapter, read the main text.
- Read the annotations on the text. These notes identify key features of the text and will be useful as you complete the questions and activities in each section.
- The main texts have been categorised as either informative, narrative or persuasive. However, some texts have features of more than one category and so the categorisation in this book depends upon the specific elements of style they contain. These, in turn, depend on each particular writer's purpose for creating that text. For example, someone writing a biographical text may have been more interested in telling a good story than merely providing factual information about the subject's life. They may have given the text all the hallmarks of a narrative.

## Step 2 Comprehension Work

- Read and answer the questions, using the hints to help you.
- Check each multiple-choice answer to ensure that it is the best response to the question.
- Re-read your longer answers to ensure that they make sense.

## Step 3 Spelling Work

- Read all of the information, rules and hints provided about spelling.
- For most questions, use the List Words provided to complete your answers.
- For open or creative questions, avoid writing basic or obvious responses.

## Step 4 Vocabulary Work

- Read all of the information and hints provided about improving your vocabulary.
- Check that you have the skills and knowledge you need to successfully complete the topic.
- Complete the questions and activities to test your knowledge and skills.

## Step 5 Grammar Work

- Read all of the information, rules and hints provided about grammar.
- Check that you have the skills and knowledge you need to successfully complete the topic.
- Complete the questions and activities to test your knowledge and skills.

## Step 6 Punctuation Work

- Read all of the information, rules and hints provided about punctuation.
- Check that you have the skills and knowledge you need to successfully complete the topic.
- Complete the questions and activities to test your knowledge and skills.

## Step 7 Writing Work

- Read the information about language forms and structures.
- Refer back to the main text to understand these forms and structures in context.
- Answer the questions to test your knowledge and understanding.

## Step 8 Writing Sample

- Study the writing sample carefully, reading all of the explanatory notes.
- Compare this text with the main text studied throughout the chapter so far, to reinforce your learning.

## Step 9 Writing Your Own Sample

- Check that you understand the terms and techniques relevant to this task.
- Using the sample text and the explanatory notes as a guide, compose a similar text inside the scaffold. You may wish to do this on separate paper or electronically, in order to give yourself more room.

## Step 10 Check Your Answers

- Check all of your answers at the back of the book.
- Whether or not you got the answers right, read through the whole answer section. Sample answers are provided along with explanations of why multiple-choice options are right or wrong.
- If you cannot understand a particular answer, revise the chapter notes and text annotations or ask your teacher for help.
- You should always attempt a question, even if you aren't confident in your answer, because in English you may still get some marks for a good attempt. Reading sample answers will help you write better answers next time.

## Step 11 Tips for the Sample Tests

- These useful tips appear on page 124. Read them before you attempt one of the Sample Tests.

## Step 12 Sample Tests

- Two Sample Tests are provided at the end of the book.
- Before attempting the Sample Tests, make sure that you have completed all of the work in the book and have worked through the answers to all questions that you answered incorrectly.
- Set aside the time allowed for the paper and complete it under test conditions—no sneaking a look at your notes!
- Work through the answers (at the end of the book) to any questions that you were unsure about. Write down your total marks for each section in the Your Score boxes at the end of each part of the paper, then add them up to get a total percentage for the test.

# HOW TO USE THIS BOOK TO STUDY FOR A CLASS TEST, HALF-YEARLY OR END-OF-YEAR EXAM

Depending on your teacher or school, you will be given a variety of tests and exams each year. There may be a single-topic test, a test that covers a number of topics, a semester test or exam, or even a half-yearly or yearly exam.

**Step 1**

### **Find out** which topics will be covered in the class test.

- To do this, look at your class workbook/textbook, laptop/tablet or online study program, and ask your teacher.
- For example, your class test may be on grammar.

**Step 2**

### **Match** the topics that your test is on to the topics in this book.

- For example, each unit has questions on grammar.

**Step 3**

### **Use** this book to study the topics being tested.

- Pages 6, 16, 26, 36, 46, 56, 66, 76, 86, 96, 106 and 118 all cover grammar. You can do the questions on these pages to study for your class test on grammar.

**Note:**

- When you are using this book to study for a **half-yearly** test, follow the same steps as above—the only difference being that you will have more topics to revise, of course.
- When you are using this book to study for an **end-of-year** test, you will more than likely need to study the whole book.

# READING

## *Types of Questions*

### Literal questions—the answer is right in front of you

This is the simplest type of reading task question that asks you to find a 'literal' answer.

**To answer these questions** you just have to locate specific facts and details to find the meaning.

For some literal questions you might have to:

* find facts, details and other forms of information from the text
* consider certain features of the text, including spelling, punctuation or common language techniques
* recount (or retell) details, sometimes in your own words
* consider the order in which facts are presented in a text
* recognise synonyms that are used for particular details and search for slightly different words from those in the question
* use your vocabulary
* use your comprehension
* identify who, what, where, when and how.

### Interpretive questions—the answer requires a synthesis of textual details

This type of question asks you to interpret the meaning of words, phrases and sentences.

**To answer these questions** you will have to combine facts and details to synthesise the meaning.

For some interpretive questions you might have to:

* synthesise meaning by putting various facts together to reach a conclusion—we synthesise meaning from texts all the time without even realising it
* consider multiple aspects of the text at once
* use logic to find additional meaning beyond the words
* interpret the meaning of facts and details as the meaning of some parts of the text may not be obvious from just a straightforward reading
* do simple calculations to find an answer
* look at language-related matters, such as meanings conveyed by certain words, phrases or symbols
* think about the connotations of words—meanings that extend beyond the words on the page
* describe, recount, explain, compare, summarise or give reasons
* make small but important distinctions between ideas. The words *bad*, *evil*, *naughty* and *diabolical* all mean a similar thing—but they have quite distinct shades of meaning. We might call a disobedient puppy naughty but not evil. Likewise, we wouldn't call a murderer naughty.

# READING
## *Types of Questions*

### Applied questions—the answer is conceptual and is not present in the text

These questions require you to understand a text's implications—the logical extension of facts and connotations. A composer can imply meaning, rather than simply state it. This allows us to extract meanings that go beyond the literal denotation (straightforward meaning) of the words a writer uses.

**To answer these questions** you have to apply multiple skills to infer the meaning.

Students sometimes confuse the terms 'imply' and 'infer'. Put simply, the composer implies meaning in a text and the responder infers meaning from the text.

For some applied questions you might have to:

- explain, prove, judge, evaluate, predict, solve, discuss or critique aspects of the text
- make an informed judgement or evaluation based on evidence from the text
- apply 'assumed knowledge'—information or understanding that the writer assumes you possess already
- interpret facts using additional knowledge from outside the text, such as allusions
- consider facts or details in specific combinations to arrive at a logical conclusion
- consider what you already know about textual features and their effects on meaning
- consider the usual rules of genre, form or type of text
- 'read between the lines' to infer meaning from the text
- 'read beyond the lines' to understand implications
- engage your senses
- apply thinking skills to develop insights and personal opinions
- consider what information may be missing from the text.

UNIT 1

# INFORMATIVE TEXT

## Online information report

READING WORK

https:/ /www.topendtourist.com

### Crocodile Safety

In partnership with Wild Australia Northern Territory Administration (WANTA)

Saltwater crocodile safety is no joke. These creatures are extremely dangerous and attacks are often fatal. Top End (Northern Territory) visitors and locals should be informed about crocs and stay vigilant when near water. If you're a Territorian, don't be complacent, and don't assume there are no crocs in an area because you haven't seen one there before.

Be WILDWARY, particularly when swimming, boating, fishing and camping. Here's how …

**Swimming**

Crocs are common in the Northern Territory (NT), but all of the fatal attacks in the past twenty years have occurred in non-designated swimming areas. Read the signs, use common sense and stay safe.

- Swim in designated waterways marked with safe swimming signs. Remember, not every waterhole in the vast Top End can be signposted. No sign does not mean no danger. ONLY swim in designated areas marked with signs.
- NEVER enter the water where you see this no-swimming sign:
- Other signs indicating that you should not swim include Crocodile Safety and Warning: Crocodile Sighting. Click on the links to learn more about these and other NT safety signs.
- Don't swim alone.
- Don't swim after dark.

**Boating and fishing**

- Don't sleep on a boat overnight.
- Take extra care when launching boats and removing them from the water.
- Avoid activities that attract crocs, such as hanging arms or legs over the side of a boat.
- When cleaning fish, remove or bury all waste far from the water's edge.
- Take particular care when fishing at night.
- If fishing from a bank, cast at least 5 metres back from the water.
- Use a long-handled net to retrieve caught fish: do not reach into the water.

**Camping**

- Don't camp alone.
- Pitch tents at least 50 meters from the water's edge.
- Keep all litter tightly wrapped and stored and take it with you when you leave.
- Don't feed, harass or try to get close to crocs.
- Be extra careful at night.
- Avoid areas where croc slide marks or nest mounds are visible.

WANTA urges everyone visiting or living in the Top End to keep on the lookout for crocs. State Wildlife Commission rangers and National Park personnel do their best to ensure visitor safety, but in the end, it's up to you to behave responsibly.

Download our Top Safety Tips for Top End Travel and SWIMS (Safe Water Indicators, Markers and Signs) info.

Report a crocodile to the WANTA Safety Team.

Learn fascinating facts about saltwater crocodiles and other dangerous Australian creatures.

- 'Partnership' with a wildlife safety organisation gives this article **authority**. The logo seems to confirm this partnership.
- Coloured **hyperlinks** appear throughout the article. Readers can click on these to find additional information and related websites.
- This **idiom** succinctly tells the reader that this is a serious issue.
- **Contractions** such as 'you're' and **idioms** such as 'Territorian' are informal and appeal to the reader.
- A single-word **slogan** sums up the subject.
- These categories will be **expanded** later in the text.
- An indented point adds emphasis to the **central message** and leads the reader's eye directly to the sign.
- **Bullet points** and **subheadings** give the article structure and make the information clear.
- A **measurement** of distance provides specificity.
- The **structure** of each section is similar to provide continuity.
- A **concluding statement** restates the subject and summarises the points.
- The **colloquial terms** 'crocs' (saltwater crocodiles) and 'Top End' (Australia's Northern Territory) have been spelt out in full earlier in the report.
- The **personal pronoun** 'our' is used in the text to suggest that the composer of this safety report is a single authority.

# INFORMATIVE TEXT

**COMPREHENSION WORK**

## Literal questions

*Hint: Read the text carefully to locate specific facts and details.*

**1** Where have all fatal Northern Territory crocodile attacks occurred in the past twenty years?

______________________________________________

**2** What are the two organisations in 'partnership' behind this text?

**a** Wild Australia Northern Territory Administration and topendtourist.com

**b** WILDWARY and State Wildlife Commission

**c** Safety Team and Wild Australia Northern Territory Administration

**3** How many hyperlinked phrases or names are included in this text? ______________________

## Interpretive questions

*Hint: These questions require you to combine facts and details to synthesise the meaning.*

**4** Which sentence in the 'Swimming' section sums up what it means to be 'WILDWARY'?

______________________________________________

**5** What is a feature shared by some of the text's imperative sentences (those that give commands)?

**a** They are short. **b** They have a sarcastic tone. **c** They are phrased as questions.

**6** Which excerpt from the opening statement indicates this text's purpose? *Hint: What type of text is this?*

**a** Saltwater crocodile safety is no joke.

**b** Top End (Northern Territory) visitors and locals should be informed …

**c** If you're a Territorian, don't be complacent …

**7** We can infer from the report that crocodiles are most active at night. What leads us to do this?

______________________________________________

**8** Who is the target audience of this text? Give evidence.

______________________________________________

**9** Finish this sentence based on the text: Swimmers are urged to read the signs because

**a** crocs are common in the Northern Territory.

**b** not every waterhole in the vast Top End can be signposted.

**c** there are other signs indicating that you should not swim.

**10** Which of these language features has not been used to make the text clear and understandable?

**a** repetition **b** colloquial language **c** rhyme

## Applied questions

*Hint: These questions require you to understand a text's implications to infer meaning from the text.*

**11** Suggest an additional two graphics that would enhance this text and explain your choices.

______________________________________________

______________________________________________

**12** This text is included on a Northern Territory tourism website ('topendtourist.com'). Why?

**a** to encourage people to visit places other than the Top End

**b** to appeal to people's sense of adventure

**c** to equip people to have a fun and safe Top End holiday

# INFORMATIVE TEXT

## Online information report

SPELLING WORK

### List Words

All of the words in the box below appear in the text 'Crocodile Safety'.

| | | | | |
|---|---|---|---|---|
| territory | fatal | vigilant | complacent | personnel |
| designated | retrieve | harass | ensure | commission |
| vast | northern | assume | bury | fascinating |

**1** Seven of the list words and five other words have been misspelt in the following passage. Circle them.

Crocodiles are fasinating creatures, and a vast number of artists, writers and movie directers have fed our intrest by depicting them in their works. They often appear cartonish and even cute, but these jaw-snapping Northern Terittory critters are no joke. Far from being vigillant about crocs, some Top End visitors are very complacent, swimming in non-designatned areas. Some camp in croc habitatts. Others even harrass them. Wildlife personell emplore tourists to be more careful. These people don't asume that their fun might be fatal.

**2** Form list words by rearranging each letter group and then adding one more letter.

**a** musas ____________ **b** sarah ____________

**c** veerite ____________ **d** suren ____________

**e** nelepsor ____________ **f** rhonter ____________

**3** Pairs of correctly spelt words appear below, but only one of each pair is correct based on its use in the context. Circle the incorrect word in each sentence. *Hint: Read the List Words in the context of the text.*

**a** It's important to bury / berry your litter or take it with you when camping.

**b** The vigilante / vigilant dealt with croc criminals in his own way.

**c** The fast / vast mud plains offered little shelter from the burning sun.

**d** I'm competent / complacent with a crocodile hook and muzzle.

**e** When a croc snatches your dog, it becomes personnel / personal.

**f** We will assume / resume water sports once the area has been declared safe.

When you see the suffixes *ent, ant, ence* or *ance,* they are usually spoken with an unstressed schwa (ə). **Schwa**, an indistinct 'uh', is a very common English vowel sound. It makes spelling difficult, since the pronunciation offers no clues. You will learn more about schwa in the Grammar Work section on page 5.

**4** Complete each word by adding the correct suffix: *ent, ant, ence* or *ance.*
*Hint: Two of the suffixes are used in the list words. Say these words aloud to hear the unstressed schwa.*

**a** My car gives me independ__________. **b** We're having a clear__________ sale.

**c** Your pres__________ is required. **d** She is a profici__________ cook.

**e** The defend__________ looked nervous. **f** Finish this sent__________.

**g** That example is not pertin__________. **h** The top quadr__________ is out of bounds.

**i** The sunset was magnific__________. **j** The jewel's magnific__________ was undeniable.

**5** Find a list word that

**a** contains two sets of double consonants. ____________

**b** nearly rhymes with 'exhume'. ____________

**c** becomes its boss when *e* and *r* are added. ____________

**d** contains a practically silent *r*. ____________

# INFORMATIVE TEXT

## Online information report

VOCABULARY WORK

### Acronym or initialism?

These two abbreviation types are sometimes confused but there is a clear difference. Both are used in the text 'Crocodile Safety'. An **acronym** is a word (not always a real one) formed using the first letter of each word in a phrase or name. It can be pronounced as a word; for example *PIN* (personal identification number). An **initialism**, however, is not pronounced as a word, but as a string of letters; for example *CNN* (Cable News Network). Here are some details about acronyms and initialisms:

- Many acronyms omit the first letter of less important words like 'and' or 'of'. For example: NASA (National Aeronautics and Space Administration). This can make acronyms more pronounceable.
- Some acronyms are printed in lower case because they have passed into common usage and become accepted as words; for example, *scuba diving* (self-contained underwater breathing apparatus) and *laser* (light amplification by stimulated emission of radiation).
- Sometimes larger parts of the phrase or name being abbreviated in an acronym are used instead of single letters; for example, *HAZMAT* (hazardous materials).
- Initialisms have grown more numerous and more popular since the advent of text messaging and other communication modes suited to abbreviated language. Some commonly used initialisms of this kind are *BTW* (by the way), *TMI* (too much information) and *BRB* (be right back).
- Many initialisms denote aspects of new technologies; for example, *LCD* (liquid crystal display).

**1** List the three acronyms and initialisms used in the text 'Crocodile Safety', along with their full forms.

| | Acronym / Initialism | Full phrase / Name |
|---|---|---|
| a | ____________ | ______________________________ |
| b | ____________ | ______________________________ |
| c | ____________ | ______________________________ |

**2** Use lines to match each well-known acronym or initialism with its description. There are two sets.
*Hint: The descriptions describe the abbreviations but they are not literally the words they stand for.*

| Set 1 | | Set 2 | |
|---|---|---|---|
| VIP | looking for alien life | ROM | a computer acronym |
| UN | dignitary or guest | ASAP | a debilitating disease |
| SETI | an inter-nation committee | FBI | denotes urgency |
| ABC | a television network | MS | a law-enforcement agency |

**3** Find words in the word list that fit the descriptions below.

**a** a common noun here, but a proper noun in the text; it means 'place' ______________

**b** a verb that can mean 'annoy' or 'intimidate' ______________

**c** an adjective meaning 'focused' and 'observant' ______________

**d** a synonym of 'captivating' ______________

**Idioms** are expressions used by a certain group or in a certain area. In the text 'Crocodile Safety', idioms are employed along with colloquial (everyday) language to connect with the reader. For example, 'no joke', 'Top End', 'bloke' and 'arvo'.

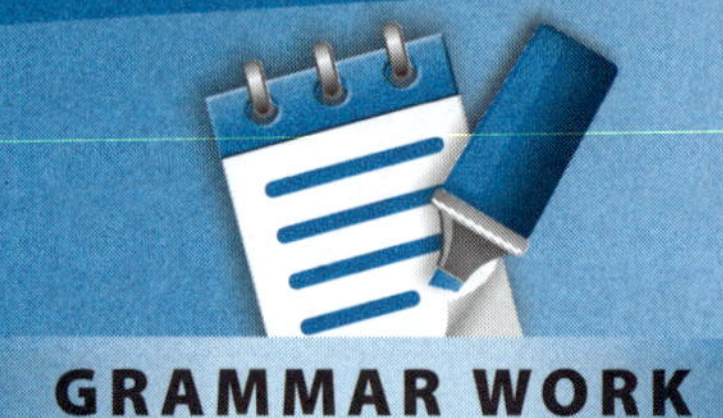

# INFORMATIVE TEXT

*Online information report*

GRAMMAR WORK

## Bullet points

Also called dot points, this common structuring tool is helpful in setting out key information in a report. Being so common, however, **bullet points** are often used inconsistently or confusingly. Knowing how to use bullet points is a grammatical skill. The guidelines below (in bullet points!) will help you.

- When using bullet points to grab attention, keep them short.
- When writing fuller, explanatory bullet points (like these), try not to write more than ten in a row.
- If a bullet point list is not preceded by a colon, use capital letters to begin each point. If these points are full sentences, end each one with a full stop. If they are not full sentences, full stops are not necessary.
- When bullet points are intended to complete an introductory sentence, maintain the tense by using appropriate participles in each point. This is the most common error made in bullet point usage.

**1** Circle the best word or phrase to complete each statement about bullet points.

**a** 'Bullet' and 'dot' are adverbs / synonyms / antonyms in this context.

**b** When aiming to make bullet points eye-catching, keep them short / full / fewer than ten in number.

**c** Capital letters are necessary in bullet points that are long / complete / incorrect sentences.

**d** To create consistent tense in a bullet point list, colons / participles / full stops must be carefully used.

## Phonemic orthography

Pho-what? This is just a technical term for the relationship between the way words are spoken and how they are written. In English, there are lots of inconsistencies in **phonemic orthography** because it is a very complex language with many origins. The list word *designated* is an example of this problem. Its word family includes *sign*, *design* (both with a long vowel sound), *signature* and *signal* (both with a short 'i').

**2** Each of these word pairs shares a three-letter combination but different sounds are created. Complete the words by adding the missing letters they have in common. *Hint: Each pair has its own letter combination.*

| | | | |
|---|---|---|---|
| **a** as __ __ me | as __ __ __ ption | **b** fa __ __ l | fa __ __ __ ity |
| **c** q __ __ ck | __ __ ay | **d** __ __ titude | __ __ tar |
| **e** m __ __ ery | __ __ __ leading | **f** __ __ __ den | b __ __ eau |
| **g** __ __ __ h | a __ __ __ itect | **h** __ __ __ age | __ __ __ ineer |

It sounds like something a backing vocalist might sing but the **schwa** is arguably the most common spoken vowel sound in English. Because it is an unstressed or lazy sound, a schwa can make spelling difficult, so it is helpful to memorise tricks for some words pronounced with this sound. Here are two examples: the list words *vigilant* and *complacent* are both spoken with an unstressed schwa suffix (word ending). Say *vigilante* to remind you of the *ant* in *vigilant*, and use the *place* in *complacent* to help you spell its suffix with an *e*.

**3** Identify any unstressed schwa sounds in these words. *Hint: There may be more than one in a word.*

| | | | |
|---|---|---|---|
| **a** about | **b** pencil | **c** occur | **d** again |
| **e** mountain | **f** fisherman | **g** president | **h** supply |
| **i** experienced | **j** importance | **k** amazement | **l** syringe |

**4** Which nine-letter adverb in the opening statement of the text modifies an adjective about crocodiles? *Hint: This adverb indicates the degree or extent of the adjective.* ____________________

# INFORMATIVE TEXT

## Online information report

PUNCTUATION WORK

### Capital letters

While not strictly a punctuation mark, capitalisation falls into the punctuation category. **Capital letters** have two general functions: to identify where a sentence begins and to draw attention to a particular element in a word, sentence or other setting. Capital letters have various specific functions in the text 'Crocodile Safety'. A capital letter in this text might indicate that a certain word is:

- opening a sentence (such as 'Don't camp alone.')
- a proper noun (such as 'Northern Territory')
- an initialism (such as 'NT') or an acronym (such as 'SWIMS'), if every letter is capitalised
- being specially emphasised, if every letter is capitalised (such as 'ONLY' and 'NEVER')
- part of a heading ('Crocodile Safety') or subheading (such as 'Fishing and Boating')
- from a sign (such as 'Warning: Crocodile Sighting').

**1** Capital letters can indicate

**a** common nouns. **b** that a subheading will follow. **c** words on a sign.

**2** In the text 'Crocodile Safety', the capitalisation of every letter in a word is used for

**a** special emphasis. **b** sentence openings. **c** both **a** and **b**.

**3** As mentioned, 'ONLY' and 'NEVER' are capitalised in the text 'Crocodile Safety' for emphasis. The more specific purpose of this is to remind the reader of the seriousness of the topic. In what other texts or contexts might capitals be used for this same purpose? Choose from the options below.

| | | | |
|---|---|---|---|
| one-way street sign | wedding invitation | cake recipe | aeroplane safety card |
| box of rat poison | can of hairspray | movie poster | twenty-dollar note |
| gas heater manual | theme park billboard | medicine bottle | train timetable |

### Capital letters and computers

Here are three pieces of **computer-related** advice on using **capital letters** that may come in handy.

- The most secure computer passwords include both lower-case characters and capitals. Numbers and special keyboard characters further enhance the effectiveness of a password.
- When in doubt regarding capitals in a certain situation, type the exact term or phrase into a search engine. Some of what you find will be wrong, but you can use the general consensus as a guide.
- Especially in electronic communications, writing entirely in capitals is the equivalent of shouting. If used carelessly or in the wrong context, using all-caps can come across as angry or even threatening.

**4** Add to the list. What is one other computer-related hint or rule you know about capital letters?

______________________________

**5** This passage is based on the text 'Crocodile Safety', but it is missing capital letters and full stops. Add them.

the saltwater crocodile is an extremely dangerous creature common in australia's northern territory wanta, or wild australia northern territory administration, in conjunction with topendtourist.com, has published a report entitled 'crocodile safety' that explains to potential top end tourists, along with locals, how to stay safe in crocodile habitats everyone in the top end must ensure that their leisure activities only take place in designated swimming areas and certainly not where signs such as 'warning: crocodile sighting' are posted

# INFORMATIVE TEXT

## Online information report



### Information reports

An **information report** is a **non-fiction informative text** that offers readers facts on a certain subject. While it can be persuasive as well as informative (as is the case in the text 'Crocodile Safety'), this type of text does not feature a personal viewpoint. Information reports are structured according to the points below.

- An initial statement introduces the subject.
- Details about place and/or time are provided that place the subject in a context.
- The information to follow is previewed.
- Body points or paragraphs address different aspects of the subject.
- Each point begins with a subheading or a topic sentence that names the focus of the point.

A concluding statement summarises the information presented. Common visual features of online information reports are:

- headers
- bullet points
- hyperlinks
- graphics
- text boxes
- embedded videos
- a comments bar
- related media and advertisements.

**1** How is an information report similar in structure to an essay?

______________________________________________

**2** The category headings below describe the **purposes** of the eight visual features listed above. Organise the visual features under the appropriate headings. One feature has been placed for you.

| a Generates funding | b Supports the information | c Structures the information | d Invites opinion |
| --- | --- | --- | --- |
| | hyperlinks | | |
| | | | |

### Purposes of an online information report

When using the internet, we constantly come across **information reports.** These texts can be written on an infinite number of subjects, which are not always serious. Just a few of the **purposes** of this kind of text are:

- to provide factual information
- to entertain
- to expose a wrong in society
- to inform people about an issue.

**3** What are the two main purposes of the text 'Crocodile Safety'? *Hint: Find the answers in the above points.*

______________________ ______________________

### Informative *and* true?

By definition, an information report should be entirely factual and correct. Unfortunately, **bias** and **error** often come into play. Internet texts can be very unreliable, because they are not always checked for accuracy and can be published by anyone. Guidelines for reading and writing online information reports are given below.

**Readers:**

- Make sure the source is authoritative.
- Read widely on the subject.
- Cross-check all important details.

**Writers:**

- Research the subject thoroughly first.
- Write in a factual and unbiased way.
- Have the piece properly checked.

# INFORMATIVE TEXT
## Online information report

WRITING WORK 2

### Writing an effective information report

As we have already discussed, readers rely on information reports to be truthful and helpful. When constructing a text of this kind, therefore, we must be very careful in selecting, organising and expressing the information. This is especially true in the case of a report such as the text 'Crocodile Safety', where people's lives may be endangered if information is incorrect. To ensure that an **information report** is **effective**, we must:

- know our target audience and the purpose or purposes of the report
- select key details to reveal about the subject and use language economically
- arrange details into paragraphs or sets of bullet points
- avoid sensationalism and bias when using superlatives or emotive language
- only use graphics and other visual elements that complement the information.

**4** Why is it important to only use graphics and other visual elements that complement the information? *Hint: Here, 'complement' is a verb meaning 'to complete or neatly match'.*

---

### Language features of an online report

The following **language features** are common in **information reports** and similar informative texts, including those published **online**. The examples provided are all from the text 'Crocodile Safety'.

- the simple present tense for key information (such as 'attacks are often fatal') and the present continuous tense for any imperatives or commands (such as 'Don't camp alone.')
- linking verbs (such as 'designated waterways marked with safe swimming signs')
- technical terms and language specific to the subject (such as 'nest mounds' and 'park rangers')
- generic or broad terms (such as 'tourists' and 'locals')

**5** From the list of options below, find four other language features evident in the text 'Crocodile Safety'.

| | | | |
|---|---|---|---|
| economical language | direct speech | onomatopoeia | run-on line |
| simile | second person | hyphenated words | explanatory parentheses |

**6** These features are all evident in the text 'Crocodile Safety'. Complete the table, using the text's annotations as a guide.

| Feature | Example(s) from the text | Effect/Purpose |
|---|---|---|
| facts | **a** | adds authority to the text |
| omission of pronouns (like 'you') and auxiliary verbs (like 'are') | • When cleaning fish<br>• If fishing from a bank | **b** |
| colloquial language | **c** | appeals to the reader and makes the information easily understood |
| emotive language | **d** | **e** |

# INFORMATIVE TEXT

## *Online information report*

WRITING SAMPLE

Here is a sample text showing you how to structure and write an information report.

## Deadly Australians

✸ **Write a literal title naming the subject.**

✸ **Include an appropriate image to catch the attention of the reader and/or to elaborate on the information.** Here, a snake epitomises the title.

An island 'girt by sea', the mainland of Australia is geographically isolated and densely occupied by fauna. Some of the planet's most dangerous wildlife lives here, from tiny bugs to reptilian giants.

✸ **Write an opening statement to introduce the subject and sum up the points that follow.** We read about the reason for the country's prolific wildlife.

### Savage serpents

✸ **Write a subheading that echoes the title.**

There are around 172 snake species in Australia. Of these, 100 are venomous and 12 can inflict a fatal bite to humans. Typically, snakes only strike when hunting, or in self-defence.

✸ **Write an introductory statement that sums up the points to follow.** Include some statistical data.

- **Eastern brown snake:** This killer can survive—even thrive—in heavily populated areas. Although it feeds primarily on rodents and pests, it will strike any human seen as an intruder.
- **Common death adder:** Of Australia's many death adder species, this is the only one found in Sydney (the nation's most populous city). Unlike most snakes, this one waits for its prey to approach.
- **Coastal taipan:** Suspicious of nearby movement, this lethal snake can deliver a shot of deadly venom deep into human flesh.

✸ **Structure a series of related facts in point form.** Here we read three facts about different species of snake. Use parentheses to provide additional relevant information—we read that 'Sydney [is] the nation's most populous city'. Use language economically to save space.

### Wet 'n' wily

✸ **Write a subheading that includes alliteration.**

Australia's coastal waters and river systems are quite literally overflowing with a proliferation of beautiful but deadly marine life.

✸ **Write an introductory statement that sums up the points that will follow.**

- **Box jellyfish:** Also known as the sea wasp, the transparent tentacles of this venomous jellyfish can extend to 3 metres. Contact with these tentacles can lead to rapid cardiac arrest.
- **Saltwater crocodile (estuarine crocodile):** An Australian icon, the saltwater crocodile is an extraordinarily powerful predator found in rivers, swamps, creeks and estuaries.
- **Bull shark:** Found in river systems around Australia, the often aggressive bull shark is the only species capable of staying in fresh water for an extended period of time.

✸ **Use technical and subject-specific terms to add to the authority of the report.** The terms 'sea wasp', 'venomous' and 'cardiac arrest' add to the report's authority. Use parentheses to provide additional relevant information. Use language economically to save space. Write at least one sentence beginning with a dependent clause to add to the economy of expression. We read about an 'Australian icon, the saltwater crocodile …'—this syntactic approach is used through most of the report.

### Suspect insects

✸ **Write a subheading that includes assonance.**

While Australian insects and arachnids terrify many people, the good news is that few such creatures have the potential to kill us. The even better news is that antivenene is available for all of them.

✸ **Write an introductory statement that sums up the points to follow.** Insects and arachnids are introduced.

- **Sydney funnel-web spider**: This fearsome spider thrives in urban areas and forests, but tales of their aggression are exaggerated. Only mature males can give fatal doses of venom.
- **Redback spider:** A close relative of the American black widow, the redback spider can live practically anywhere, although they are unlikely to attack unless a hand falls upon their web.
- **Honey bee:** Honey bees pose a deadly risk to anyone allergic to them. Statistically, they have claimed more lives than any spider.

✸ **Use some emotive language to make the content engaging.** Here we read that the funnel-web is 'fearsome' and 'fatal'. Make three related points to give balance to the report. Correct a misconception about the topic: we read that 'tales of [funnel-web] aggression are exaggerated'.

### Staying safe

✸ **Make the final subheading literal and serious.**

To avoid becoming a victim of a deadly Australian, travellers and locals alike are urged to take precautions, read warning signs and, mainly, stay at a safe distance. But should you be bitten or stung, seek immediate medical attention.

✸ **Write a concluding statement that offers practical advice based on the report.** Use second person address. For example, 'should you be bitten or stung' appeals to the reader directly.

# INFORMATIVE TEXT

## *Online information report*

**WRITING YOUR OWN SAMPLE**

Plan your sample on the lines provided.

- Write a literal title naming the subject.
- Include an appropriate image to catch the attention of the reader and/or to elaborate on the information.
- Write an introductory statement that sums up the points to follow. Include some statistical data.
- Write a subheading that echoes the title.
- Write an introductory statement that sums up the points to follow. Include some statistical data.
- Structure a series of related facts in point form. Use parentheses to provide additional relevant information. Use language economically to save space. Write at least one sentence beginning with a dependent clause to add to the economy of expression.
- Write a subheading that includes alliteration.
- Write an introductory statement that sums up the points that will follow.
- Use technical and subject-specific terms to add to the authority of the report. Use parentheses to provide additional relevant information. Use language economically to save space. Write at least one sentence beginning with a dependent clause to add to the economy of expression.
- Write a subheading that includes assonance.
- Write an introductory statement that sums up the points to follow.
- Use some emotive language to make the content engaging. Make three related points: you should have done this in the other sections also. Correct a misconception about the topic.
- Make the final subheading literal and serious.
- Write a concluding statement that offers practical advice based on the report. Use second person address.

# INFORMATIVE TEXT

## *Review*

### *Abbey Road* remastered

Music Review
*Abbey Road* (Vinyl Remasters)
The Beatles

**Everything old is new again**

And the newest of the new is old. LP (long-play) records—'vinyls' to the faithful—have made a quiet but powerful re-emergence, and the result is a loud *kerching* of a comeback for many beloved, long-retired bands. In early 2016, music news site Consequence of Sound reported that Pink Floyd's *The Dark Side of the Moon* and The Beatles' *Abbey Road* topped the charts for 2015 vinyl record sales in the rock'n'roll genre. Both albums are more than forty years old. Both bands have dead guys in them. What's going on? Possibly more impressive: across *all* vinyl record sales in all genres, these two classic outfits were beaten out by only two other artists: Adele, who moved 116 000 vinyl copies of the album *25*, and Taylor Swift, with 74 000 vinyl sales of *1989*. Reissues and remastering are the order of the day, and the diehard fans are loving it almost as much as whoever is collecting the royalties.

**A fourteen-album comeback**

In a literal case of back to the future, Capitol has released The Beatles' 'Vinyl Remasters': fourteen classic records on LP, including *Revolver* and *Sgt. Pepper's Lonely Hearts Club Band*. Available individually or as a box set (accompanied by a swanky, glossy, 252-page book), the Fab Four's entire inventory has been remade the way it should be: on glorious vinyl. While the albums are back in their original physical form, they boast digitally remastered content. So now fans can own the anthology in the form of both the oldest and the latest technology at the same time. From the roll of fourteen, let's take a closer look at the one sheathed in arguably the most iconic album cover of all time: *Abbey Road*.

**_Abbey Road_ on 180 gram mono vinyl**

Pressed in 180 mono, the production has got it going on at both ends: there's a warmer bass and also a richer high end than we've heard from *Abbey Road* before. Now if you're an analogue snob, you might have more than a little digital prejudice. But put that hate aside: drop the needle on this baby and you'll be surprised and excited by the fullness of the sound that's emerged at the hands of some remastering masters. The first 1960s pressings may have a sweet nostalgic appeal, but at some point you'll come to terms with the fact (as I did … eventually) that, in matters of sound, original isn't always best. Sometimes, old isn't 'matured'; it's just old.

Of course, this new pressing may not be for you, for an entirely different reason. If it's primarily the nostalgia factor that floats your yellow submarine—and that's an absolutely cool attitude—don't let me stand between you and your original Beatles LPs. If not, read on.

Through headphones, the listener can appreciate the way that *Abbey Road* has been given plenty of breathing space in this format. It's especially noticeable on Side One. Much of the music is double-tracked, offering a lovely richness. Even when it's pared back, with nothing but piano and bass, the high end remains crisp. None of the tinniness of the original has lingered, individual lilts and licks are discernible, and the presence of John's vocals is enhanced. Paul's bass—especially on 'Come Together'—is massively improved from earlier editions, and in 'Something' George's guitar dances lightly over the fluid bass line.

Even if you've got *Abbey Road* on MP3, CD, original vinyl … wax disc, papyrus scroll, etc., you're very likely to love it in its latest format. So should you go down this new road? That's a question only you can answer, fellow vinylphile, and that's not a cop-out. I'm not here to tell you how to enjoy a classic album. Vinyl is an utterly individualistic passion. Now that you know the basics, and you've heard the confessions of one serious fan, stand at the crossing, look both ways and walk your own path.

- This line functions as both a title for the review and its first subheading. It is a **cliché** (common saying).
- A **key term** is defined at the beginning. Readers will need to understand this term before they continue.
- A blunt, irreverent statement sets the **tone**, which is highly informal and personal.
- **Data** about album sales is provided to give credibility to the review.
- An **allusion** is made to a popular film, *Back to the Future*, to complement the casual style.
- This is another name often given to The Beatles.
- The composer is unashamedly a fan of vinyl records. **Adjectives** like 'glorious' make this clear.
- The composer **personifies** the albums (in phrasing like 'they boast') to describe their features.
- The jargon-filled subheading is **abbreviated** in the first line of this section.
- The composer uses highly **colloquial** language, which is created using features including contractions (such as 'you're'), direct address (such as 'put that hate aside') and idioms (such as 'drop the needle').
- **Jargon** is used throughout the review, which suggests that this text is targeted at readers with a reasonable knowledge of vinyl records.
- Many specific qualities of the album are given in this section. The composer goes into **detail** to show a deep understanding of the work being reviewed.
- A list of types of recordings begins sensibly and then dissolves into **hyperbole**. The purpose of this is to suggest that a true Beatles fan will own their music in many forms.
- The composer **sums up**, in one brief sentence, the reason why this review is not aimed at selling a product. It is informative and persuasive to the extent of identifying the product's qualities, but the reader is left to decide whether this product is right for them.

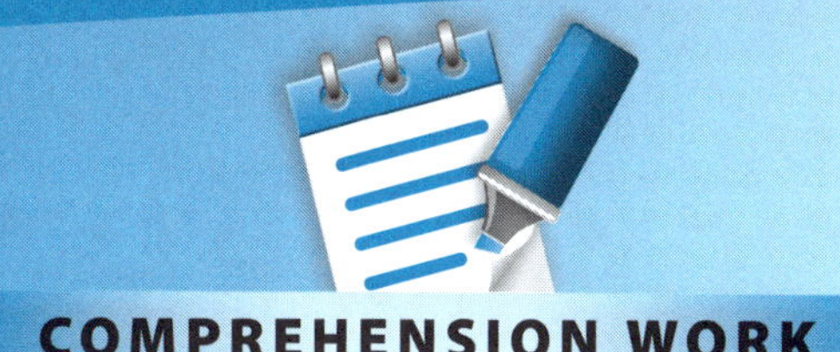

# INFORMATIVE TEXT

## Review

**COMPREHENSION WORK**

### Literal questions

*Hint: Read the text carefully to locate specific facts and details.*

**1** How many vinyl copies of her new album did Adele sell in 2015?

**a** 25 **b** 116 000 **c** 74 000

**2** What is '*Revolver*'? ______________________________

**3** What, according to the writer, is 'an absolutely cool attitude'?

______________________________

### Interpretive questions

*Hint: These questions require you to combine facts and details to synthesise the meaning.*

**4** What is 'possibly more impressive' than Pink Floyd and The Beatles topping the 2015 vinyl sales?

**a** Both bands are more than forty years old and have dead guys in them.

**b** Adele and Taylor Swift beat these bands in vinyl sales.

**c** The bands came close to topping vinyl sales in all genres.

**5** In the first section, what is meant by the word 'moved'?

**a** shifted **b** sold **c** emoted

**6** Explain how a language feature in the review refers to the famous Beatles song 'Yellow Submarine'.

______________________________

**7** What is meant by 'the confessions of one serious fan'?

**a** this review **b** a police statement **c** a cop-out

**8** What are three phrases that are puns on 'road' (based on the album title *Abbey Road*) in the text?

__________ __________ __________

**9** According to the composer, what does an 'analogue snob' hate?

**a** analogue sound **b** needles **c** digital sound

**10** Re-read the review and choose the trio of terms that have the same meaning as 'the roll of fourteen'.

**a** entire inventory, anthology, box set

**b** remasters, box set, earlier editions

**c** entire inventory, copies, royalties

### Applied questions

*Hint: These questions require you to understand a text's implications in order to infer meaning from the text.*

**11** Only the first names of the members of The Beatles are used in the review. Why?

______________________________

**12** Based on its use in context, what is the meaning of the made-up word 'vinylphile'?
*Hint: More than one answer may be close to correct. Choose the best answer based on the context.*

**a** someone who loves vinyl **b** someone who loves LPs **c** someone who hates vinyl

# INFORMATIVE TEXT

*Review*

SPELLING WORK

## List Words

All of the words in the box below appear in the text '*Abbey Road* remastered'.

| | | | | |
|---|---|---|---|---|
| iconic | fourteen | diehard | album | bass |
| anthology | genres | discernible | lilts | literal |
| vocals | technology | vinyl | fluid | guitar |

**1** One of the list words is also a number. What is it? ______________________

Write these numbers (and number derivatives) as words:

**a** 11 ______________________ **b** 60 ______________________

**c** 80 ______________________ **d** 100 ______________________

**e** 144 ______________________ **f** 2040 ______________________

**g** ½ ______________________ **h** 8th ______________________

Many words have **deceptive spellings**; that is, they don't look quite as they sound. For example, the list word 'vocals' is pronounced *voh-cools*. The second syllable is really an unpronounced vowel sound called a schwa.

**2** Write these musical terms correctly based on the phonetic spellings given. *Hint: Two are list words.*

| Sound | Correct spelling | Sound | Correct spelling |
|---|---|---|---|
| **a** guttar | ______________ | **b** kord | ______________ |
| **c** chello | ______________ | **d** base | ______________ |
| **e** rithum | ______________ | **f** him | ______________ |

## Onomatopoeia

The word itself is tough to spell but examples of it are simpler because their spellings and sounds match.

**3** **a** What word in the music review text is an example of onomatopoeia? k______________________

**b** What is meant by this word? ______________________________________________

______________________________________________

**4** Write these music-related onomatopoeic words beside the sounds or instruments they describe.

| | | | | |
|---|---|---|---|---|
| warble | buzz | clang | plunk | oompah |
| tish | boom | croon | doof-doof | tinkle |

**a** hand (or crash) cymbals ______________ **b** small cymbal (hi-hat) ______________

**c** amplifier feedback ______________ **d** gentle, high-pitched bells ______________

**e** unpleasant singing voice ______________ **f** smooth singing voice ______________

**g** large bass horn ______________ **h** techno bass beat ______________

**i** plucked string ______________ **j** bass drum ______________

**5** Every list word but one is strung together in these two lines. Extra letters have been added that, when shuffled, spell the remaining list word. Separate the words with slashes and write out the shuffled word.

**a** liconicgenrestechnologydililtsfluidguitarvocalssc

**b** anthologyfourteenrnalbumibbassediehardvinylliterale

Remaining list word (made from the shuffled extra letters): ______________________

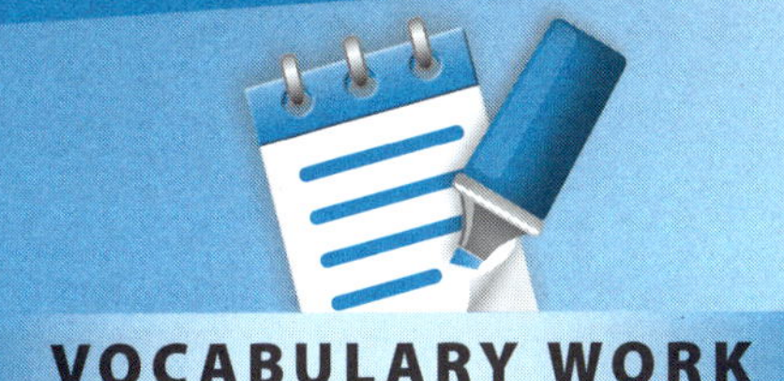

# INFORMATIVE TEXT

## Review

## VOCABULARY WORK

### Homophones

Many words sound a bit like others but they are not **homophones** unless they sound exactly alike. Test your understanding of homophones by distinguishing them from pairs of words that commonly cause mix-ups.

**1** Identify whether each of these is a pair of homophones (H) or just a confusable pair (CP).
*Hints: One word in each pair appears in the music review text. Say each word aloud to help you with this task.*

| Word pair | H or CP? | Word pair | H or CP? |
|---|---|---|---|
| **a** sliver / slither | ______ | **b** bass / base | ______ |
| **c** bitten / beaten | ______ | **d** album / albumen | ______ |
| **e** watts / what's | ______ | **f** maid / made | ______ |
| **g** guys / guise | ______ | **h** bands / bans | ______ |

**Jargon** and **idiom** are often confused for each other, because both describe expressions used by certain groups. When telling them apart, it helps to remember that most idioms have no direct link to the literal denotation of the words they comprise. For example, we read in the text '*Abbey Road* remastered' the suggestion to 'drop the needle on this baby', which actually means 'play this album'.

**2** Show your understanding. Correctly categorise six terms and expressions from the music review as jargon and six as idiom. *Hint: To answer accurately, you must read these expressions in their context in the review.*

| | | | | | |
|---|---|---|---|---|---|
| swanky | LP (long play) | rock'n'roll | the order of the day | bass line | vinyl |
| diehard | what's going on | remastered | reissues (plural noun) | masters | the faithful |

**Jargon** ______ ______ ______
______ ______ ______

**Idiom** ______ ______ ______
______ ______ ______

**Compound words** are words made up of two or more parts. Often these words are hyphenated (for example, *noise-cancelling*). Many adjectives are compound words, since the combined words offer specificity.

**3** Look in the text '*Abbey Road* remastered' to find the hyphenated compound adjectives described below.

**a** The length of the book included in the box set: ______

**b** The size of the box set based on albums: ______

**c** The types of groups making a comeback: ______

**d** The type of dual voice recording on some songs: ______

**4** Look in the text '*Abbey Road* remastered' to find the unhyphenated compound nouns described below.

**a** Personal listening accessory: ______

**b** A notable return to a particular arena: ______

**c** Another word for 'anyone': ______

**d** A word for 'groups' that can also mean 'sets of clothing': ______

**5** Write a definition of the list word 'discernible' that begins with the meaning of its suffix.

______

# INFORMATIVE TEXT

*Review*

**GRAMMAR WORK**

## Clauses

This unit of language is the essential building block of sentences in English. Here are some **clause** basics:

- There are four types of clause: independent (or main), dependent (or subordinate), adjectival and noun.
- A clause differs from a phrase, in that it must contain a verb.
- To prevent a sentence from being a fragment, it must contain at least one independent clause.
- An independent clause consists of a subject (usually a noun phrase) and a verb or verb phrase.
- The rule of independent clause construction is subject plus verb equals whole thought or idea. For example, the words 'the diehard fans' (noun phrase) 'are loving it' (verb phrase) make up a clause.

**1** Identify whether each group of words from the music review is a phrase or a clause.
*Hint: Revise the points and examples above to be sure of getting these right.*

**a** beloved, long-retired ____________ **b** music news site ____________

**c** *Abbey Road* topped the charts ____________ **d** Consequence of Sound reported ____________

**e** both bands have dead guys in them ____________ **f** possibly more impressive ____________

When writing clauses that include **time-related words** like *when*, *until* and *after*, we often use the present tense to refer to future events. For example: *I'll come back when I finish shopping. They are arriving after five o'clock.*

**2** Rearrange the words below into their correct order to form time-related clauses from the text '*Abbey Road* remastered'.

**a** now basics that you the know ________________________________

**b** can the way the listener appreciate ________________________________

We usually omit **second uses** of the word ***will*** in time clauses; also in clauses containing the word *if*. For example, in *I will see you after I will finish work* is incorrect—the second *will* should be omitted. The clause *I will be happy if you will buy the car* may seem correct, but the second *will* is unnecessary and creates awkward expression.

**3** Construct 'if' clauses from the text 'Abbey Road remastered' by correctly placing the words in each group of words below on the line. Each word group is missing at least two words; be careful to add these when completing the clauses.

**a** snob you're analogue if ________________________________ will

**b** the that it's if ________________________________ floats

**4** You should already be familiar with the main parts of speech, such as nouns and pronouns. Highlight or circle parts of speech in the bank of options below. *Hint: Not all of the English parts of speech appear below.*

| adjective | and | fragment | adverb | comma |
|---|---|---|---|---|
| conjunction | preposition | full stop | article | |

**5** Circle all of the adjectives and underline all of the adverbs in this sentence from the music review.

If it's primarily the nostalgia factor that floats your yellow submarine—and that's an entirely cool attitude—don't let me stand between you and your original Beatles LPs.

**6** Circle all of the nouns (all types) and underline all of the verbs in these excerpts from the music review.

**a** the Fab Four's entire inventory has been remade the way it should be: on glorious vinyl.

**b** a question only you can answer, fellow vinylphile, and that's not a cop-out

**c** stand at the crossing, look both ways and walk your own path.

# INFORMATIVE TEXT

*Review*

## PUNCTUATION WORK

### Colon (:) or conjunction?

The composer of the text '*Abbey Road* remastered' makes use of the **colon** (:) as a **conjunction** substitute.

What does this look like?

- The colon can function as a conjunction (joining word), but only if it makes sense in the context (for example, 'put that hate aside: drop the needle on this baby').
- Not every use of colons in the text fits this description. Some colons used by the writer perform their traditional functions of beginning lists and dividing sentences into statements and explanations.

Why do it?

- Using a colon to join sentences or fragments can be an economical choice when constructing a text.
- Rather than use words like *and*, *because*, *if* and *but,* or longer conjunction phrases like *rather than*, *which is* and *even though,* we can save space and keep expression tidy by using one punctuation mark.
- Conjunction substitution, like other stylistic features of writing, can help a composer create a certain tone in a text. In '*Abbey Road* remastered', the tone is very casual and sometimes cheeky. The conjunction substitutions contribute to this tone.

**1** Show your understanding of colon usage by stating whether each example below is correct or incorrect on the line provided. *Hint: These examples do not appear in the review text.*

**a** I don't want to go on a picnic: I can't find my basket. ____________

**b** Where are you going: don't leave without me. ____________

**c** You shouldn't stand there: it's an ant nest. ____________

**d** This is the worst: or maybe the second-worst cake I've tasted. ____________

**2** Rewrite these excerpts from the music review, replacing the colon with an appropriate conjunction or conjunction phrase from the bank of options provided.
*Hint: Various combinations may make sense, but only a correct answer will show a replacement of the colon.*

| is that | and | because | rather than | which is | but | such as | instead of |
|---|---|---|---|---|---|---|---|

**a** the way it should be: on glorious vinyl ____________

**b** put that hate aside: drop the needle ____________

**c** more impressive: across all vinyl record sales ____________

**3** Which punctuation mark is often used near a conjunction in a sentence? *Hint: It is not the colon.* ____________

**4** This passage has not been taken from the text, but it is about the same subject. It is missing four colons. Insert these marks where they are missing. *Hint: The colons may perform different functions.*

There's a new kid on the music industry block the old bloke. The LP. It's been a very long time, but it was worth the wait the best of The Beatles has been remastered. How? You guessed it on vinyl. The box set includes the following all fourteen Beatles' albums, static-resistant sleeves and a commemorative book.

**5** Show your understanding of appropriate colon-for-conjunction usage: circle any conjunctions that could be replaced by colons in these sentences. *Hint: Some sentences may not contain any conjunctions.*

**a** Because you disobeyed the teacher, you won't be going to the zoo.

**b** Looking at them, I can't tell which is which.

**c** You're acting like that because you're jealous.

**d** I won't be eating that because it's turned rotten.

**e** Drop everything and look at this amazing deal!

# INFORMATIVE TEXT
## *Review*

**WRITING WORK 1**

### Reviews
An informative **review** is a **non-fiction text** that presents details about an artistic or literary work, product, performance, business, process or system. Practically anything can be reviewed, and anyone can be a reviewer, particularly in the opinion-saturated environment of the internet.

**1** From the bank of review subjects, circle all of those that you have read, listened to or viewed.

| movies | travel destinations | recipes | tech gadgets | music |
|---|---|---|---|---|
| cosmetics | cars | books | restaurants | toys |

**2** If you were to review something or someone, what or who would it be? Perhaps you've already done so.

_______________

Give a specific reason for your choice. _______________

_______________

### Informative or persuasive?
While we are exploring informative reviews in this chapter, it is more common to encounter reviews that are persuasive, like film critiques. A review can also be primarily **informative** and partly **persuasive**. This is the case with '*Abbey Road* remastered', whose composer is 'not here to tell [the reader] how to enjoy a classic album' or whether they should buy The Beatles' music on LP. Rather, an assessment is made of the album and the box set to which it belongs, and factual information is provided about the resurgence of interest in vinyl records. While the remastered music is evaluated positively, there is no direct persuasion; we are not coerced into buying a product. The writer is 'a serious fan', not a music producer or advertiser aiming to sell records.

**3** There is often a strong link between advertising and reviews. In what ways is this evident on the internet?

_______________

### Main features of an informative review
The review of the remastered *Abbey Road* LP is intended for inclusion in a magazine or website featuring similar texts about a range of well-known albums and music acts. In it, we find the basic **features** of a **review**:

- an informative title, the name of the person or group who made the work or product (such as The Beatles) and any other basic information that the reader may find useful
- subheadings or paragraphs of information presented in a logical order
- an introductory statement that may include contextual details, statistics about the sales and success of the item, a brief anecdote and/or a reason for this review
- initial thoughts and expectations of the reviewer
- comments on the overall style and quality of production
- a detailed evaluation of some individual aspects of the work or product
- a concluding statement.

**4** What is another feature (not listed above) that you can see in the text '*Abbey Road* remastered'?

Feature: _______________ Example: _______________

### Additional features of a persuasive review
In a **persuasive review**, you are likely to encounter some or all of the following features:

- a rating (such as *4 out of 5 stars*) and/or a persuasive statement (such as *Grab it now!*)
- quotes from the composer of the work or from authoritative people about the work
- commands and imperatives (such as *Don't waste your money.*)
- emotive language and superlatives (such as *the most gorgeous version of this song you'll ever hear*)

**5** Even when expressing an opinion, it is important that we remain fair and sensible when writing a review. Reword these exaggerated, nasty or weak statements to make them more reasonable and convincing.

- **a** I'd rather die than hear this album again. ____________________
- **b** It's a miracle that The Beatles ever had fans. ____________________
- **c** I don't know why but I love this band. ____________________
- **d** If you don't buy this box set, you're stupid. ____________________

**6** Give two reasons why writing direct insults in a review might be ineffective or risky.

____________________

____________________

## Language features commonly used in reviews

- First person for most of the text
- Conditional clauses
- Second person when addressing the reader directly
- Informal (colloquial) and sometimes very casual register

## Conditional clauses

These are clauses that place limits (or conditions) on events. We often read **conditional clauses** in reviews because these texts are based on personal interests and views; those of both the composer reviewing the product and the reader considering the product. When writing these clauses, we often use the present tense as we do for time clauses. For example, *We won't go if I am tired. I'll walk to the café unless it is raining.*

**7** Complete these conditional clauses from the text '*Abbey Road* remastered'. *Hint: In the text, they may begin with a capital letter.*

- **a** you're very ____________________ it
- **b** this new pressing ____________________ you
- **c** even ____________________ *Road*

## Reviewing with authority

As we've already noted, anyone can write a review. But to write one **authoritatively**, we must:

- make reasonable and well-informed judgements, avoiding manipulation and nastiness
- give detailed explanations, examples and evidence
- use clear expression and avoid redundancy (padding and useless words)
- use jargon appropriate to the subject
- know the audience for whom we are writing, and choose details and words accordingly.

**8** The language features listed below all contribute to the tone of the text '*Abbey Road* remastered'. Complete the table. *Hint: The entire third column requires answers based on your own ideas and opinions.*

| Language feature | Example(s) from the review | Effect and/or purpose |
|---|---|---|
| contractions | **a** ____________ | **b** ____________ |
| **c** ____________ | LP, vinyl, bass line, vocals | **d** ____________ |
| statistical data | **e** ____________ | **f** ____________ |
| puns (on 'road') | **g** ____________ | **h** ____________ |

Here is a sample text showing you how to structure and write a product review.

## Tech Review: Intel NUC 6i7KYK

✱ **Write a title that is literal and contains no figurative, persuasive or rhetorical techniques.** Simply name the product and state that this is a review. In this case it is a technology ('tech') review.

Intel's super-compact NUC is what your IT friend means by *bare bone kit*. It's a semi-finished PC. But don't get bored yet. This pocket rocket computer is ready to perform, right out of the box. It has all the ports required for a keyboard, mouse and even up to three HD TVs. It offers instant connectivity and the double bonus of inbuilt wireless and Bluetooth.

✱ **Use a casual writing style to appeal to a general readership.** We detect this style when we read 'But don't get bored yet', because a conjunction begins the sentence and a contraction ('don't') is used. Create or borrow a metaphorical catchphrase to sum up the product's key qualities. A 'pocket rocket' suggests that the NUC PC is both compact and fast.

The NUC range of PC kits may have had its debut a while back, but it's only now that they are being packaged with serious graphics processing power, largely to address rampant growth across online gaming, e-sports, digital content creation and video editing.

✱ **Write an entirely informative sentence to inform readers about the product's background.** Write a detailed list to spark the interest of certain readers. In this list (from 'online gaming' to 'video editing') we read about NUC being developed due to growth in areas like 'e-sports'.

As a fully functioning, power-packed computer, the new NUC 6i7KYK has two exclusive attributes: maximum mobility and minimum visibility. It's tiny (a ludicrous 116 x 211 mm), yet by no means does this undermine its power. The NUC can breeze through most desktop applications, but it also has enough grunt to tackle some of the most popular titles in e-sports. In its earlier incarnation, the graphics processor wasn't up to a host of challenges, but this latest version boasts Iris Pro Graphics 580, which is not only exciting gamers and graphic content creators, but has massively ramped up NUC's allure in general.

✱ **Use hyphenated compound words, to help keep language usage economical.** An example here is 'power-packed'. Heighten the casual tone by using exaggeration (like 'ludicrous'), idiom (like 'breeze through') and slang (like 'grunt', meaning power). Use personification to give the product a distinct identity and to add interest to the review. We read 'this latest version boasts …'

Intel partners with resellers like MWave, Umart and JW Computers to complete the NUC with RAM, SSD and a Microsoft Windows OS. The true tech-head still enjoys the thrill of building a PC from the motherboard up, but really, you'd need to be pretty keen. The NUC offers similar build-appeal without you having to start from anywhere near scratch.

✱ **Provide information about who sells the product.** Use jargon here and elsewhere in the review to add detail and authority. We read computer jargon like 'RAM', 'SSD' and 'motherboard'. Reach out to the reader using direct address, using the second person. We see this in 'without you having to …'

While its versatility gives widespread appeal, NUC's miniscule size allows resellers to pitch it directly to a range of otherwise unreachable customers for a plethora of new applications. Digital signage at POS (point of sale), office and home entertainment are all settings where the NUC really comes into its own. Its unobtrusive, space-saving body makes it ideal for rear-mounting on displays like menus, or for use in home theatre systems.

✱ **Repeat the product's key quality using a stronger adjective than those already used.** Here, we read that the product is not just small, but 'miniscule'. List groups of adjectives before nouns to give detail. For example: 'unobtrusive, space-saving body'. Suggest one or two specific applications of the product. Here, we read about using the product in 'home theatre systems' and elsewhere.

Due in large part to the superior graphics processing of this model, two other key product markets have emerged: entry-level mainstream gaming (with a focus on PC portable gamers) and digital content creators (meaning everyone from microbloggers to newsjackers).

✱ **Use one or more technical terms that are nouns with specific meanings.** An example here is 'gaming'. Include one or more compound words with or without hyphens (such as 'entry-level' or 'newsjackers').

A surprisingly powerful GPU and CPU make this machine the little engine that could. Check out Intel's family of resellers to buy the NUC either instore or online.

✱ **Close the review by giving a concise summary of the product's key selling points.** The composer has summarised the review with a 'surprisingly powerful GPU and CPU'. Try to make a catchy allusion or create a catchphrase: here the product is described as 'the little engine that could'. Use the final sentence to remind interested readers where they can buy this product.

# INFORMATIVE TEXT

*Review*

**WRITING YOUR OWN SAMPLE**

Plan your sample on the lines provided.

- **Write a title that is literal and contains no figurative, persuasive or rhetorical techniques.** Simply name the product and state that this is a review.
- **Use a casual writing style to appeal to a general readership.** Create or borrow a metaphorical catchphrase to sum up the product's key qualities.
- **Write an entirely informative sentence to inform readers about the product's background.** Write a detailed list to spark the interest of certain readers.
- **Use hyphenated compound words, to help keep language usage economical.** Heighten the casual tone by using exaggeration, idiom and slang. Use personification to give the product a distinct identity and to add interest to the review.
- **Provide information about who sells the product.** Use jargon here and elsewhere in the review to add detail and authority. Reach out to the reader using direct address, using the second person.
- **Repeat the product's key quality using a stronger adjective than those already used.** List groups of adjectives before nouns to give detail. Suggest one or two specific applications of the product.
- **Use one or more technical terms that are nouns with specific meanings.** Include one or more compound words with or without hyphens.
- **Close the review by giving a concise summary of the product's key selling points.** Try to make a catchy allusion or create a catchphrase. Use the final sentence to remind interested readers where they can buy this product.

UNIT 3

# INFORMATIVE TEXT

## Biographical article

**READING WORK**

### Beatrix Potter

**Children's author and illustrator, 1866–1943**

Beatrix Potter is best known for creating, illustrating and writing stories about the beloved character Peter Rabbit. Born Helen Beatrix Potter on 28 July 1866 in South Kensington, England, she was the only daughter in a very conservative household. Her mother had great plans for her only daughter to enter into Victorian society and marry into a well-connected, well-moneyed family. The shy but strong-minded and artistic Beatrix tried her best to fit into society events, but she didn't belong.

The family often picnicked and holidayed in the countryside, and the young Beatrix whiled away a lot of the time sketching animals—real and imagined—in their natural setting and became 'friends' with them. She had been doodling from an early age and showed a genuine talent for it. We know from her diary that this unapologetic daydreamer was most happy in the country, and when back in her own bedroom she spent most of her time writing and illustrating stories about the adventures of her little friends, particularly a rabbit called Peter (based on her real pet buck rabbit, Peter Piper).

Generations of children have enjoyed the stories about mischievous Peter Rabbit and his adventures in Mr McGregor's garden, where he would feast on his favourite treats: lettuce and beans. Many times Peter just managed to escape under a fence or through the hedge before Mr McGregor could grab him. His sisters—Flopsy, Mopsy and Cottontail—were not nearly as daring as Peter, who was often sent to bed without his tea by his mother when he had been especially naughty and lost a button off his jacket or torn a sleeve.

Beatrix had other animal friends and wrote delightful stories about them: Jemima Puddle-Duck, Benjamin Bunny, Tabitha Twitchit, Squirrel Nutkin and Tom Kitten, to name just a few of her anthropomorphic characters. On delving into her books with their lovingly drawn illustrations, the reader can find that these characters become almost as real to them as they were to Beatrix.

*The Tale of Peter Rabbit* was her first book and was published in 1902 by F Warne & Co. After much effort and frustration, the work of this patient, tenacious woman was finally in print, but practically everyone believed the book would mark both the beginning and the end of her writing career. As it turned out, however, she continued to write, and would eventually make both herself and the Warne publishers very rich.

Beatrix Potter used her wealth for good causes, mainly in conservation work. She purchased Hill Top Farm in 1913 and married William Heelis shortly after. The couple then bought a 1900-acre sheep farm and Beatrix became a respected conservationist. Their last purchase was Castle Cottage, across the road from Hill Top, which was to be their home for thirty years.

The children's writer was elected as the first woman President of Hardwick Sheep Breeders Association, but would die in December 1943 before she could take office. After her husband died two years later, all the properties were bequeathed to the National Trust. She had continued to write about Peter Rabbit and other characters until her death. Some unpublished stories were printed after this time and new readers today are as enchanted with Potter's books as the generations of children before them. She has been lauded as one of the most successful author-illustrators of all time.

- Title lines include the **name** of the subject (that is, the person about whom the article is written), her main claim to fame and the dates of her birth and death.
- Life events are **condensed** and strung together. Details are expressed very economically.
- Unusual **verbs** create interest.
- Specific ages and dates are not always necessary in a biographical text.
- The writer takes a brief break from describing Potter's life and **celebrates** her most famous creation: Peter Rabbit.
- A **technical term** about Potter's characters adds to the authority of the article.
- Potter's first publication is noted.
- A single, simple statement **sums up** Potter's successful publishing career.
- Another **unusual detail** is provided. Because this event occurred very close to the time of Potter's death, it is of great interest to her fans.
- The article **ends in a similar way** to how it opens, about the most familiar aspect of Beatrix Potter's life.

# INFORMATIVE TEXT

## Biographical article

COMPREHENSION WORK

### Literal questions

*Hint: Read the text carefully to locate specific facts and details.*

**1** For what does the text say Beatrix Potter is best known?

**a** creating and illustrating stories **b** writing stories **c** Peter Rabbit

**2** What two important things did Potter do in one year? ____________________

**3** Using only the events and dates in this text, make a partial timeline of Beatrix Potter's life.
*Hint: Abbreviate the wording of each event to make the descriptions as brief as possible.*

____________________

### Interpretive questions

*Hint: These questions require you to combine facts and details to synthesise the meaning.*

**4** According to the text, which words best describe Peter Rabbit?

**a** lovingly-drawn, published and rich

**b** unapologetic, strong-minded and artistic

**c** naughty, daring and mischievous

**5** Which features of Potter's books are most likely to have been inspired by the countryside around her?

**a** talking animals **b** hedges and fences **c** lettuces and beans

**6** Why might Beatrix have made up animal characters with whom she became 'friends'?

____________________

**7** How old was Beatrix Potter when she was first published by F Warne & Co.? ____________________

**8** What are two likely reasons why Beatrix was elected President of the Sheep Breeders Association?

____________________

**9** Based on its use in the text, which word has the closest meaning to 'well-connected' in the first paragraph?

**a** linked **b** influential **c** strong

**10** Which of these language features are frequently used in the text to inform the reader about Beatrix Potter?

**a** adjectives, common nouns and lists **b** adverbs, similes and questions

**c** onomatopoeia, meter and rhyme

### Applied questions

*Hint: These questions require you to understand a text's implications to infer meaning from the text.*

**11** In the context of the text, 'society' refers to the upper classes and to circles of privileged people who tend to value money, fashion and gossip very highly. Why do you think Beatrix 'didn't belong' in 'society'?

____________________

**12** This text is from a biography website. Which of these other contexts would it best suit?

**a** as a poster in the young children's section of a library

**b** as a short feature article in a nature magazine

**c** as a speech in British parliament

# INFORMATIVE TEXT

## Biographical article

## SPELLING WORK

### List Words

*All of the words in the box below appear in the text 'Beatrix Potter'.*

| | | | | |
|---|---|---|---|---|
| countryside | delightful | treasured | anthropomorphic | acre |
| beloved | illustrations | beginning | conservation | delving |
| wealth | bequeathed | enchanted | unapologetic | career |

**1** Using the line provided, correct the misspelt word in each sentence.

**a** The beloved character of Peter Rabitt has enchanted generations of children. ____________

**b** Beatrix Potter bequethed most of her money to conservation societies. ____________

**c** When reading about anthromorphic characters, we need to suspend our disbelief.

____________

**d** Beatrix Potter was unapolagetic about pursuing a writing career. ____________

**e** To a city-dweller, an acre of land probally seems like a small country. ____________

**f** Most people today are more intrested in conversation than conservation. ____________

**2** One word in each set below is not a real word. Cross it out. *Hint: Each set is derived from a list word.*

| | | |
|---|---|---|
| **a** anthropomorphism | anthropologist | anthropographer |
| **b** enchantful | enchanter | enchantingly |
| **c** illustrative | illustrationer | illustrational |
| **d** conservationist | conservative | conservatious |

**3** Add letters before or after these word portions to form complete words.

| | | |
|---|---|---|
| **a** ____________ nicked | **b** ____________ ural | **c** dayd ____________ |
| **d** ____________ cters | **e** ____________ thor | **f** ____________ rty |
| **g** ten ____________ | **h** ____________ eve | **i** ____________ eyed |

**4** Add three letters to the beginning or the end of a list word to make

**a** an adverb meaning 'without being sorry.' ____________

**b** a synonym for 'disillusioned.' ____________

**c** a noun meaning 'someone who protects and preserves.' ____________

**d** a noun meaning 'an area of land.' ____________

**e** a present tense verb meaning 'moving quickly and out of control.' ____________

**Compound words** are made up of two or more words that can also stand alone, such as *flowerpot.* Some compound words are hyphenated, such as *power-hungry.* Compound words without hyphens are called closed compound words. Increasingly, hyphens are being dropped from common compound words. Many closed compound words were once hyphenated, such as *bumblebee, today, wetsuit, crybaby, leapfrog.*

**5** **a** Join word halves to make five closed compound words. Write them on the line, separated by commas. *Hints: Hyphens are not required. Only one compound word can be found in the list words.*

| | | | | |
|---|---|---|---|---|
| country | lunch | side | free | day |
| fall | birth | week | box | end |

____________

**b** Write another three closed compound words. ____________

# INFORMATIVE TEXT
## *Biographical article*

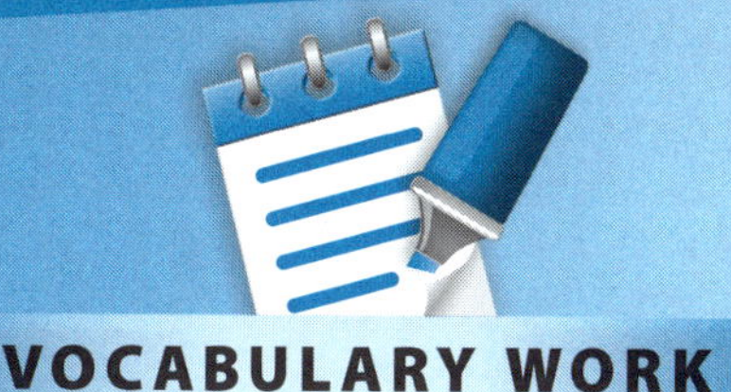

## VOCABULARY WORK

**1** The answers to these questions are all found in the list words.

**a** Which adjective can be used to describe Beatrix Potter's charming illustrations? ____________

**b** Name three land-related nouns. ____________

**c** Find two synonyms associated with affection. ____________

**d** Which word means the same as 'unashamed'? ____________

**e** What is a verb meaning 'donated'? ____________

A key technical term**, anthropomorphism**, is used in the article about Beatrix Potter to add to the credibility of the information. This literary and artistic technique involves giving animals human qualities, such as speech, clothing and houses. Beatrix Potter's characters, including Peter Rabbit, are anthropomorphic because they dress and behave like humans. **Zoomorphism** works in the reverse: the composer gives animal characteristics to humans and non-human things. For example, calling a timid person a *mouse* is a zoomorphic image.

**2** Write *A* or *Z* beside each example to show whether it can be categorised as anthropomorphism or zoomorphism. *Hint: Peter Rabbit and Beatrix Potter's other animal characters are anthropomorphic.*

| Example | A or Z? |
|---|---|
| **a** I sing in the shadow of [God's] wings (Psalm 63:7). | ______ |
| **b** Nick Bottom becomes a donkey in Shakespeare's *A Midsummer Night's Dream.* | ______ |
| **c** A corrupt government is run by pigs in George Orwell's *Animal Farm.* | ______ |
| **d** My brother eats like a horse. | ______ |
| **e** A toad drives a car and a mole rides a horse in Kenneth Grahame's *The Wind in the Willows.* | ______ |
| **f** Walt Disney's Mickey Mouse dances and sings songs. | ______ |
| **g** The ocean roars. | ______ |

Small groups (also called **stems** or **roots**) of words inside larger English words often come from Latin or Greek. Knowing what word roots mean can help a lot with extending our vocabulary.

**3** Write words containing Greek roots by completing the blanks below.

**a** *Anthropomorphism* contains two Greek roots: *anthro* (meaning *human*) and *morph* (meaning *shape*).

anthro__________gy    ph______anthro_____    morph______g    m_______morph_____is

**b** *Biography* and *autobiography* are non-fiction texts about people's lives. These words contain the Greek roots *bio* (meaning 'life') and auto (meaning 'self').

autom_______c    autom________le    bio______c    bio_____gy

A **suffix** is a group of letters that ends a word. Changing a word's suffix changes its meaning, tense or part of speech. For example, when the suffix *ly* is added to the adjective *quick* it becomes the adverb *quickly.*

**4** Connect these suffixes with their meanings by drawing lines. There are two sets of suffixes and meanings.

**Set 1**

| Suffix | Meaning |
|---|---|
| **a** *ed* | full of |
| **b** *ful* | with the features of |
| **c** *ic* | verb form |
| **d** *ing* | past tense |

**Set 2**

| Suffix | Meaning |
|---|---|
| **a** *less* | native of |
| **b** *ous* | capable of |
| **c** *able* | with the qualities of |
| **d** *ese* | without |

# INFORMATIVE TEXT

## *Biographical article*

**GRAMMAR WORK**

### Tense

**Tense** tells us whether events (shown as **verbs** in sentences) belong in the **past**, **present** or **future**. Did you know there are at least a dozen different tenses? This is because there are four types of each main tense: simple, perfect, continuous and perfect continuous. Here are just three definitions from the world of tenses:

- The simple past tense is used to describe things that have happened and are no longer occurring. For example, *My grandfather* died *in 1999*.
- The present perfect tense is used when an action started in the past but is still happening or relevant. It combines the word *have* or *has* with a past participle. For example, *We* have lived *here for thirty years*.
- The future continuous tense links an action in the future to another action or time. It combines *will, be* and a present participle (with the suffix *ing*). For example, *I* will be flying *to New York on Thursday*.

**1** Complete these statements about tense to show your understanding.

**a** There are ____________ main types of tense. **b** A present participle ends with ____________.

**c** ______________________________ tense links the past with the present.

### Which tense?

Because it is usually chronological (in a timeline-based order), most of the material in a biographical article—especially one about a person from history who has died—is written in the **past tense**. Some situations require the use of a certain tense. For instance, when analysing literature, we imagine that time is suspended. Literature exists in its own **timeless present**, so it is usually discussed using the present tense. For example, *Shakespeare often alludes to the Bible in his plays.* Of course, there are always exceptions, such as the references to Peter Rabbit's escapades in the biographical article. The past tense works better in that instance.

The most important tense rule is **consistency**. It is easy to slip in and out of tenses, and you must be keenly aware of this when writing. For example, this sentence might seem correct at first glance: *If the sun would just come out, we can go swimming.* But it should read: *If the sun would just come out, we could go swimming.*

**2** Change these words from the biographical article from past to present tense or from present to past tense.

**a** enchanted ______________________ **b** delving ______________________

**c** treasured ______________________ **d** bequeathed ______________________

**e** beginning ______________________ **f** whiled ______________________

**3** This passage is meant to be entirely in the present tense. Circle all of the inconsistent uses of tense.

Dear Diary … Now I wandered over the hills again, and gaze with delight upon the endless array of greens that stretched from the McGregor farm to the horizon. It will have been a constant source of inspiration to me, this landscape. I am never tiring of its wonders. Its tiny residents, while they weren't much troubled by me, showing some interest in my presence and popped their dear little noses in and out of their holes as I passed.

Deciding where **commas** should be used in sentences can be tricky. As a result, some people overuse them so their sentences end up looking cluttered and awkward. Others go by the rule 'when in doubt, leave it out'.

**4** This passage has been taken directly from the text 'Beatrix Potter'. Mark all of the unnecessary commas.

After much effort, and frustration, the work of this patient, tenacious, woman was finally in print, but practically everyone believed, the book would mark both the beginning, and the end of her writing career. As it turned out, however, she continued, to write, and would eventually make both herself, and the Warne publishers, very rich.

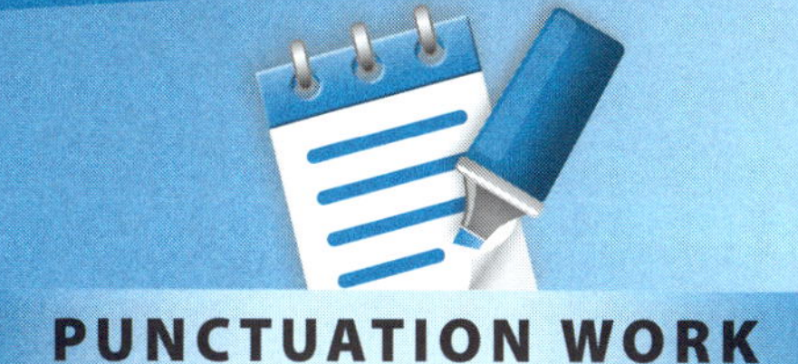

# INFORMATIVE TEXT

## Biographical article

## PUNCTUATION WORK

### Commas

The **comma** is one of the most commonly used punctuation marks. Its chief purpose, in all situations, is **separation**. Under this general function, however, are many usage rules. Just some of these are listed below.

- Use commas to separate words and groups of words in a list of three or more items. For example, *My favourite clothes are cardigans, vests, tight jeans and op-shop dresses.*
- Separate adjectives in lists using commas. For example, *He is a sincere, smart, capable man.*
- Do not use a comma instead of a full stop, or the result will be a comma splice. For example, *Dogs are always excited at the beach, they love running on sand.* This comma splice can be fixed by replacing the comma with a full stop or semicolon, adding a conjunction or dropping the comma and replacing *they* with *and.*
- When using a dependent clause at the start of a sentence, place a comma after it. For example, *If you have any questions, don't hesitate to ask.*
- Place a comma after a single word that introduces a sentence. For example, *No, I don't think you can.*
- Separate cities from states or countries using commas. For example, *He's from Mt Isa, Queensland.*
- Use a comma to introduce or interrupt a piece of direct speech. For example, *Anna yelled, 'Get out!'*
- End a quotation with a comma if it comes before the speaker and/or manner of speech. For example, *'We can go if you like,' Mum shrugged.* Exceptions are when a question mark or exclamation mark is required. For example, *'You have no idea how angry I am!' fumed Iggy.*

**1** Insert commas correctly into these sentences. *Hint: Use the rules listed above as you complete the task.*

**a** Beatrix Potter was feisty funny and fearless.

**b** Popular for many decades the *Peter Rabbit* books are still best-sellers.

**c** Born in Kensington England Beatrix Potter showed artistic talent at an early age.

**d** 'Go back to your room Beatrix' insisted her mother but the fearless young lady marched right past her.

**2** This passage has not been taken from the text, but it is about the same subject. It contains no commas. Insert the commas where they are missing. *Hint: No other punctuation corrections are required.*

Beatrix Potter one of Britain's most admired children's author-illustrators inspired women of her day to pursue their career goals and she continues to do so today. She is celebrated not only for her talent but also for her tenacity and perseverance making her a heroine for many girls with an interest in earning a living from art. Potter's creativity childlike imagination and sparkling originality make her an enduringly popular composer.

A stumbling block for beginning writers is knowing which words to **capitalise**. Test yourself on this punctuation skill by completing the following task. You will need to look back at the text for the context of each word or phrase, which will indicate whether or not capital letters are needed.

**3** Circle each word or phrase requiring capital letters, based on its context in the biographical article.

| william | victorian | illustrator | castle cottage | career | hill top farm |
|---|---|---|---|---|---|
| sheep farm | national trust | writing | natural setting | family | tom kitten |

**4** Circle any incorrect uses of capital letters in these sentences. *Hint: This passage includes omitted capital letters.*

**a** My Great Aunt madge says I'm a Great writer.

**b** Beatrix Potter married William Heelis in 1913.

**c** Peter rabbit wore a blue jacket.

**d** The potter family enjoyed the English Countryside.

**e** Beatrix's Stories were published by F. Warne & co.

**f** The Buck Rabbit Peter Piper inspired Beatrix.

# INFORMATIVE TEXT

WRITING WORK 1

## Biographical articles

A **biographical article** is a **non-fiction** informative text that provides life details about a **real person**, living or deceased. This person is called the **subject** of the article. Biographical texts come in many forms, including feature articles in magazines and e-zines, full-length books and even poems of honour and celebration, such as odes and elegies. The text about Beatrix Potter is intended for inclusion in a book or website of similar texts about a range of well-known people. In article form, these are the basic features of a biography:

- a literal, informative title
- date and place of birth
- date of death if applicable
- main career and life achievements
- education
- family and personal life
- quotes by or about the subject
- a selection of little-known facts.

Biographical articles also commonly include at least one picture as a point of reference.

## Tense in biographical articles

As we noted in the Grammar Work section on page 25, most of the material in a **biographical article** about a person from history is written in the **past tense**. If, however, the subject is alive at the time of writing, the article may be written in a variety of tenses. The composer may begin in the present tense to introduce the subject, then move to the past tense as events from the subject's background are recounted, then include some statements in the future tense as the subject's plans or upcoming projects are mentioned, and then perhaps sum up and close in the present tense.

**1** Rewrite each excerpt from the biographical article based on the tense instructions provided.

| Excerpt | Rewrite in | |
|---|---|---|
| **a** Beatrix Potter is best known for | Past tense | ________________ |
| **b** children have enjoyed | Present tense | ________________ |
| **c** the reader can find | Past tense | ________________ |
| **d** before Mr McGregor could grab him | Future tense | ________________ |

**2** Complete the table about types of tense by writing the missing content into the empty cells.

| Main tense | Specific tense | Example from the biographical text |
|---|---|---|
| **Past** | **a** S________________ past | 'Her mother had great plans' |
| | **b** Past ________________t | 'She had continued to write' |
| | Past continuous | **c** 'she spent most of her time ________________' |
| | Past perfect continuous | **d** ________________ doodling |
| **Present** | Simple present | **e** 'We know ________________' |
| | **f** Present ________________c | **g** '________________ as one of the most successful author-illustrators' |

# INFORMATIVE TEXT

## *Biographical article*

### Writing an effective biographical article

Compared to finding content, it can be a more difficult task deciding what to leave out of this kind of text. Selecting life events and personal details will depend on the subject of the article, and what they are best known for. For example, a **biographical article** about a famous actor should focus on their most well-known roles on the stage and/or screen. It will also interest readers, however, to learn about the subject's other talents or interests. If the subject is involved in charity work or known as a philanthropist (someone who gives large amounts of money and aid to those in need), readers will enjoy reading about these things.

To ensure that a biographical article is effective, we must:

- know the audience for whom we are writing, and choose details and words accordingly
- judiciously (with great care) select facts to reveal about the subject
- use language economically, providing only the most essential details
- limit our use of figurative and emotive language.

**3** Why is it important to limit figurative and emotive language when writing a biographical article?

___

### Adding interest to a biographical text

To add interest to a **biographical text**, we can:

- divide the information under subheadings
- provide captioned graphics (photographs, illustrations or other visual aids) related to the main events
- frame the information by providing selected details about the historical and/or cultural context
- intersperse the information with quotes from texts written by or about the subject
- include both positive and negative experiences and events in the subject's life
- offer suggestions about further reading or internet links.

**4** What are three main events in the article about Beatrix Potter that would best suit captioned graphics?

___

**5** Apart from a picture of Beatrix Potter, what is an effective image that could be used to headline the article?

___

**6** The features listed in the table below all contribute to the interest, clarity and detail of the text about Beatrix Potter. Complete the table by writing content into the empty cells. There are no set answers.

| Feature | Example from the text | Effect/Purpose |
|---|---|---|
| **a** dated events | | |
| **b** adjectives about the subject (Beatrix Potter) | | |
| **c** little-known facts | | |
| **d** dashes used as parentheses | | |

# INFORMATIVE TEXT

## *Biographical article*

WRITING SAMPLE

Here is a sample text showing you how to structure and write a biographical article.

| Sample text | Notes |
| --- | --- |
| **JK Rowling**<br>**Author 1965–** | **Write the title lines, which include the subject's name, date of birth and what he or she is famous for.** Title lines are literal and simple. At the time of writing, Rowling was still alive, which is why a dash follows her birth date. |
|  | **Insert a recent picture of the subject.** A recent picture of JK Rowling (at the time when the article was written) is included for the reader's reference. |
| Joanne Rowling (pronounced *roll-ing*), known as 'Jo', was born on 31 July 1965 in Gloucestershire, England. The writing career of the wildly successful *Harry Potter* creator began with a novel called *Rabbit*. She wrote it at the age of six. Early in life, Jo showed ability as a student of English and other languages, and later studied French at university. | **Begin with a statement about the birth of the subject.** Include the date, place and full birth name. Make a note on a highly relevant topic that will anchor the rest of the article. We learn that Rowling wrote her first 'novel' as a child. |
| After her mother's death, Jo moved to Portugal for a new start and worked as a teacher. She had a brief and volatile marriage to Jorge Arantes, and the pair had a daughter, Jessica. Rowling returned to Britain when the marriage ended. She was unemployed and suffered financial hardship for some time while a single parent. | **Describe key moments in the subject's life and break them into chronological chunks that are easy for the reader to follow.** Choose the most important events to include and express each one economically to save words. |
| The first book in the *Harry Potter* series, *Harry Potter and the Philosopher's Stone,* was written by Rowling at a café table while her infant daughter napped beside her. Jo has been quoted as saying that 'there's always room for a story that can transport people to another place', and while the *Harry Potter* series certainly proves that this is the case, Jo also benefited from this truth herself while crafting her first novel at the lowest period in her life. Writing lifted her morale and gave her back some momentum after enduring some very tough times, including her mother's death, the collapse of her marriage, financial stress and depression. | **Provide facts about the subject's main claim to fame near the beginning of the article.** These details would be of great interest to Rowling's fans. Include a quote (preferably by the subject). The biographer has showed how it is relevant on different levels. Mention the subject's personal experience. Rowling's experience gives the reader a sense that they are really getting to know their heroine by reading this text. |
| The first *Harry Potter* book was turned down by no fewer than twelve publishers and, considering the money-making machine that the series was destined to be, this would become a major regret for all of them. The book was eventually bought by Bloomsbury for a very modest sum in 1997 and the published author JK Rowling was born. With no middle name of her own, she borrowed the 'K' from her grandmother, Kathleen. | **Include one or two surprising facts.** We read about the multiple rejections of *Harry Potter* by publishers. Give some other interesting information about the subject, such as their stage name or pen name. Here we read of Rowling's pen name (the name under which she publishes books). |
| From this moment, Jo's life took a dramatic upturn. The tales of Harry's wizarding adventures would go on to become the biggest-selling book series of all time (also a movie franchise) and make Jo Rowling one of the wealthiest people on earth. | **Use the subject's first name and surname at different times, depending on the context.** The subject's first name (Jo) and surname (Rowling) are used in different situations. In the first sentence here, her life is more the focus than her books, so she is called 'Jo'. |
| Not one to forget her humble roots, and having a keen empathy for people in financial and other distress, Jo Rowling is known as one of the world's most generous philanthropists and has lost her billionaire status because she has given so much money to those in need. | **Conclude the article with a brief note or epilogue.** Use a different topic from the subject's main claim to fame. The article's conclusion has nothing to do with *Harry Potter*. This change of direction still engrosses fans of the books because it shows a different side to the author and celebrates one of her qualities. |

# INFORMATIVE TEXT

## *Biographical article*

**WRITING YOUR OWN SAMPLE**

Plan your sample on the lines provided.

- **Write the title lines, which include the subject's name, date of birth and what he or she is famous for.** If the person has died, also include a death date. If not, follow the birth date with a dash.
- **Insert a recent picture of the subject.** If they have died, use the most recognisable image of them that you can find.
- **Begin with a statement about the birth of the subject.** Make a note on a highly relevant topic that will anchor the rest of the article..
- **Describe key moments in the subject's life and break them into chronological chunks that are easy for the reader to follow.** Choose the most important events to include, and express each one economically to save words. You will need to leave a lot out.
- **Provide facts about the subject's main claim to fame near the beginning of the article.** These details must be of great interest to fans of the subject. Include a quote. If possible, show how it is relevant on different levels. Mention the subject's personal experience. This gives the reader a sense that they are really getting to know their hero or heroine by reading this text.
- **Include one or two surprising facts.** Give some other interesting information about the subject, such as their stage name or pen name.
- **Use the subject's first name and surname at different times, depending on the context.**
- **Conclude the article with a brief note or epilogue.** This change of direction should show a different side to the subject and celebrate one of their qualities.

UNIT 4

# INFORMATIVE TEXT

## *Procedure*

READING WORK

### Make your own modelling clay

*Making your own unique, durable clay trinkets and accessories doesn't need to be expensive. Try this simple craft 'recipe' and you might just be hooked!*

**Ingredients**

½ cup cornflour
1 cup bicarb soda (baking soda)
¾ cup water

**Method**

1. Mix cornflour and soda in a medium/large saucepan.
2. Gradually add water and mix well. Ensure there are no lumps of flour.
3. Turn stove heat to medium.
4. Cook the mixture, stirring occasionally, until it nears boiling point. Continue cooking until it resembles pale clay/modelling dough.
   Note: It will look like mashed potato for a while. Don't be alarmed! Keep stirring.
5. Remove clay from pot and leave on a plate or board to cool.
6. Knead clay until smooth and pliable.
7. Model clay into shapes as desired.
8. Optional: Press decorative heatproof objects (e.g. shells, metal pieces, thick glass beads) into the clay.
9. Air-dry clay shapes in a just-warm oven (on 'keep warm' setting or max. 100 °C) for approx. ½ hour or until white and hardened.
10. Remove shapes from oven and leave to cool.
11. Paint and decorate.

Hint: If you are planning to string or hang your clay shapes, remember to pierce holes in them before drying!

- A simple, **literal** title identifies what **type** of procedure this is.
- An **introduction** elaborates on the **purpose** of this procedure.
- **Ingredients** are listed.
- **Abbreviations** are used throughout the procedure.
- A series of **steps** shows how to complete the procedure.
- **Economical language** is used. Here, 'the' is omitted.
- A **note** explains why the procedure may not seem to work at first.
- Steps are **divided** into brief, simple instructions to avoid confusion.
- An **optional step** is suggested.
- An **explanation** of a term ('just-warm') is given.
- The **absence of elaboration** allows the reader or user of the procedure to decide how this step will be done.

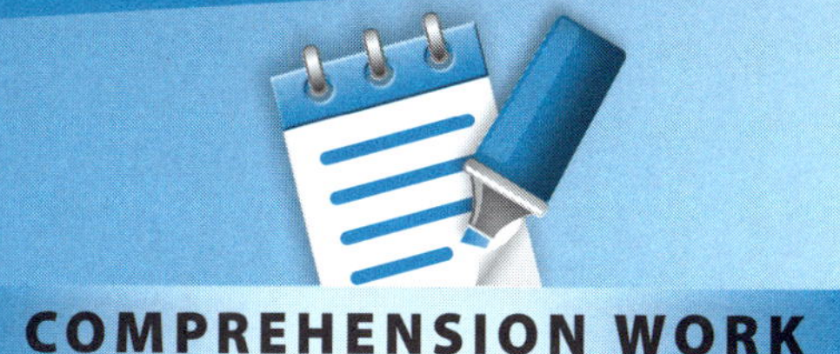

## Literal questions

*Hint: Read the text carefully to locate specific facts and details.*

**1** What is a synonym for bicarb soda?

**a** cornflour **b** soda **c** baking soda

**2** What is the usual maximum temperature of an oven's 'keep warm' setting? ______

**3** What are three things that might indicate that the clay is set?

______ ______ ______

## Interpretive questions

*Hint: These questions require you to combine facts and details to synthesise the meaning.*

**4** In Step 7, what is the best substitute for the word 'model'?

**a** sample **b** construction **c** shape

**5** From its use in the context, what word does the forward slash ( / ) represent?

**a** or **b** and **c** but

**6** Why is the word 'recipe' in quote marks in the introduction to the procedure?

______

**7** What are two adverbs in Step 2 that the reader should note to 'ensure there are no lumps of flour'?

______

**8** What are three aspects of this procedure that are optional or based on the reader's own ideas?

______ ______ ______

**9** Based on its use in the text, which word has the closest meaning to the word 'trinkets'?

**a** accessories **b** clay **c** craft

**10** Which of the following is a list of clay items that the reader may make using this procedure?

**a** models, shapes, paints

**b** trinkets, accessories, hanging objects

**c** shells, metal pieces, glass beads

## Applied questions

*Hint: These questions require you to understand a text's implications to infer meaning from the text.*

**11** What are two things that suggest this procedure is not targeted at children?

______ ______

**12** Which of the following would be the most appropriate addition to this procedure text?

**a** an advertisement for ovens

**b** a link to a procedure for making clay jewellery

**c** a picture of shells on a beach

# INFORMATIVE TEXT
## Procedure

## SPELLING WORK

### List Words

All of the words in the box below appear in the text 'Make your own modelling clay'.

| durable | accessories | recipe | cornflour | saucepan |
|---|---|---|---|---|
| gradually | modelling | occasionally | smooth | heatproof |
| pierce | stirring | ensure | dough | pliable |

**1** Cross out the word that does not fit in each sentence.

**a** Making accessorise / accessories from clay is a cheaper option than buying them.

**b** When buying an expensive product, always keep the recipe / receipt.

**c** It is important to ensure / insure your child's safety around the oven.

**d** Clay is required to make a pottery piece / pierce.

**e** Keep string / stirring to get a smooth consistency.

**f** I'm not sure if this paint is durable / endurable enough.

The **spelling of some words containing *l* and ending in *ing*** varies between countries. For example, in the USA a single *l* is often used instead of a double. Most British spellings of words containing *l* and *ing* are the same as Australian ones.

**2** Circle the British/Australian spelling of these words. *Hint: Some words are fake and not used in any country.*

**a** travelling traveling
**b** ailing ailling
**c** totalling totaling
**d** modeling modelling
**e** rolling roling
**f** fledgling fledglling

You have probably heard the ***i* before *e* rule** before but more often than not, some of the rule is left out. This means that there are so many exceptions to the rule that it becomes almost useless. The actual rule is: *i* before *e* except after *c* with the sound of 'ee'. When this full rule is applied, there are far fewer exceptions.

**3** Using the full *i* before *e* rule, write *i* and *e* in the correct places to complete the partial words below. *Hint: Check for* c *with the sound of 'ee' (as in 'deceive'). Words containing* ch *do not have this sound.*

**a** I will p _ _ rce my ears.
**b** It is more rewarding to give than rec _ _ ve.
**c** Th _ _ ves broke into my house.
**d** That is an amazing ach _ _ vement!
**e** I bel _ _ve your story.
**f** The police ch _ _ f had great authority.
**g** My c _ _ ling leaks when it rains.
**h** Have another p _ _ ce of cake.

**4** Reshuffle the letters to form list words.

**a** snuree ________________
**b** ughdo ________________
**c** poforhate ________________
**d** recipe ________________

**5** Cross out the mismatching word in each trio below to leave pairs of homophones (words that sound exactly the same). *Hint: The letters gh can make different sounds in different words.*

**a** bough borrow bow
**b** rough ruff rouge
**c** through threw trough
**d** draft drought draught
**e** flue flew flow
**f** dough do doe

# INFORMATIVE TEXT

## Procedure

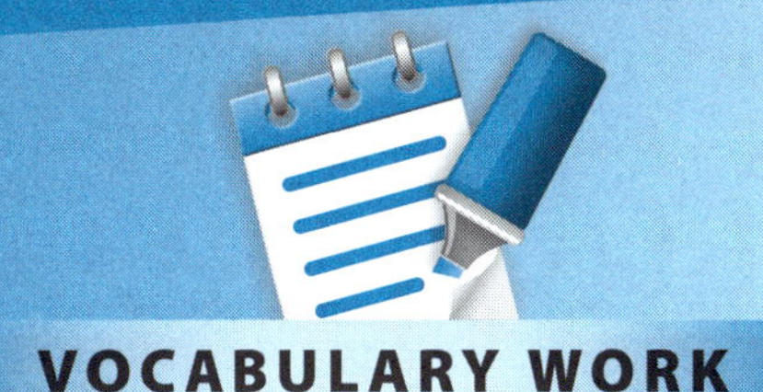

**VOCABULARY WORK**

### Adjectives

In narrative and persuasive texts, **adjectives** are used to create interest and impact. In informative texts, however, adjectives are more likely to be used for explanatory and clarifying purposes, to increase the likelihood that the procedure will work. We see this in the text 'Make your own modelling clay'.

**1** Fill in the blanks to complete adjectives from the text 'Make your own modelling clay'.
*Hints: Adjectives describe nouns. Some adjectives are words that can also be used as verbs.*

**a** h _ _ _ p _ _ _ _ **b** m _ _ _ ed **c** ha _ _ _ _ ed

**d** w _ _ t _ **e** s _ _ _ th **f** al _ _ _ _ d

**g** pa _ _ **h** _ _ _ _ _ ling **i** pl _ _ _ _ _

**2** Define these adjectives based on their use in the text 'Make your own modelling clay'. Give full meanings.

**a** expensive ____________________

**b** unique ____________________

**c** smooth ____________________

**d** decorative ____________________

**e** optional ____________________

Many words that are **nouns can also function as verbs**. To further complicate things, many of these nouns are also adjectives.

**3** Circle the words that can function as either a noun or a verb. *Hint: All of these words appear in the text.*

| | | | | |
|---|---|---|---|---|
| model | smooth | object | stirring | shape |
| lumps | mixture | warm | cook | craft |

**Synonyms** (words that share a similar meaning) do not need to be the same part of speech. Often the same word can be a noun, verb, and/or adjective.

**4** Each set of words below contains three synonyms. Circle the mismatching word in each set.

| | | | |
|---|---|---|---|
| **a** nears | reaches | accepts | approaches |
| **b** cooking | stirring | blending | mixing |
| **c** plan | fashion | shape | model |
| **d** construct | craft | consider | assemble |
| **e** pliable | washable | malleable | elastic |

**5** For each list word below, write one or two synonyms, depending on how many empty cells are provided. Some synonyms have been provided. *Hint: This question increases in difficulty with each word.*

| List word | Synonym | Synonym |
|---|---|---|
| **a** recipe | | |
| **b** durable | | lasting |
| **c** saucepan | | vessel |
| **d** occasionally | | |
| **e** ensure | | ascertain |

# INFORMATIVE TEXT

## Procedure

GRAMMAR WORK

### Abbreviations

**Abbreviations** are **shortened words** and terms. There are many types and purposes of abbreviations, including:

- measurements and quantities
- titles and qualifications
- months and days
- jargon and slang.

Abbreviations can be created by:

- simply cutting a word short or condensing it (such as *vs* or *v* for *versus*)
- using a full stop (.) to shorten a word or phrase (such as *beg.* for *beginning* or *etc.* for *et cetera*)
- telescoping a phrase into a single word, with or without a hyphen (such as *sci-fi* for *science fiction* and *smog* for *smoke and fog*)
- initialising a title, term or phrase (such as *PM* for *Prime Minister* or *GP* for *general practitioner*)
- converting words into numbers (such as ¾ for *three-quarters*).

**1** Give an example of an abbreviation, including its full form, in each category below.

| Category | Abbreviation | Full form |
|---|---|---|
| **a** measurement | ______ | ______ |
| **b** month | ______ | ______ |
| **c** day | ______ | ______ |
| **d** title | ______ | ______ |
| **e** slang | ______ | ______ |

**2** Expand each of these common abbreviations into its full form.

**a** cm ______ **b** Q. ______

**c** tsp ______ **d** ASAP ______

**e** cont. ______ **f** brunch ______

**g** 1st ______ **h** romcom ______

**3** These abbreviations all appear in the procedure 'Make your own modelling clay'. Express them in full.

**a** max. 100 °C ______

**b** ¾ cup water ______

**c** approx. ½ hour ______

**Text speak** is a whole language of different abbreviations. In this age of electronic and online communications, we use these abbreviations very frequently, particularly when creating basic informative texts. This is a point of contention for English sticklers, who often complain that such uses of abbreviations are destroying the language. On the other side of the debate, keen abbreviators argue that as long as they (and their audience) understand the meaning of what is being said, there is no harm done.

**4** Identify the meaning of each abbreviation below according to the way it is commonly used today.

**a** IMO ______ **b** 143 ______

**c** thx ______ **d** gr8 ______

**e** b4 ______ **f** CYA ______

**g** ppl ______ **h** YOLO ______

# INFORMATIVE TEXT

## Procedure

**PUNCTUATION WORK**

### Full stops

You will be very familiar with the use of the **full stop** (also called a full point or period) in sentences, since it appears at the end of many of them. Apart from ending a sentence, a full stop also abbreviates a word or phrase (such as *Feb.* for *February* and *est.* for *established in* or *estimated to be*).

We use many Latin words and phrases in English because much of our language comes from Latin. While many of these words have been absorbed into the language, others remain in their original form. Some of these are used as abbreviations. In the points above, the example *MD* was given. The full Latin term for which this stands is *medicinae doctor,* meaning 'teacher of medicine.'

**1** Here are some commonly used Latin abbreviations which are often written containing one or two full stops. The Latin words are provided. You need to provide the meaning of each abbreviation.

| Abbreviation | Latin words | Meaning |
|---|---|---|
| **a** e.g. | *exempli gratia* | ______________________ |
| **b** i.e. | *id est* | ______________________ |
| **c** c. | *circa* | ______________________ |
| **d** p.a. | *per annum* | ______________________ |
| **e** etc. | *et cetera* | ______________________ |

You already know that, when **ending a sentence with a question mark (?) or an exclamation mark (!)** we omit the full stop, but did you know that the same rule applies when either of those marks is attached to a word, a title or a piece of direct speech? Look at the examples below for an explanation.

Correct: I've always used the search engine Yahoo! Incorrect: I've always used the search engine Yahoo!.

Correct: You were great in the play *Whassup, Doc?* Incorrect: You were great in the play *Whassup, Doc?*.

**2** Circle any incorrect uses of full stops in these sentences. *Hint: This includes incorrectly omitted full stops.*

- **a** Once upon a time. There were three little foxes who lived in a burrow.
- **b** In this procedure, the mixture must be reheated. Not once. But twice.
- **c** The prime minister both began and ended her speech by exclaiming. 'Freedom!'
- **d** Rubbing her arms vigorously, she asked, 'Why is it so cold in here?'.
- **e** For example. The colour blue represents calm

**3** Look again at these uses of the full stop in the text 'Make your own modelling clay' and write the function of each one. *Hint: There are three different functions. Two will be used more than once in your answers.*

- **a** 9. ______________________
- **b** approx. ______________________
- **c** leave to cool. ______________________
- **d** max. 100 °C ______________________
- **e** Keep stirring. ______________________

# INFORMATIVE TEXT

*Procedure*

**WRITING WORK 1**

## Procedures

A **procedure** is an **informative text** that provides clear, easy-to-follow steps that result in a particular outcome or product. A common type of procedure is a recipe. The text 'Make your own modelling clay' is very similar in style and structure to a recipe, but the product is a craft item. Increasingly, the most likely place where a craft procedure like the sample text is found is online. People with common craft interests share their ideas and creations in procedure texts for free, or sometimes for a small fee. Other contexts where craft procedures are found include printed publications like hobby books and leisure magazines.

Aside from craft and cooking, a procedure can be written to explain to the reader how to make or do almost anything. For example, game rules, instruction manuals and experiment guidelines are all procedure texts.

## Main features of a procedure

The basic features of any procedure text are:

- a literal, informative title
- a logical structure, including subheadings and clear steps (preferably numbered)
- a progression of actions or a method leading to the outcome or product named in the title
- limited use of the definite article (*the*)
- the simple present tense
- assumed knowledge of some informative and economical language features (such as measurements and abbreviations); key procedural words (such as *ingredients* and *method*); standard equipment relevant to the type of procedure (such as *saucepan* and *oven*); and key verbs commonly used in procedures (such as *stir* and *cook*).

**1** Look back at the text 'Make your own modelling clay' and briefly summarise the method.

______________________________________________

______________________________________________

## Writing an effective procedure

To ensure that a procedure is effective, we must:

- use language economically, providing only the most essential details
- use clear expression, accurate punctuation and consistent simple present tense
- use action verbs
- give factual descriptions
- avoid employing figurative language unless necessary (for example, the simile 'It will look like mashed potato for a while' in the text is helpful and specific—it is the only use of figurative language in the whole text).

**2** Why is it important to use language economically in a procedure?

______________________________________________

**3** How would the text be different if it was written for children under 10 years of age?
*Hint: Look back at Comprehension Work Questions 8 and 11 for ideas.*

______________________________________________

## Adding interest to a procedure

To add interest, clarity and detail to a procedure text, we can:

- include a brief **introduction** (this is the case in the main procedure in this unit but not the sample procedure)
- add explanatory **pictures** or diagrams and provide optional extra steps or hints
- occasionally use a **conversational tone** that addresses the reader in a friendly manner (for example, 'Don't be alarmed!').

# INFORMATIVE TEXT
## *Procedure*

The text 'Make your own modelling clay' contains a number of specific language features that are well suited to the informative text form of procedure.

**4** Complete this table by writing the missing content in the white cells. *Hint: Use the text's annotations.*

| | Feature | Example(s) from the text | Effect in the text |
|---|---|---|---|
| Elements of informative language | action verbs | **a** | **Specific action verbs** help the reader understand precisely what to do in the procedure. |
| | **b** s________<br>p________<br>t________ | 'Ensure there are no lumps of flour.'<br>'Leave on a plate or board to cool' | This mode of expression is the best one for giving instructions. It gives the procedure **immediacy** and helps the reader understand what to do at each stage of the procedure. |
| | **c** p________ words | 'Ingredients'<br>'Method' | These informative words provide **structure** and distinguish between what materials are needed and what to do with them. |
| Elements of economical language | abbreviations | **d** | These keep the procedure **uncluttered** and easy to read. Because the readers of a procedure text are likely to be familiar with common procedure abbreviations, it saves them reading time when abbreviations are used. |
| | measurements | '¾ cup'<br>'½ hour' | **e** |
| | limited use of the definite article (*the*) | **f** | Limiting use of the definite article in a procedure keeps the language **highly economical and informative**. |
| Structural features | title | 'Make your own modelling clay' | **g** |
| | clear, numbered steps | '6 Knead clay until smooth and pliable.<br>7 Model clay into shapes as desired.' | **h** |

# INFORMATIVE TEXT

**WRITING SAMPLE**

Here is a sample text showing you how to structure and write a procedure.

## DIY shadow puppet theatre

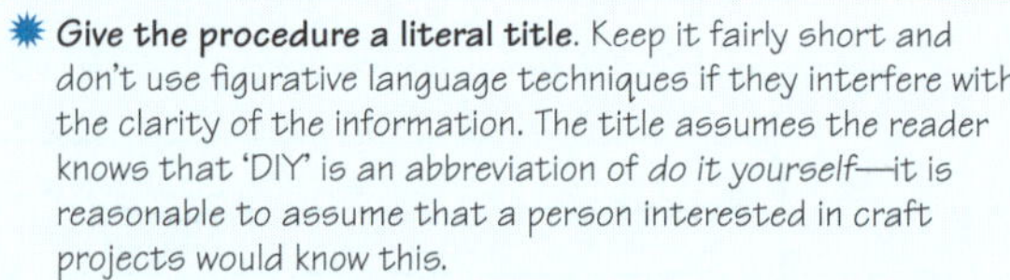

**Give the procedure a literal title.** Keep it fairly short and don't use figurative language techniques if they interfere with the clarity of the information. The title assumes the reader knows that 'DIY' is an abbreviation of *do it yourself*—it is reasonable to assume that a person interested in craft projects would know this.

**Materials**

Cardboard box
White tissue paper
Adhesive tape or stapler
Torch
Cardboard or foam character shapes (homemade or bought)
Puppet sticks (thin wooden craft sticks or short skewers)
Small piece of packing foam (optional)

**Write the materials list.** The writer has used generic names for materials, for two reasons. First, some terms need to be understandable in different countries, so idioms have been avoided. We see this in terms such as 'adhesive tape' rather than *sticky tape*. Second, it's correct to avoid advertising products in a text like this by using brand names. Adjectives and common nouns can easily take their place (such as 'thin wooden craft sticks'). In this section of a procedure, it is common, but not compulsory, for the composer to include at least one appropriate picture. Pictures both enhance the visual appeal of the text and improve reader understanding.

**Make the stage**

1 Find an empty cardboard box without a lid (a shoebox is perfect) 20 x 20 cm or larger.
2 Cut base out of box and replace with one or two sheets of white tissue paper taped or stapled to sides of box.

**Write the method.** Bold headings have been used throughout the procedure to break it into clear, understandable steps. Information is provided in parentheses ( ) to add detail and advice to the basic instructions. In procedures, abbreviations are used for information like measurements (for example '20 x 20 cm').

### Make the puppets

1 Draw and cut out puppet character shapes from spare cardboard, or use ready-made shapes (cardboard or foam) bought from a craft or toy store.
2 Attach a stick to each shape using adhesive tape or heavy staples.

Hint: Don't waste time colouring the shapes! They'll only appear as shadows. If you want colour, you'll need some cellophane … and another set of instructions, like the ones you'll find here!

www.callingallcrafters.com/colouredshadowpuppets

**Continue to describe the method in simple steps.** Two hints appear in the procedure. The first one is here. Hints contain important information that might not easily fit elsewhere. They also allow the writer to address the reader in a colloquial manner and to make the text friendly and engaging. Exclamation marks reinforce this tone. Another bonus of this hint is that it functions as an advertisement for another of the writer's craft procedures. A web link has been included that makes it easy for the reader to access the second text. The link suggests that the puppet procedure text is most likely to appear online but it is also common to find links in printed publications like magazines. Key words in the hint explain what this procedure is about: 'colour' and 'cellophane'.

### Stage the show

1 Place stage on a table where you can sit directly behind it. Optional: Place packing foam inside stage to position puppets when they're not being moved around.
2 Place torch behind stage.
3 Assemble your audience and turn out the lights.
4 Use your puppets to act out a story, dance to music or just muck around! Experiment with moving them closer to and further from the screen to change their size and appearance.

Hint: It's a good idea to video your shows so that later you can enjoy them too!

**Write the final steps of the method.** Use the second person to make the text suitable for readers of any age (for example, 'Use your puppets to act out a story'). This style makes the text suitable for an adult or a younger reader. Both readers are targeted because this is a craft project designed to involve kids. Include an optional extra step or two. Slang (such as 'muck around'), contractions (such as 'they're') and exclamation marks keep the tone light and fun, which is appropriate for a text about kids' craft. In a procedure text, there is no need to write a conclusion, but the writer may choose to include one if it enhances the overall appeal of the text. Here, the second hint functions as a conclusion and reinforces the friendly tone.

Plan your sample on the lines provided.

* **Give the procedure a literal title.** Keep it fairly short and don't use figurative language techniques if they interfere with the clarity of the information.

* **Write the materials list.** Use generic names for materials, avoiding idioms and brand names. In this section, you may include at least one appropriate picture if you wish to. Pictures both enhance the visual appeal of the text and improve reader understanding but they are not compulsory.

* **Write the method.** If possible, divide the method under bold subheadings to break it into clear, understandable steps. Provide information in parentheses ( ) to add detail and advice to the basic instructions. Use abbreviations for information like measurements. Limit your use of the definite article (*the*).

* **Continue to describe the method in simple steps.** If appropriate, use subheadings. Write at least one hint. Hints contain important information that might not easily fit elsewhere. They also allow you to address the reader in a colloquial manner and to make the text friendly and engaging. Add a web link to an imaginary second procedure text or for a real procedure text you have found online. Before and/or inside the link, use some key words that explain what the procedure is about.

* **Write the final steps of the method.** Remember to use the second person to make the text suitable for readers of any age. Include an optional extra step or two to expand on the procedure and make it work better. Try using slang, contractions and exclamation marks to keep the tone light and fun. In a procedure text, there is no need to write a conclusion but you may choose to include one if it enhances the overall appeal of the text.

# UNIT 5 PERSUASIVE TEXT

## Speech

**READING WORK**

### Sporting heroes

*The following persuasive speech was written as a response to a debate topic: 'Do sports stars make good heroes?' and presented as one of three negative responses to the topic. An opposing team of three speakers answered for the affirmative (that is, 'Yes, sports stars make good heroes.'). This informal debating style is often used as a type of stand-up comedy. The winning team is usually decided by audience vote or 'clap-o-meter' (applause volume).*

Ladies and gentlemen, our topic today is 'Do sports stars make good heroes?'

Nope.

Thank you and good day.

But seriously, do they?

Not so long ago, Lance Armstrong was the world's best-ever cyclist; in fact, one of the best athletes of all time. Many of his millions of fans could more accurately be called disciples. This AHH-sum American's humble origins, his inspirational recovery from cancer, his humanitarian work and, of course, his seemingly endless string of world cycling titles, made him the ultimate sporting hero. Now everyone hates him.

Turns out he took performance-enhancing drugs. A lot. He didn't really win anything fair and square. But why are we all so heartbroken about it—especially when we know there are so many drug cheats, thugs, casual crims and mischief-makers out there? I decided to try and find out.

OJ Simpson, Mike Tyson, Tiger Woods, Oscar Pistorius. And ladies, you're not off the hook: hello, Marion Jones. If you've heard of these athletes, you've probably also heard the word 'disgraced' or 'downfall' in the same sentence. Which is one thing. But it's another thing entirely to see how utterly horrified fans have been to discover that their one-time idol could possibly let them down. Why the horror?

Back to Lance Armstrong for a moment. I read this in *Atlantic* magazine: '... Armstrong's career has followed the typical arc of celebrity worship: first we raise our heroes to the pedestal then pull them down, throwing them onto the trash heap. Once disillusionment sets in, idealisation gives way to hatred and contempt.'

So the problem is not so much the fall from grace as the height of the fall. And the height is determined by us, the fans, in the first place.

I kept hunting, and came across an *Independent* article suggesting that sport is at the 'centre of our moral universe' and that, in the mind of the average person, 'athletes are a force for good' in this universe. The image that immediately sprang up for me was a bunch of The Avengers hurling things about in downtown New York City, making a dreadful mess but generally being awesome. But are we really expecting sports stars—ordinary human beings with slightly-better-than-ordinary human abilities, and absolutely ordinary human failings—to live up to that kind of standard? Is that fair?

No, which is why we should stop doing it. Sure, we can admire a sporting *achievement*, but taking it to the next level and idolising the *achiever* is dangerous and, in many cases, very disappointing. We need to stop mythologising these people. Even if they have razor-cut abs. Do we even understand what we mean by the word 'hero' anymore?

Part of the problem with that word is the increasingly popular archetype of the superhero. So we're back to The Avengers again. Hey, they're more than happy to take the weight of all your expectations upon them, because THEY'RE NOT REAL. By all means, make one of *them* your hero. Enjoy your delusion!

And here's a thought ... what about your mum? Your dad? Your great-great aunty? Let's see a brattish tennis ace or overpaid soccer god—or an Avenger, for that matter—change a nappy and keep a smile on their face. Maybe the most worthy heroes are closer to home than we think.

Thank you.

- A **salutation** indicates the general audience.
- The **topic** is clearly established.
- A single **slang** word is offered as a full response to the topic. The effects are: humour, an oversimplification of the topic and a persuasive implication that the answer is very simple.
- The speaker resumes and will now give a real answer.
- A 'once upon a time' styled phrase **implies** that sporting heroes may as well be fairytale characters.
- **Informal and economical language** is used throughout.
- **Understatement and truncation** give this two-word sentence impact. Truncation is used similarly throughout the speech.
- Sentence **fragments** like this question are broken off from the rest of the sentence to show that they are building on the idea.
- The speaker **personalises** the quest to unwrap the mystery of idolising athletes.
- A **list** of sporting celebrities adds to the persuasive power of the argument.
- The **first point** is completed here after a brief interruption involving references to athletes other than Armstrong.
- Two articles from reputable publications are **quoted** to add to the argument. This is the second.
- The speaker returns to the **simplicity** of the opening.
- A **colloquial hyperbole** conjures a superhero-type image.
- Many **rhetorical questions** are used in the speech to get the audience thinking. Some of these questions also point out the obvious to the audience.
- These **capital letters** indicate a forceful (yet still comical) tone. The speaker may have delivered this line with cupped hands around the mouth like a megaphone for greater impact.
- A suddenly **sarcastic tone** changes the pace and adds to the humour, especially as the sarcasm doesn't seem derisive.
- An **ellipsis** introduces a 'crazy' new thought.
- A 'take-home' **lesson** is given at the very end.
- A simple, polite **sign-off** is offered.

## Literal questions

*Hint: read the text carefully to locate specific facts and details.*

**1** Who, according to the speaker, 'could more accurately be called disciples'?

**2** What image 'immediately sprang up' for the speaker while reading the *Independent* article?

**3** What example of the increasingly popular archetype of the superhero is given?

**a** Lance Armstrong **b** The Avengers **c** your mum

## Interpretive questions

*Hint: These questions require you to combine facts and details to synthesise the meaning.*

**4** According to the speaker, what are 'we all so heartbroken about'?

**a** that Lance Armstrong was a drug cheat

**b** that some athletes do not win 'fair and square'

**c** that many people now hate Lance Armstrong

**5** What everyday task makes someone a hero in the speaker's eyes?

**6** A few lists are used by the speaker. Copy the list in which two examples of alliteration are used in a row.

**7** What 'height' is referred to as being 'determined by … the fans'?

**a** an athlete's height **b** the height of a fall from grace **c** a drug high

**8** What are two effects of the speaker beginning the speech as though it is ending?

**a** sincerity and authority **b** comedy and surprise **c** irony and anger

**9** What do a brattish tennis ace, an overpaid soccer god and your great-great aunty have in common?

**10** Select the correct order of attitudes experienced by a fan when he or she loses faith in a sports hero.

**a** disillusionment, hatred, contempt **b** hatred, grace, idealisation

**c** hatred, contempt, disillusionment

## Applied questions

*Hint: This question requires you to understand a text's implications to infer meaning from the text.*

**11** What does the speaker claim is unfair?

**a** that ordinary people are held to superhero standards

**b** that sports stars have ordinary human failings

**c** that a soccer god can't change a nappy

**12** What is meant by the made-up word 'AHH-sum' and what is its purpose?

# PERSUASIVE TEXT

## SPELLING WORK

### List Words

All of the words in the box below appear in the text 'Sporting heroes'.

| | | | | |
|---|---|---|---|---|
| heroes | humanitarian | accurately | seemingly | origins |
| pedestal | celebrity | achiever | increasingly | disillusionment |
| superhero | archetype | expectations | overpaid | mythologising |

**1** Circle true or false for each statement about list words and their spellings.

| | | |
|---|---|---|
| **a** 'Heroes' is a plural of superhero. | True | False |
| **b** 'Mythologising' can also be spelt with a z. | True | False |
| **c** 'Humanitarian' ends with a suffix meaning one who is in need. | True | False |
| **d** The *ch* in 'archetype' is pronounced 'ck'. | True | False |
| **e** The *stal* in 'pedestal' is pronounced 'still'. | True | False |
| **f** There is a silent letter in 'overpaid'. | True | False |

The list word 'heroes' is an *oes* **plural**. It can be difficult to get word endings right when making plurals, especially for words ending in *o*. This is made more difficult by the fact that there is no spelling rule for *os* and *oes* plurals. There is, however, a punctuation rule: no plurals require apostrophes. Making a plural using *'s* is always incorrect.

**2** Add *s* or *es* to make plurals of these words ending in o. *Hint: For some words, either ending is correct.*

**a** memo____ **b** tornado____ **c** potato____ **d** zero____ **e** halo____

**f** studio____ **g** photo____ **h** tattoo____ **i** tomato____ **j** yo-yo____

**3** Correct the misspelt words in each sentence on the lines provided. Separate the words using commas. *Hint: Some of the words used in the sentences are derived from list words.*

**a** We shouldent place sporting heroes on pedestalls if we don't want to be dissapointed by them.

______________________________

**b** Fans of sporting starrs are becomming increasingly disallusioned with drug used in sport.

______________________________

**c** Atheletes can acheive amazeing things in the sporting areana, but they can't help been human.

______________________________

**d** Playing a sport can garner you celeb-rity stattus these days, but this can add alot of anziety to you're game.

______________________________

**4** Shuffle each letter group to form words that are in the families of list words. For example, words in the family of *heroes* include *hero*, *heroic* and *heroism*. To make it easier, no new prefixes have been used (such as *anti*hero).

**a** hanitumy ____________ **b** mese ____________

**c** mentiaveech ____________ **d** hymt ____________

**e** curcacya ____________ **f** galnorii ____________

**5** Every list word is hidden in these two lines. Separate the words and cross out any extra letters using slashes.

**a** superherocachieverdcelebritypedestallheroesohumanitarianarchetypeaccuratelyly

**b** aseeminglyincreasinglyexpectationsorgoriginsadisillusionmentoverpaidmythologisings

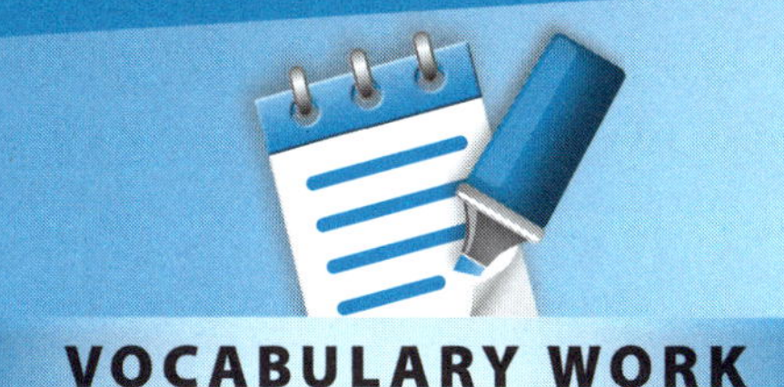

# PERSUASIVE TEXT

## Speech

## VOCABULARY WORK

### Diction

**Diction** simply means '**word choice**'. This is an easy term to remember, because it is in the word *dictionary.* Effective writing and speaking involves choosing and using words that are:

- properly understood by the writer/speaker
- not superfluous (that is, unnecessary or verbose)
- appropriate in the context
- easily understood by the target audience.

In order for our diction to be effective—that is, to choose the best words for use in a certain context—we need to have access to lots of words. This means that we need to build a strong, full **vocabulary** of words to choose from.

**1** Circle the words and phrases related to diction. *Hint: Register is discussed in the Writing Work section on page 47.*

| register | language | pause | stammer | colloquialism |
|---|---|---|---|---|
| idiom | syntax | volume | comma | jargon |

**Idioms** are used in a particular place, nation, group or era. Their meaning cannot usually be deduced from each individual word's definition. For example, the idiom *over the moon,* meaning *very happy,* has nothing to do with outer space. Test your knowledge of idioms and other types of expressions in the task below.

**2** Organise these words and phrases from the text 'Sporting heroes' under the correct expression types. *Hint: Use the number of rows as a guide. That is, there can be no more than four of any type of expression.*

| off the hook | tennis ace | being awesome | crims | fair and square |
|---|---|---|---|---|
| for that matter | mum | here's a thought | hey | |

| Idioms | Abbreviations | General colloquialisms |
|---|---|---|
| | | |
| | | |
| | | |
| | | |

The **modality** of a word or phrase is the strength or force with which it is used. Low modality expressions include *could, might* and *maybe,* while high modality expressions include *never, must* or *will.* The modality of some words and phrases depends on their context. For example, *should* can sound either uncertain or insistent. High modality words, especially verbs, are often used in persuasive texts.

**3** Show your understanding by placing these modal verbs on the line in order from weakest to strongest.

| must | might | will | should | can |
|---|---|---|---|---|

________ ________ ________ ________ ________

**4** Identify whether each phrase from the text 'Sporting heroes' is an example of low, medium or high modality. For each phrase circle *low, medium* or *high.*

**a** should stop low medium high
**b** probably also heard low medium high
**c** can admire low medium high
**d** need to stop low medium high

In the text 'Sporting heroes', **inclusive language** is used. For example, 'determined by us, the fans'.

**5** Find another three inclusive expressions used in the speech text and write them on the lines.

____________ ____________ ____________

# PERSUASIVE TEXT

## *Speech*

**GRAMMAR WORK**

### Relaxed syntax

When speaking **colloquially**, as the speaker does in the text 'Sporting heroes', syntax tends to relax along with diction. Syntax refers to the way in which sentences are constructed. Evidence of **relaxed syntax** in the speech includes truncation (shortened sentences), fragments (partial sentences) and the use of conjunctions (joining words such as *because* and *but*) at the beginning of sentences. These features add to the speech's friendly tone.

**1** Give examples of relaxed syntax from the speech text under the headings below.

**a Truncated sentence/Fragments**

______________________________
______________________________
______________________________

**b Sentences beginning with conjunctions**

______________________________
______________________________
______________________________

### Saying more with less

Breaking up or extending sentences in unusual ways through truncation and the use of fragments does more than create a friendly, conversational tone in a text. This technique can also have the effects listed below:

- language economy (using words concisely)
- irony or sarcasm
- humour
- surprise
- understatement
- suspense
- rhythm
- breathlessness
- urgency
- realism.

**2** Did you notice that all of the effects of truncation and fragments listed in the first column are present in the text 'Sporting heroes'? For each of these effects, give an example of a truncated sentence or fragment from the text. *Hint: Some examples have more than one effect, so you may use the same example twice if you're struggling.*

**a** language economy ______________________________

**b** irony or sarcasm ______________________________

**c** humour ______________________________

**d** surprise ______________________________

**e** understatement ______________________________

In the text 'Sporting heroes', the past tense verb 'sprang' is used by the speaker. In this **tense family** are the past participle *sprung*, the present tense *spring* and the future tense verb phrase *will spring*.

**3** Test your knowledge by completing these tense families. *Hint: One word in each family is used in the text 'Sporting heroes'.*

| Past | Present | Future |
|---|---|---|
| saw | **a** ______________ | **b** will ______________ |
| **c** ______________ | string | **d** will ______________ |
| **e** ______________ | **f** ______________ | will horrify |

**4** Unscramble these words related to tense. *Hint: Most are auxiliary verbs (sometimes called 'helping verbs').*

**a** pepractili ____________ **b** liwl ____________ **c** saw ____________

**d** renteps ____________ **e** ear ____________ **f** ash ____________

# PERSUASIVE TEXT

## Speech

## PUNCTUATION WORK

### Apostrophes in contractions

One function of the **apostrophe** is to show **ownership** (also called possession). The other is to create **contractions** by replacing one or more letters in a pair or group of words in order to contract them (that is, pull them together). This punctuation feature is frequently used in the text 'Sporting heroes' to suit the colloquial approach.

**1** These phrases, which feature contracted words, have been taken from the text. Rewrite the phrases, undoing the contractions by removing apostrophes and writing each word in full.

- **a** Let's see a brattish tennis aces ______
- **b** you're not off the hook ______
- **c** If you've heard of any ______
- **d** here's a thought ______
- **e** it's another thing entirely ______
- **f** Hey, they're more than happy ______
- **g** we're back to The Avengers ______

**2** How can these phrases be rewritten to contain contractions? *Hint: The phrases will become very informal.*

- **a** the height is determined by us ______
- **b** Which is one thing ______
- **c** there are so many drug cheats ______

Many **compound words** (some with hyphens) are used in the text 'Sporting heroes'. This is due to two main factors. First, the speaker is mostly using colloquial (or casual) language, and compound adjectives are common in this register. Second, the use of compound words with hyphens can contribute to economical language usage, which is important in a speech.

**3** Find the following hyphenated compound words in the text 'Sporting heroes' and write them on the lines provided.

- **a** Three adjectives ______ ______ ______
- **b** One plural noun ______

**4** Find five compound words without hyphens in the text 'Sporting heroes' and write them below. *Hint: Some are adjectives.*

______ ______ ______ ______ ______

**5** Name each punctuation mark or feature used in these extracts from the text 'Sporting heroes'. *Hint: Include capital letters but not italics.*

- **a** soccer god—or an Avenger ______
- **b** Thank you. ______
- **c** THEY'RE NOT REAL. ______
- **d** Armstrong's career ______
- **e** world's best-ever ______

**6** Which punctuation mark is missing from this sentence?

Here's a thought what about your mum? ______

# PERSUASIVE TEXT
## *Speech*

**WRITING WORK 1**

### Speeches

A **speech** is a spoken text that is usually planned and written first. It **answers a question**, **argues a case** or **addresses a topic** in the form of an extended response. Here is some general information about speeches.

- They fall into three main categories: informative, commemorative and persuasive. The form of speech presented in this chapter is persuasive.
- The formal term for all public speaking is oration and a speechmaker is called an orator.
- Rhetoric is the general term for language techniques commonly used in persuasive speeches.
- Persuasive speakers often make three types of rhetorical appeals to their audience: ethos, pathos and logos. Ethos is an appeal to the audience's ethics and values, pathos to emotions and logos to logic.

### Essential elements of persuasive speeches

Clarity and structure are very important in **persuasive speeches**. So are these **elements**:

- an attention-grabbing opening
- an argument that is logical, flows and, ideally, builds to a climax
- authoritative evidence, such as facts, statistics or quotes.

**1** What four-letter adjective in the *oration* word family means 'spoken' or 'relating to the mouth'? ____________

**2** Complete these word families based on the three rhetorical appeals.
*Hint: Unless shown otherwise, the new words begin with the same letter as the root word.*

| | | | |
|---|---|---|---|
| **a** ethos | ____________ ics | e ____________ lly | un ____________ al |
| **b** pathos | ____________ tic | s ____________ thy | p ____________ gical |
| **c** logos | ____________ al | ____________ tics | i ____________ ally |

### Register

There are five main language styles. These styles are called **registers** (in the past, they were also known as levels of usage). Each register is suited to different situations but some crossover works if it is done thoughtfully. Some registers are highly inappropriate in certain contexts. For example, a 'pet' language shared between siblings or spouses should not be used in a formal job interview. The choice of language register depends on purpose, audience and topic, and can determine the tone and impact of a text. The five main registers are:

1 static register, which never changes; it is used in ceremonies and very formal settings like a courtroom
2 formal register, required in many situations, ranging from business letters to university lectures
3 consultative register, which is a step down in formality; it is used by consultants (including lawyers and therapists) and in media contexts like television news bulletins
4 casual register, which is informal (colloquial), often includes slang and is used between friends
5 intimate register, reserved for use by people in close relationships like parents and their children.

**3** What is another word for level of usage? ____________

**4** What is the most formal language style? ____________

**5** What language style is most likely to be used in these settings?

**a** job interview ____________ **b** hockey team training session ____________

**c** family holiday ____________ **d** baby's christening ____________

**e** doctor's surgery ____________ **f** documentary ____________

# PERSUASIVE TEXT

## Speech



### Language features and techniques used in persuasive speeches

Here are some specific **features** and **techniques** that can have a powerful impact in a **persuasive speech**:

- repetition
- lists
- inclusive language
- vivid imagery
- selective use of the first, second and third person
- emotive language (such as *bloodshed* and *integrity*)
- truncation (short, cut-off sentences)
- one or more brief, relevant anecdotes (personal stories)
- analogies (detailed comparisons between things)
- allusions (references to other works, people or events)
- imperatives and challenges (such as *We must stop this, now!*)
- questions, especially rhetorical ones (such as *Is that fair?*).

'Do we even understand what we mean by the word "hero' anymore?" This is a **rhetorical question** used in the text 'Sporting heroes'. It doesn't require an answer; it's intended to get the audience thinking.

**6** Find three other rhetorical questions used in the text 'Sporting heroes' and write them below. You will need to abbreviate the questions using ellipses (...) if they are very long. *Hint: Not all questions are rhetorical.*

______

______

______

**7** Very briefly describe how the rhetorical question 'Do we even understand ...?' and the sarcasm 'By all means, make one of them your hero ...' in the text have different effects.

______

______

**8** Give at least one example of each of these features and techniques from the text 'Sporting heroes'.

**a** inclusive language ______

**b** vivid imagery ______

**c** truncation ______

**9** What does the composer of the text 'Sporting heroes' seem to want the audience to

**a** know? ______

**b** think? ______

**c** do? ______

**10** What are two visual, audio or audiovisual aids that would enhance the delivery of the text 'Sporting heroes'? Describe each one.

______

______

**11** Suggest a forum where this speech could be given.

______

# PERSUASIVE TEXT

## WRITING SAMPLE

Here is a sample text showing you how to structure and write a speech.

### Responsible pet ownership

✸ **Write a literal, straightforward title that names the issue.**

I would like to thank the RSPCA for hosting today's fundraiser, and for championing the cause of responsible animal ownership. We are here today to do the same. Many of you run veterinary practices, volunteer at local animal shelters or simply have a moral objection to the way in which this nation's pets are mistreated and discarded.

✸ **Open by establishing the context and the purpose of the speech.** In the opening sentence the speaker establishes that the context is a fundraiser hosted by animal care group the RSPCA and its purpose is 'championing … responsible animal ownership'. Some sections of the audience are also identified: vets, volunteers and concerned citizens.

It is an old, yet increasingly pertinent truism: *A dog is not just for Christmas.* Each year the RSPCA rehomes 20 000 animals who have been abandoned by their owners. The biggest spike in abandonment occurs in January, as post-Christmas reality sets in, and cries like these go up all over the country:
'Change a litter tray? You must be joking!'
'I thought he'd *like* living in a high-rise!'
'She looked much cuter in the pet shop!'

✸ **Begin the main argument with a well-known saying or a similar feature that sums up the issue.** A statistic—20 000 animals rehomed annually—adds to the authority of the speech. To add authenticity, the speaker vocalises some common attitudes of irresponsible pet owners.

In today's throwaway culture, pets are often considered accessories. A photogenic puppy makes great internet fodder (not to mention a nice handbag stuffer), but it is a dignified being and should be treated as such. We refuse to tolerate pet abandonment as 'another harsh reality of life'. This is something that we, as a society, can rein in through regulation. How, specifically?

✸ **Use emotive, strong adjectives.** Examples are used in phrases such as 'today's throwaway culture' and 'dignified being' . Shocking images, like a 'photogenic puppy' being a 'nice handbag stuffer', remind listeners of the selfish and cruel behaviour behind this issue. A question is set up that the speaker will answer.

Pet licenses. The State Government needs to introduce a system of formal permits for pet owners. This won't make all of our pet issues magically vanish, but it is a significant step up from the only current fix: rehoming. Pet licensing would serve two main purposes.

✸ **Propose a solution concisely and in simple language.** The speaker has delivered the solution as a truncated sentence. The speaker is honest about the fact that the problem is a large one and that the issues will not 'magically vanish'—this generates trust.

First, it would assist in educating potential pet owners about the practical responsibilities involved in domestic animal ownership. This needs to happen at point of purchase *and* beforehand. It's very simple: if you want a pet, you need to understand exactly what that means. Second, a pet permit would hold accountable those who have abandoned animals in the past, and those charged with acts of animal cruelty. It is clear that many people are unfit to provide shelter to animals and if we can create a national registry for pet ownership, we can stop at least some of them from doing so.

✸ **Give reasons for your proposed solution in two parts, providing clarity and structure.** The language moves from formal to colloquial when a contraction ('it's') and second person direct address ('you need to understand') are used. This change has an impact on listeners' sense of involvement. Inclusive language, such as 'we can create' and 'we can stop' reminds listeners that this is everyone's problem.

The Department of the Environment already requires permits for the keeping of certain exotic animals. This system is in place to protect our native wildlife and their habitats. Angling licences are required to preserve our fish stocks. But what about protecting our supposed best friends—our domestic pets? Frankly, at this point, nothing.

✸ **Give an additional point to support your argument and make this point an appeal to logic.** Other animal-related legislation exists, so why not this? The speaker alludes to a common idiom for a dog (man's best friend) to heighten the outrage.

We have a petition here today. A petition that will put this issue onto the desks of the policymakers. Right now, only one thing is missing that could make that happen: your name.
Thank you.

✸ **Repeat a key word.** The repetition of the word 'petition' informs listeners that there is a way they can help fix the problem. The speech ends with a direct challenge to listeners.

# PERSUASIVE TEXT

## Speech

WRITING YOUR OWN SAMPLE

Plan your sample on the lines provided.

- **Write a literal, straightforward title that names the issue.**
- **Open by establishing the context and the purpose of the speech.** Identify the target audience or sections of it.
- **Begin the main argument with a well-known saying or a similar feature that sums up the issue.** Quote a statistic to add authority. To add authenticity, vocalise some common attitudes associated with the issue being discussed.
- **Use emotive, strong adjectives.** Include one or more shocking images to remind listeners of the seriousness of the issue. Set up a question that you will answer.
- **Propose a solution concisely and in simple language.** Be honest about the scale of the problem in order to generate trust in listeners.
- **Give reasons for your proposed solution in two parts, providing clarity and structure.** Shift the language from formal to colloquial with a contraction and second person direct address in order to give listeners a greater sense of involvement. Use inclusive language to remind listeners that the issue is everyone's problem.
- **Give an additional point to support your argument, and make this point an appeal to logic.** Make an allusion or use a common idiom to heighten the impact of your call to action.
- **Repeat a key word.** This informs listeners that there is a way they can help fix the problem. End the speech with a direct challenge to listeners.

# PERSUASIVE TEXT

## *Advertising script*

**READING WORK**

### Castle in the Clouds Funerals

**Campaign: Castle in the Clouds Funerals**

Project: 30 sec TVC

Version: Draft 2

| SCENE | TIME | VISION | AUDIO |
|---|---|---|---|
| 000 | 1 sec<br>00:01 | | *Music box style track begins and continues until end of scene 004.* |
| 001 | 2 secs<br>00:03 | Fast fade in to illuminated fairytale text 'Once Upon a Time …' on parchment page of a large, leather-bound book; page is slowly turning.<br>*Transition: fast dissolve as page turns.* | VO 1: Once upon a time … |
| 002 | 2 secs<br>00:05 | Silhouette of two people holding hands on page; page is slowly turning.<br>*Transition: fast dissolve as page turns.* | VO 1: There was a beautiful couple … |
| 003 | 2 secs<br>00:07 | Silhouette of two adults and two children with arms around each other on page; page is slowly turning.<br>*Transition: fast dissolve as page turns.* | VO 1: A loving family … |
| 004 | 2 secs<br>00:09 | Silhouette of two people in profile on page, laughing and holding glasses. | VO 1: A treasured friendship …<br>*Music box track ends.* |
| 005 | 1 sec<br>00:10 | *Transition: misty 'dream' dissolve into live action footage.* | *Gentle piano and guitar music track begins and continues until the end.* |
| 006 | 6 secs<br>00:16 | Leafy, sunny cemetery with people walking and comforting each other, placing flowers on graves, etc.<br>Onscreen text: Castle in the Clouds Funerals 1300 RIP (1300 747) | VO 2: Sadly, the reality of life is that all fairytales must eventually end.<br>Make that ending as pain-free as possible with Castle in the Clouds Funerals. |
| 007 | 4 secs<br>00:20 | Montage of caring staff comforting grieving people, placing flowers, speaking at a service, etc. that continues until end of scene 009.<br>Onscreen text: Compassionate | VO 2: Our family team offers the most compassionate care at the most difficult time. |
| 008 | 2 secs<br>00:22 | Onscreen text: Experienced | VO 2: With more than thirty years experience … |
| 009 | 4 secs<br>00:26 | Onscreen text: Conveniently located<br>*Transition: misty 'dream' dissolve.* | VO 2: … and fifty convenient locations, Castle in the Clouds Funerals can help you cope as the fairytale ends. |
| 010 | 3 secs<br>00:29 | Parchment page with a picture of a castle in the clouds; book closes to show ornate leather cover with the golden title 'Castle in the Clouds'.<br>Onscreen text:<br>Call Castle in the Clouds Funerals 1300 RIP (1300 747)<br>www.citcfunerals.com | VO 1: And they had their 'happily ever-after', with Castle in the Clouds.<br>*Music ends.* |

- A **buffer** of up to one second has been left for music and visuals to be faded in at the beginning and out at the end.
- **AUDIO** means sound features.
- This **style of music** suits the fairytale theme. The theme has been chosen in keeping with the company name.
- *'VO 1'* is an **abbreviation** for *Voiceover 1*. This is one of two voices used in the advertisement. One voice tells a story and the other speaks on behalf of the company.
- **Transitions** describe how one scene cuts to the next. A 'dissolve' is a cross-over fade into the next image.
- **Ellipses** in Scenes 002–004 show that only some words from the fairytale are being spoken. They also complement the page-turning and the dissolves between scenes.
- The **number of seconds** that the scene will run is noted, then the time at the end of the scene (in minutes and seconds).
- The **slow page-turning** is offset by the fast transition.
- **Three broad types** of relationships are mentioned to show that Castle in the Clouds Funerals understands people's loss.
- This is a **transition** from pictures to live action, and from fantasy to reality. The word 'reality' follows straight after.
- 'Gentle' music is appropriate for a **serious and emotional subject** like funerals. The 'music box style track' is also gentle.
- The **company's details** appear over appropriate footage.
- A **montage** is a series of overlapping brief scenes set to music. This montage sums up what the company offers.
- **Inclusive**, welcoming language inspires viewer confidence.
- ***Onscreen text*** persuades viewers about three of the company's best qualities.
- The company's name is frequently **repeated**.
- A return to the fairytale completes the ad and suggests that this funeral service offers mourners peace and closure. A play on words makes Castle in the Clouds a place as well as the company's name.
- This scene **ends the story**. The title, which is also the company's name, implies that the company 'wrote the book' when it comes to funerals. This means they are experts.
- The **music ends** to match both the story and the ad ending.
- Another **contact detail**—a website—is given at the end.

# PERSUASIVE TEXT
## *Advertising script*

COMPREHENSION WORK

### Literal questions

1 How many people are shown as silhouettes in the advertisement? ______

2 What, specifically, is 'convenient' about Castle in the Clouds' office locations? ______

______

3 With what technical element does the advertisement begin and end?

**a** music **b** timing **c** a voiceover

### Interpretive questions

*Hint: These questions require you to combine facts and details to synthesise the meaning.*

4 How many times has this script been edited so far?

**a** none **b** once **c** twice

5 Give two visual or language features that make this advertisement emotive.

______ ______

6 There are three hyphenated compound words in the advertisement. Two of them have connotations of peace. What are these words? *Hint: A compound word is made up of two parts.*

______ ______ ______

7 What visual element complements the phrase 'as the fairytale ends' in Scene 009?

**a** the onscreen text 'conveniently located'

**b** the 'misty "dream" dissolve'

**c** the 'leafy, sunny cemetery' footage

8 What is the first transition prescribed in the table?

**a** a fast fade **b** a voiceover **c** a dissolve

9 What does each time stamp in the 'TIME' column denote? ______

______

10 There is only one negative adjective and one negative adverb in the advertisement. What are they?

**a** difficult (adjective) and sadly (adverb)

**b** sadly (adjective) and ending (adverb)

**c** cope (adjective) and difficult (adverb)

### Applied questions

*Hint: These questions require you to understand a text's implications to infer meaning from the text.*

11 The script title includes the abbreviation 'TVC'. What does this abbreviation stand for?
*Hint: Think of a synonym for the word 'advertisement'.*

**a** television commercial **b** television visual context **c** televised vision capture

12 Why do connotations of a 'Castle in the Clouds' make it an effective image for a funeral services advertisement?

______

______

# PERSUASIVE TEXT
## *Advertising script*

**SPELLING WORK**

**List Words** All of the words in the box below appear in the text 'Castle in the Clouds Funerals'.

| | | | | |
|---|---|---|---|---|
| footage | silhouette | illuminated | dissolve | transition |
| onscreen | funerals | treasured | castle | cemetery |
| grieving | convenient | montage | scene | compassionate |

**1** These sentences contain common spelling errors in highlighted text. Correct them on the corresponding lines. *Hint: Some of the errors are List Words and some others come from the text and annotations.*

A regular **a** **telvision** **b** **advertisment** consists of live **c** **footidge**, still **d** **immages** and transitions **e** **beetween** **f** **scences**. Ad composers need to use language **g** **economically** in this time-constrained **h** **contecxt**.

a ______________________ b ______________________

c ______________________ d ______________________

e ______________________ f ______________________

g ______________________ h ______________________

**2** Some of the highlighted words below are spelling errors and some are already correct. Correct or simply rewrite each word on the corresponding lines. *Hint: Some of these words are from the list and the others come from the text and annotations.*

Composers of **a** **commercials** use many **b** **pesuasive** techniques to **c** **reech** their target **d** **audience**. These include **e** **retorical** questions, **f** **reppeated** catchphrases, **g** **onscreen** text and **h** **emmotive** music.

a ______________________ b ______________________

c ______________________ d ______________________

e ______________________ f ______________________

g ______________________ h ______________________

**Synonyms** are words with the same or similar meaning. **Antonyms** are opposites.

**3** Write *true* or *false* for each statement about list word synonyms and antonyms.

| Statement | True or False? |
|---|---|
| **a** A synonym of *cemetery* is *graveyard*. | ______________ |
| **b** A synonym of *montage* is *model*. | ______________ |
| **c** A synonym of *compassionate* is *sympathetic*. | ______________ |
| **d** An antonym of *convenient* is *handy*. | ______________ |

**4** Circle the incorrect words in each sentence. *Hint: The words may or may not appear in this chapter.*

**a** Advetising a buisness is important for its survivle.

**b** Evryone reacks to death and greif in diffrent ways.

**c** A cemetary can be a peacefull place to visit.

**5** Circle the correct words in each sentence. *Hint: Whether a word has correct spelling is partly based on context.*

**a** Castels, fairytals and clowds might seam unconventional funerel immages, but there effectave.

**b** Tellevision adds abbout funerels doen't nead too be deppressing.

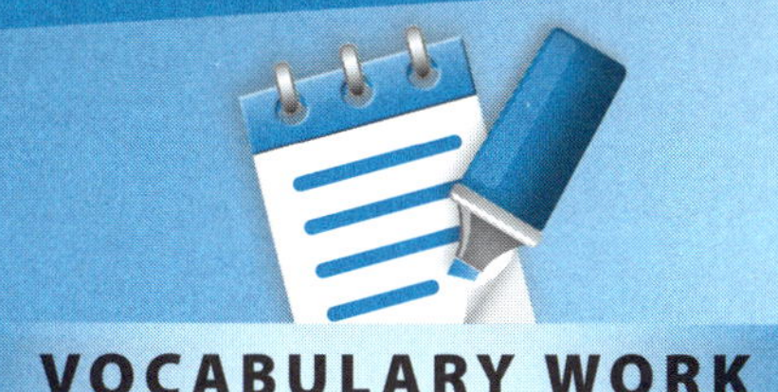

# PERSUASIVE TEXT

## Advertising script

VOCABULARY WORK

### Homonyms

There are various types of **homonyms**. The word *homonym* comes from the Greek and means 'same' (*homo*) 'name' (*nym*), so homonyms are simply words that are the same in some way. They may be different in other ways. For example, a **homophone** (meaning 'same sound') is a type of homonym that sounds the same as another word but has a different meaning. A **homograph** (meaning 'same writing') is a word with the same spelling as another but a different meaning. **Heterophones** (words with different sounds) and homophones are types of homographs.

**1** Complete these homophone pairs. *Hint: Homophones must sound the same.*

**a** bough b________ **b** key ________y **c** tier ________

**d** way ________ **e** right ________ **f** sight ________

**2** Provide a definition for each homograph below. *Hint: These homographs are also homophones.*

**a** bat ____________________ bat ____________________

**b** treat ____________________ treat ____________________

**c** stalk ____________________ stalk ____________________

**3** Using capital letters, write different pronunciations for these heterophones. How you write the pronunciations is up to you, as long as they work. For example, wind can be pronounced 'winned' or 'wined'.

**a** bass ____________________ bass ____________________

**b** tear ____________________ tear ____________________

**c** bow ____________________ bow ____________________

**d** desert ____________________ desert ____________________

**4** Write *true* or *false* for each statement about homonyms. *Hint: Homographs can also be homophones.*

**a** The words *memories* and *memorise* are homophones. ____________

**b** The words *cemetery* and *cemetary* are homographs. ____________

**c** The words *scene* and *seen* are homophones. ____________

**d** The words *salt* and *assault* are homonyms. ____________

**5** Match these words and meanings from the text 'Castle in the Clouds Funerals' and its annotations. *Hint: Some of these words have been defined in the text's annotations and elsewhere.*

| | | | |
|---|---|---|---|
| scene | track | dissolve | illuminated |
| fade | parchment | footage | montage |

**a** ________________ antique paper

**b** ________________ a gradually disappearing image

**c** ________________ lit up or highlighted in some way

**d** ________________ moving images captured by cinematography

**e** ________________ a single unit of action

**f** ________________ a fading scene transition

**g** ________________ a single song or piece of music

**h** ________________ overlapping images or brief scenes

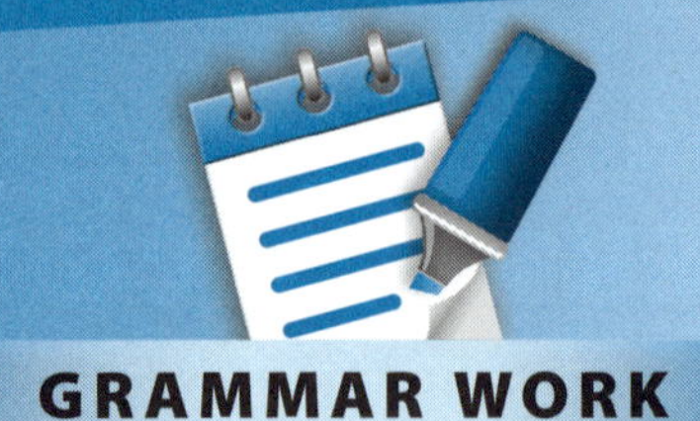

# PERSUASIVE TEXT

## Advertising script

GRAMMAR WORK

### Second person address

In a range of texts and media, we read and hear language expressed in the **second person**. This form of address:

- differs from the first person (which includes pronouns like *I* and *me*)
- differs from the third person (which includes pronouns like *he* and *she* and also proper nouns, such as *James Bond*); third person address is common in storytelling
- is commonly employed in the persuasive text forms of advertisements and speeches
- is used for most instructions; for example, *Put masking tape on the edges before painting*
- often appears in song lyrics; for example, *Don't you break my heart.*

The second person speaks and appeals directly to the target audience, which is why it is so effective in advertising. Some of the text 'Castle in the Clouds Funerals' is expressed in the second person and some in the third. The third person is mainly used in the sections where the fairytale is narrated.

**1** Write *yes* or *no* to show whether each phrase from the text is in the second person.

**a** There was a beautiful couple ____________

**b** Montage of caring staff ____________

**c** Make that ending as pain-free as possible ____________

**d** Castle in the Clouds Funerals can help you cope ____________

**2** Change these first and third person statements and questions to the second person.

**a** They want a boat. ____________ **b** Where is she? ____________

**c** Jack is going. ____________ **d** Let's take a chance. ____________

**e** Everyone laughed. ____________ **f** 'Go now!' I yelled. ____________

Advertisers use plenty of adjectives in their writing. These add to the persuasive power of advertisements and complement other persuasive language features such as emotive language. We read many **persuasive adjectives** in the text 'Castle in the Clouds Funerals'.

**3** Circle the adjectives used in the 'VISION' column of the text.

| sunny | leafy | illuminated | clouds | book | fairytale |
|---|---|---|---|---|---|
| leather-bound | caring | placing | cope | ornate | fade |

**4** Change the words below into adjectives. Some may not need changing to work as adjectives.
*Hint: Check for accuracy—add 'person', 'place' or 'thing' to see if your word works as a description.*

**a** beauty ____________ **b** sadness ____________

**c** death ____________ **d** friendship ____________

**e** flowers ____________ **f** illuminated ____________

**g** clouds ____________ **h** happily ____________

**i** fairytale ____________ **j** funeral ____________

**5** Fill in the blanks below with adjectives from the 'AUDIO' column of the text 'Castle in the Clouds Funerals'.

**a** b ____________ **b** lo ____________ g **c** tr ____________ d

**d** g ____________ e **e** p ______ - ______ **f** c ____________ t

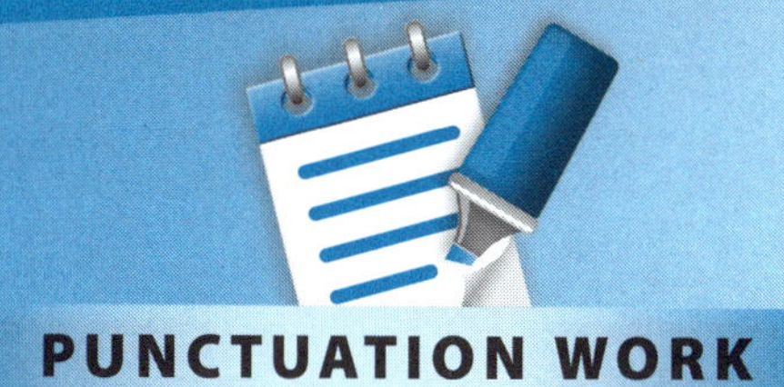

# PERSUASIVE TEXT

## Advertising script

PUNCTUATION WORK

### The ellipsis (...)

This punctuation mark's name comes from the Greek for falling short. An **ellipsis** (plural **ellipses**), which is a trio of full stops, shows that a word, sentence or section of a text has been purposely omitted. This is done in order to:

- save words or space
- seamlessly incorporate a quote
- show hesitation in a speaker
- create a trailing-off.

In the text 'Castle in the Clouds Funerals', ellipses show that only some words from the fairytale are being read. They also complement the turning book pages and the transitional dissolves between scenes.

**1** Show your understanding of the ellipsis by writing *correct* or *incorrect* beside each example of its use.

- **a** Jason said that we … can't borrow his car. __________
- **b** I still need to buy two things … a textbook and a uniform. __________
- **c** 'You look like you have bad news …' she said anxiously. __________
- **d** A proverb says 'Listen to advice … be counted among the wise.' __________

**2** Rewrite these sentences using correct punctuation. *Hint: They do not appear word-for-word in the script text.*

- **a** castle in the cloud's funerals offer: compassion peace of mind and dignity, to grieving family's
- **b** when youre at your lowest point why trust your loved ones funeral to just anyone call us
- **c** heres one of our customers tai jackson, castle in the clouds is, the best in the business
- **d** a television advertisement script should include—voiceover's music and scene timing's!

**3** This passage has been taken from the text but is incorrectly punctuated. Rewrite it correctly to match the text.

Vo 2 … sadly the reality of life is that all, fairytales, must eventually end make that ending a's pain free as possible with castle in the cloud's funeral's our family team offers the most compassionate care at the most difficult time

**4** What function do colons have in the 'TIME' column of the text? __________

**5** Which punctuation mark is used to show the numbers for '1300 RIP'? __________

**6** What is another punctuation mark used in the advertisement and what is its specific function?

# PERSUASIVE TEXT

## Advertising script

WRITING WORK 1

### Advertisement scripts

An **advertisement** (or commercial) **script** is a persuasive text that details a **written plan for an advertisement's production**. Visual, audio and written features are all included in this text form if it is intended for distribution on television. All of these elements work together to persuade the target audience to buy a particular product or company service. Only audio features, including voice over lines, sound effects and music, are used in a radio advertisement. Both advertisement forms generally run for thirty seconds with small time buffers at both ends.

### Main features of advertisement scripts

- Detailed descriptions of scene content, laid out in columns and rows
- Instructions for transitions between scenes
- Scripted voice over and/or dialogue lines
- Additional audio content, including music and sound effects
- Duration of scenes, shown in minutes and seconds, and time stamps for the end of each scene

### Additional features of television advertisement scripts

- Camera directions, including shots, angles and movements
- Detailed descriptions of footage, which may include a montage
- Onscreen text, such as phone numbers and product names

**1** What are three specific ways in which an advertisement for television can differ from one for radio?

______________________________

**2** Why is an advertisement script divided into rows? ______________________________

**3** Why has a montage been used in the advertisement for Castle in the Clouds Funerals?

______________________________

**4** Why do all advertisement scripts need small time buffers at both ends? *Hint: Re-read the text's annotations.*

______________________________

**Persuasive adjectives**, which are commonly used in advertising, were mentioned in the Grammar Work section on page 55 because adjectives are one of the main parts of speech. Check your adjective knowledge by answering the question and completing the task below.

**5** Circle the persuasive adjectives in these statements.

**a** With our convenient locations and our compassionate service, you'll feel right at home.

**b** Castle in the Clouds is a family-run business that offers your loved one a respectful farewell.

**6** Improve this passage by adding persuasive adjectives. It can advertise anything you choose.

Visit one of our ______________ stores today to experience our ______________ service. Speak to our ______________ staff about our ______________ products. We offer ______________ prices and ______________ advice. You will be ______________ and ______________ by what's on offer.

# PERSUASIVE TEXT

## Advertising script

### Other persuasive language features in advertisements

In the text 'Castle in the Clouds Funerals', the composer has used some specific **language features** designed to **persuade** the target audience. These include:

- second person address, including pronouns like *you;* for example, 'help you cope'
- repetition; for example, 'Castle in the Clouds Funerals' (this is the company's name)
- emotive language; for example, 'beautiful couple'
- high modality words and imperatives; for example, *must* and *most.*
- a command or direction; for example, the onscreen text 'Call Castle in the Clouds Funerals'
- descriptive and specific language; for example, 'more than thirty years experience'
- music that complements the subject, audio and visuals; for example, 'music box style track'
- euphemisms; for example, 'as the fairytale ends' is a euphemism for death.

**Euphemisms** are expressions that 'dilute' an unpleasant subject by rephrasing it in a more palatable way. Many expressions associated with political correctness are euphemisms. At other times, euphemisms are used for the sake of politeness or sensitivity.

**7** Complete the blanks to explore some common euphemisms.

**a** Jen is **vertically challenged.** means ______________________

**b** ______________________ means He is dead.

**c** I seem to have **misplaced** your coat. means ______________________

Some **special language features** of television advertisement scripts include:

- scene numbers and time stamps
- film-related abbreviations such as 'VO' (voiceover) and film jargon such as 'dissolve', 'montage' and 'track'.

**8** What other film jargon is used in the text 'Castle in the Clouds Funerals'?

______________________

______________________

**9** How is repetition used to help viewers remember the most vital detail in the text 'Castle in the Clouds Funerals'? *Hint: A clue is given in the bullet point notes above.*

______________________

______________________

**10** What contrasting images are used and with what effect?

______________________

______________________

**11** What emotions is the composer trying to manipulate in the text and how is this done?

______________________

______________________

**12** What addition could be made to the advertisement to make it more effective?

______________________

______________________

# PERSUASIVE TEXT

**WRITING SAMPLE**

Here is a sample text showing you how to structure and write an advertising script. This one is for radio.

## Campaign: Move Me Homes

Project: 30 sec RC

Version: Draft 1

| SCENE | TIME | AUDIO |
|---|---|---|
| 000 | 1.5 secs<br>00:01.5 | *SFX: An auctioneer's voice taking bids and saying phrases associated with buying a home. Sound dissolves into Scene 001 and fades out by the end of the scene.* |
| 001 | 2 secs<br>00:03.5 | VO: When you're buying a new home, you're not just looking for a building … |
| 002 | 0.5 secs<br>00:04 | *SFX: Flourish of a harp to suggest a dream* |
| 003 | 1 sec<br>00:05 | VO: You're *building* a dream. |
| 004 | 6 secs<br>00:12 | VO: Don't trust your dream to just anyone. At Move Me Homes, we have the industry contacts and new home know-how to bring your dream to life. |
| 005 | 0.5 secs<br>00:12.5 | *SFX: Doorbell* |
| 006 | 3.5 secs<br>00:16 | VO: From securing the right finance to laying the welcome mat, Move Me Homes will guide you every step of the way. |
| 007 | 3 secs<br>00:19 | VO: We even offer testimonials from families in neighbourhoods of your choice. |
| 008 | 5 secs<br>00:24 | VO: Janine and the trusted team at Move Me Homes are waiting to take you on your new home journey. |
| 009 | 4.5 secs<br>00:29.5 | VO: Call 1300-MOVE-ME. That's 1300 66 83 63. Call now! Be moved … with Move Me Homes. |

- **Write the headings SCENE, TIME and AUDIO to show the purpose of each column.**
- **Write the number of seconds for each scene and the time stamp by the end of each scene in the rows.** The timing is very specific: at the beginning, a buffer of 0.5 seconds is left for a volume fade-up. The other 1 second allows for sound effects (SFX) to begin; these sounds are shown in italics. Here, an auctioneer is heard selling a home.
- **Continue to describe all sound elements, including sound effects and voiceover lines (VOs) in detail.** The scenes are divided according to natural breaks in the information or changes in the sound.
- **Insert a brief sound effect.** Here, a harp flourish lasting half a second, suggesting a dream, precedes the word 'dream' in the script.
- **Write VO lines appealing to the listener using second person address.** An emotive word, 'dream', is linked to home ownership and repeated throughout the advertisement.
- **Continue to make second person appeals to listeners.** Economical language is used here: 'industry contacts and new home know-how' sum up the skills and knowledge offered by Move Me Homes.
- **Insert a brief sound effect.** Here a doorbell connotes both an image and an idea (or dream) of coming home.
- **List things offered by the company or product, implying that many other wonderful things are on the list.** The list of things offered by Move Me Homes is suggested by the words 'from', 'to' and 'every step of the way', as though many other wonderful things are on that list. 'Laying the welcome mat' is both a literal and a metaphorical reference related to moving into a home.
- **Mention a special feature of a company product and/or a bonus offer.** A part of Move Me Homes's service, 'testimonials from families in neighbourhoods of your choice', is made into a special feature by the words 'We even offer'.
- **Name a contact person to make the company sound relatable and friendly or to inspire confidence about the product.** Telling the audience about their 'new home journey' is the final emotive appeal before contact info is given.
- **Give a phone number, a persuasive command, a slogan and the company or product's name at the end of the advertisement.** This advertisement urges the listener to 'Call now!', and gives the slogan 'Be moved' and the company's name 'Move Me Homes' at the end. A buffer of 0.5 seconds is left for a volume fade-down.

# PERSUASIVE TEXT

## *Advertising script*

**WRITING YOUR OWN SAMPLE**

Plan your sample in the spaces provided.

**Campaign:** ______________________________

Project: 30 sec RC

Version: Draft 1

| | | |
|---|---|---|
| 000 | | |
| 001 | | |
| 002 | | |
| 003 | | |
| 004 | | |
| 005 | | |
| 006 | | |
| 007 | | |
| 008 | | |
| 009 | | |

- **Write the headings SCENE, TIME and AUDIO to show the purpose of each column.**
- **Write the number of seconds for each scene and the time stamp by the end of each scene in the rows.** At the beginning, leave a buffer of 0.5 seconds for a volume fade-up. Write voiceover (VO) lines for most scenes. Show sound effects (SFX) in italics to distinguish them from the VOs.
- **Continue to describe all sound elements, including sound effects and voiceover lines (VOs) in detail.** Most of the advertisement should consist of VOs. Divide scenes according to natural breaks in the information or changes in the sound.
- **Insert a brief sound effect.**
- **Write VO lines appealing to the listener using second person address.** Using the word *you* is the best way. Include an emotive word or phrase.
- **Continue to make second person appeals to listeners.** Use economical language to sum up the positive qualities of the company or product.
- **Use a final sound effect.**
- **List things offered by the company or product, implying that many other wonderful things are on the list.** Use a metaphor or pun related to the company or product.
- **Mention a special feature of a company product and/or a bonus offer.**
- **Name a contact person to make the company sound relatable and friendly or to inspire confidence about the product.** Make a final emotive appeal to the audience.
- **Give a phone number, a persuasive command, a slogan and the company or product's name at the end of the advertisement.** Leave a buffer of 0.5 seconds for a volume fade-down.

UNIT 7

# PERSUASIVE TEXT

## *Playbill*

**READING WORK**

### Antigone

*The following visual text is a playbill (poster advertising a play) promoting a high-school production of* Antigone, *the ancient Greek tragedy by Sophocles. The play was staged in a chapel which was temporarily converted into an indoor amphitheatre using tiered seating. The production featured a main cast of six actors, a twelve-member Greek chorus, a large dance troupe and a live music ensemble. In total, more than fifty students from Year 8 to Year 12 performed. Prior to each of the shows, patrons were invited to purchase Greek food and drinks from a bazaar set up outside the performance space.*

ANTIGONE

*"I will be a pure and holy criminal"*

St Agnel's College
Bedesville

School Chapel: raised amphitheatre seating

Wednesday 17th March
Thursday 18th March
Friday 19th March
Saturday 20th March

7:30pm

Authentic Greek food & drinks available from 5:30pm

Online ticket sales:
www.bookme.ed/antigone

Door sales from 5:30pm performance nights

- A large, stylised A for *Antigone* **alludes** to Mount Olympus and the Greek gods.
- A large Greek-style font is used in the **banner**.
- A **key quote** from the play is the only italicised text in the playbill.
- The noose alludes to the **climax**.
- The school and suburb are **named**.
- A noose in place of a head creates **mystery** about the heroine.
- **Venue and seating information** are given.
- Show **dates** and days are listed.
- A white gown **symbolises** purity and innocence; grey smoke stains suggest doom and the shadow of death.
- The **starting time** is in large font.
- **Details** about food bazaar are white to attract extra attention.
- **Vectors** created by flames lead the viewer's eye to the heroine figure and up to the noose.
- **Ticketing information** is in coloured type to match other show details.
- **Stylised** flames represent both destruction and the catharsis (cleansing) central to Greek tragedy.
- A hand-drawn, cartoon **style** and rough lower border edge soften the gruesome **images**.

# PERSUASIVE TEXT

## Playbill

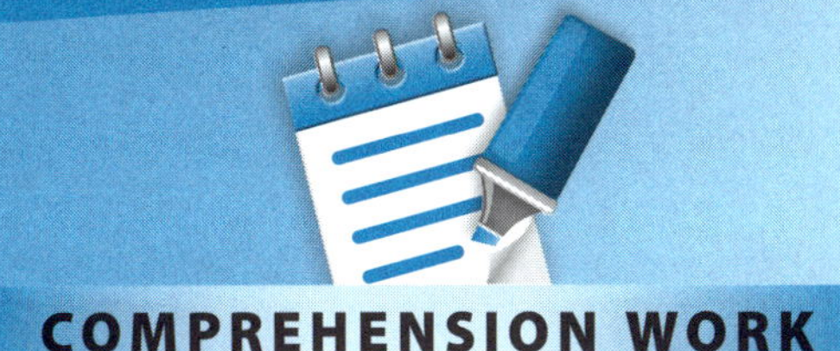

COMPREHENSION WORK

### Literal questions

*Hint: Read the text carefully to locate specific facts and details.*

1 When can tickets be purchased at the door?

a from 5:30 on performance nights    b at 7:30 on performance nights    c at any time online

2 In which suburb is the venue located? ______

3 When is opening night? ______

### Interpretive questions

*Hint: These questions require you to combine facts and details to synthesise the meaning.*

4 Where is the temporary amphitheatre?

a inside the chapel    b outside the chapel    c there isn't one

5 Which two words beginning with *a* suggest that the event will be presented in true ancient Greek style?

a 'amphitheatre' and 'authentic'    b 'Agnel's' and 'amphitheatre'    c 'authentic' and 'available'

6 What is the connection between the noose and the quote from the play?

______

______

7 What is one effect of the contrasting fonts (printed text styles)?

*Hint: The correct term for a text style is typeface. In common usage, however, font is acceptable.*

______

______

8 What is wrong with the way the quote from the play is punctuated?

______

______

9 Which adjective in the text indicates that everyone in the audience will have a good view?

a 'authentic'    b 'seating'    c 'raised'

10 Which option below lists three visual features that create a sense of doom in the playbill?

a flames, black background and criminal    b noose, flames and black background

c flames, dress and quote

### Applied questions

*Hint: These questions require you to understand a text's implications to infer meaning from the text.*

11 The heroine (main female character, more properly called a protagonist), Antigone, is the 'pure and holy criminal' in the play. How do we know this? Give a specific answer that refers to features of the playbill.

______

______

12 What is the most likely reason why the composer of the playbill has not given details about the story?

a In order to avoid spoiling the shock of Antigone's hanging.

b The play is ancient so the story is already well known.

c The play is ancient so nobody cares what happens.

# PERSUASIVE TEXT

*Playbill*

## SPELLING WORK

### List Words

All of the words in the box below appear in the text 'Antigone' and the introduction above it.

| | | | | |
|---|---|---|---|---|
| promoting | troupe | ensemble | bazaar | tiered |
| prior | college | authentic | criminal | amphitheatre |
| online | pure | holy | seating | performance |

**1** The passage below requires ten list words to be complete. Find the words and write them correctly in order in the spaces provided. *Hint: The playbill text will be useful as a guide to the meaning of each word.*

The staff and students of St Agnel's ______________ staged an ________________ ancient Greek-style ________________ of Sophocles's tragedy *Antigone.* To enhance the experience, a ______________ featuring Greek food and drink was open ____________ to the show. The audience's seats were raised and _____________ to maximise everyone's view. The actors, dance t____________ and _______________e of musicians all wowed the crowd with their skill, and the lead actress played the role of Antigone, the 'pure and holy _____________', with great passion. Following each show, the director posted a photo __________ featuring the talented St Agnel's students in action.

When the order of letters in a word is changed, we can call this a jumble or a scramble, but when a word's letters are shuffled to form another word, the result is called an **anagram**. Every second word in the following question is an anagram.

**2** Unscramble the letters to form list words.

**a** riorp ________________ **b** teasing ________________

**c** motorping ________________ **d** pouter ________________

**e** enolin ________________ **f** dieter ________________

**3** Make new words using the letters in the following list words. You may only use each letter once. For each list word, try to give at least ten new three-letter words and at least three new words containing four letters or more. The first one has been done for you as a guide. *Hint: An anagram of one word appears in Question 2.*

| List Word | New three-letter words | New four-letter words or longer |
|---|---|---|
| **a** college | leg, cog, gel, log, eel, lee, ego, ole, col, cel | cell, cleg, ogle, Lego, cello |
| **b** authentic | | |
| **c** troupe | | |
| **d** performance | | |

**4** Each sentence below contains a pair of words with correct spelling but only one word fits in the context. Circle the word that best fits in each sentence. *Hint: The correct words are not necessarily list words.*

**a** A playbill is a traditional way of promoting / prompting a theatrical show.

**b** Sam's parents strongly desired to give him a college / collage education.

**c** The holy / holly bush, with its bright red berries, is associated with Christmas.

**d** Versace created a spectacular tiered / tired gown for the actress.

**e** The troupe / toupé of clowns was a favourite with the circus audience.

**f** It was the most bazaar / bizarre movie she'd ever seen.

**g** 'I'm pleased to announce the ensemble / assemble of cast members,' said the director.

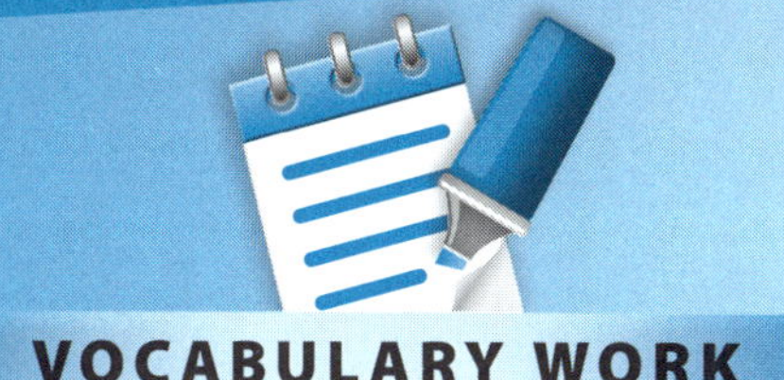

# PERSUASIVE TEXT

## Playbill

## VOCABULARY WORK

**1** Complete these sentences by using a list word. The meaning of each word is provided.

- **a** The company spent a lot of money ______________________ their products. (advertising or pushing)
- **b** This olive oil is the most _______________ one available. (untainted and unchanged)
- **c** His business activities can only be described as ________________________. (against the law)

**2** Are these word meanings correct? Write *true* or *false* next to each meaning given below.
*Hint: Look back at how the words are used in the playbill text for clues.*

| Word | Meaning | True or False? |
|---|---|---|
| **a** tiered | layered or stacked | ______________ |
| **b** online | along a line | ______________ |
| **c** holy | full of holes | ______________ |
| **d** college | educational institution | ______________ |

It can be difficult choosing just the right word for use in a sentence. The question below features pairs of list words that are the same part of speech (either **adjectives** or **nouns**), which can easily lead to confusion.

**3** Cross out the list word that does not fit in each sentence below. The sentences refer to the production of *Antigone* at St Agnel's College. Either word can fit into each sentence, but only one word makes sense based on the information provided in the text. *Hint: Look back at the playbill to help you with this question.*

- **a** Food and drinks were sold at the Greek bazaar / performance before *Antigone*.
- **b** A temporary college / amphitheatre was the performance space for the show.
- **c** Patrons enjoyed the convenience of online / authentic ticketing.
- **d** The performance / seating layout ensured that everyone in the audience got a good view.
- **e** The heroine's white costume symbolised her pure / holy heart.
- **f** The audience was given prior / pure warning about exactly when the show would start.
- **g** It was quite a task, creating an amphitheatre / performance indoors.

**4** Define these non-list words from the Spelling Work section. Do not simply give single-word synonyms.
*Hint: Looking back at Question 4 of the Spelling Work section will help you define some of these words.*

- **a** prompting ________________________________________________
- **b** collage ________________________________________________
- **c** holly ________________________________________________
- **d** tired ________________________________________________
- **e** toupé ________________________________________________
- **f** bizarre ________________________________________________
- **g** assemble ________________________________________________

**5** These words appear in the notes on the text. Match up synonym pairs by drawing connecting lines.

**Set 1**

| | |
|---|---|
| climax | refers |
| alludes | peak |
| symbolise | represent |

**Set 2**

| | |
|---|---|
| vectors | sightlines |
| attention | enigma |
| mystery | focus |

# PERSUASIVE TEXT

## Playbill

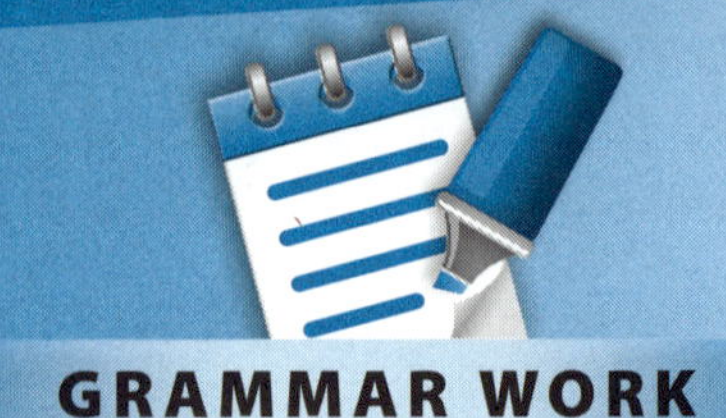

GRAMMAR WORK

### Economical language

Particularly in a text like a visual advertisement, **using language economically**—that is, conveying ample information in as few words as possible—is very important. Using language economically in a visual text:

- keeps the text uncluttered
- helps the viewer take in details quickly
- complements a balanced layout
- makes the text easy to understand.

The text 'Antigone' offers good examples of economical language usage, including dates and times, carefully chosen phrases and a key quote from the play. While it is a persuasive text, it appears to be simply informative and not manipulative. This is partly due to its language economy.

**1** Write a full sentence in each category to form a summary of the information given in the text 'Antigone', using the word presented. The first one has been done for you as an example. Give specific details but keep your language economical. Use the present tense.

**a** School The school whose students are staging the play is St Agnel's College in Bedesville.

**b** Play ______

**c** Venue ______

**d** Show dates ______

**e** Show time ______

**f** Tickets ______

**g** Heroine ______

**2** More than five of the list words contain three or more syllables. What are they? Write them on the line below, separated by commas. Show the syllable divisions in each word using dashes, like this: syll–a–ble.

______

A **malapropism** is the term we can give to a word that has been **used incorrectly based on context**. This term comes from the character Mrs Malaprop in the comedy *The Rivals* by Richard Sheridan. An example of a malapropism from the play is 'she's as headstrong as an allegory [alligator] on the banks of the Nile.' Having a good vocabulary helps us choose the best word for each situation and avoid malapropisms.

**3** Write *yes* or *no* to indicate whether the list word in each sentence has been used as a malapropism.

**a** We went to the bazaar to buy some tasty flatbread. ______

**b** Prior to getting this retail job, I'd never sold clothing. ______

**c** The scan showed that Baruk had an online fracture in his arm. ______

**d** He was beyond tiered after the three-day hike. ______

**e** You look familiar: you ensemble my cousin. ______

**f** I delivered all my lines and didn't need any promoting. ______

**4** One of the words in each sentence is a malapropism. Circle it, then write the word that should have been used. *Hint: Some of the malapropisms are list words and some of the correct words are list words.*

**a** We can learn about this ancient Greek amphibian from its ruins. ______

**b** I need to find a prior who will give me a good price on my car. ______

**c** Going to the gym can help you become more authentic. ______

**d** The legal system should be tougher on minimal behaviour. ______

**e** I really like this steered birthday cake. ______

# PERSUASIVE TEXT

*Playbill*

PUNCTUATION WORK

## Colons

Students of English are familiar with seeing a colon before a list but they are often unsure about how to use one in a sentence. It helps a lot to know that this punctuation mark essentially stands for *this is what I mean*. It is also important to know that, while they look similar, the **colon** (:) and the **semicolon** (;) must not be used interchangeably. A colon appears in the next sentence because a list follows. When using colons, we must keep in mind that:

- a colon only precedes a list when the list is in a series of dot points (like this one), not when the list is incorporated into a sentence (for example, *Janie wanted to study art, music and dance.*)
- two independent clauses in a sentence may be divided by a colon when the second clause explains the first (for example, *I'll take my umbrella: it looks like it will rain any minute.*)
- a key phrase or word at the end of a sentence can be given emphasis by a colon and this key item is not capitalised (for example, *The jury had reached their unanimous verdict: guilty.*)

## Other functions of the colon

Did you notice that **colons** can also have **non-grammatical functions**? We can use them when:

- showing the time (for example, *5:30 pm*)
- expressing a ratio or odds (for example, *The Spartans were outnumbered 5:1 by the invading army.*)
- showing volumes or chapters in a text reference (for example, *Photographic Quarterly, 5:81–84*)
- dividing two details that do not form a full sentence (for example, *Fairmont Pavilion: rear stalls*)
- writing electronic or written correspondence (usually formal) (for example, *Attn: The Manager, cc: Barry Smith, PS: Please do not respond to this automatically generated message.*)

**1** Find where colons are used in the playbill text and write *yes* or *no* beside the various functions listed below. *Hint: Look back over the examples in the two lists above to help you answer.*

**a** showing the time ________

**b** expressing a ratio ________

**c** dividing two independent clauses in a sentence ________

**d** dividing two details that do not form a full sentence ________

**e** emphasising a key phrase or word at the end of a sentence ________

**2** Read the following passage carefully then insert all missing punctuation marks, including colons and capital letters.

*Antigone* by sophocles is a play in a key theatrical tradition greek tragedy This masterpiece features the following classical tragedy conventions a family of nobles a heroine a chorus and a plot that unfolds over one or two days The blind prophet tiresias is a character who appears in this and other greek tragedies Many people leave a performance like this one in tears it can be a moving experience

**3** Circle any incorrect uses of colons in these sentences.
*Hint: Include any times that a colon has been omitted where it should have been used.*

**a** Jackson got what he'd worked so hard for: a recording contract.

**b** In this instance: it's vital that: you do not stir the mixture.

**c** Take it easy you've just had: surgery.

**d** I'm telling you: for the last time leave it alone.

**e** When you go to the shop, please buy: bread, cheese and cat food.

# PERSUASIVE TEXT

## *Playbill*

### Playbills

A **playbill** is a **persuasive visual text** that advertises a **play**. Traditionally only printed posters, playbills in today's internet age can also be electronic texts that you will find online. Playbills can be found just about anywhere, from theatre foyers to telegraph poles. Anywhere that people can be advertised to, a playbill can be posted. This type of text is very similar to a movie poster because a movie is a play shown on-screen instead of live in a theatre. Theatre playbills, however, will usually contain more details about the venue, times and ticketing for the show. Movies play in many different cinemas so this kind of information is too variable to include in movie posters. Playbills can be bought and sold as collectors' items. Vintage playbills in good condition can fetch a lot of money. While the features of playbills vary widely depending on the production and the target audience, some aspects are always the same. Certain features of this persuasive text form are also simply informative.

### Features of a playbill

The main **features** of any **playbill** are:

- the title of the play
- show dates and times
- venue information
- ticketing information
- a relevant image, font or design feature related to the production.

Other common features of playbills include:

- the name of the playwright
- the names of the actors, especially if they are well known and likely to attract fans to the show
- the director and/or producer
- a short blurb about the play
- a key quote or two from the play
- favourable quotes from theatre critics and/or a star rating
- some details about the production company, director or play genre, to suggest a target audience.

**1** What are some other persuasive or informative features that can be included in a playbill?

______________________________________________

### Making an effective playbill

To ensure that a **playbill** is **effective** in promoting the play, the composer of the text must:

- persuade the viewer/reader to see the play
- use clear and economical expression and accurate punctuation
- position words and images in a balanced layout
- choose images that complement the text and convey the intended tone of the play
- ensure that patrons are clear about how to go about seeing the show.

**2** Define these words from the three lists you've just read. Make sure that the definitions suit the context.

**a** features ______________________

**b** playwright ______________________

**c** director ______________________

**d** critics ______________________

**e** complement ______________________

**3** Look back at the text 'Antigone'. How has balance been created in the layout?

______________________________________________

______________________________________________

## Writing about playbills

A **playbill** is a visual text so we use the language of **visual literacy** when describing and evaluating it. We can see that the *Antigone* advertisement contains a number of visual literacy features that are well suited to the text form of playbill. These include:

- contrast
- symbolism
- hand-drawn images
- balanced layout
- vectors
- different fonts
- seamless border
- texture

**4** Describe what you think is the most effective visual feature of the text 'Antigone' and explain its impact. Look back at the text and the explanatory notes to be reminded of its main visual features.
*Hint: You may refer to features other than those listed above.*

______________________________________________

______________________________________________

Of course, we must also refer to the words and their impact when discussing a playbill, and we need to consider the ways that **words and images complement** (add to or support) each other. Look at the text 'Antigone' and consider how words and pictures work together to create a persuasive text.

**5** What is one specific way that a visual feature complements the words in the text 'Antigone'? For example, the banner of the playbill is in an ancient Greek-style font because the play is an ancient Greek tragedy.

______________________________________________

______________________________________________

**6** What is one feature in each category that could be added to the text to improve it?

**a** Visual: ______________________________________________

**b** Written: ______________________________________________

**7** Complete these sentences to construct a brief discussion of the *Antigone* playbill. Fill each space provided.
*Hint: There is no set answer and some of the features below have not been mentioned yet.*

The composer of the text 'Antigone' has chosen to symbolise ______________________________________________
in the text, through the visual elements of ______________________________________________.
Contrast has been created in the playbill by ______________________________________________.
One effect of this contrast is ______________________________________________.
The banner at the top attracts the viewer's eye because ______________________________________________
and ______________________________________________.
Vectors also lead the eye up to the banner. These are created by ______________________________________________.
The most important informative words on the playbill are ______________________________________________.
The quote 'I will be a pure and holy criminal' is significant because ______________________________________________.
The position of the quote is important because ______________________________________________.
The persuasive impact of this playbill is subtle yet effective. It is persuasive because ______________________________________________
______________________________________________.

# PERSUASIVE TEXT

## *Playbill*

WRITING SAMPLE

Here is a sample text showing you how to structure and write a playbill.

**Watch this space . . .**

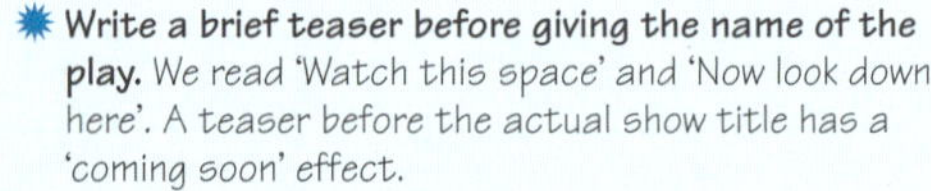

✷ **Write a brief teaser before giving the name of the play.** We read 'Watch this space' and 'Now look down here'. A teaser before the actual show title has a 'coming soon' effect.

Now look down here

✷ **Include an appropriate image from or related to the show.** A vintage image of a pointing hand alludes to Monty Python skits and similar types of silly sketch comedy, suggesting a lot about the show *The Theatrical Menagerie*. An unexpected phrase completes the teaser and echoes the silly tone.

**THE THEATRICAL MENAGERIE**

Variety Show

✷ **State the name of the play and present it in an appropriate and eye-catching typeface.** 'Menagerie' in the show title suggests an eclectic collection of comedy acts.

**Coming to Lionsford Community Playhouse really quite soon**

✷ **Name the venue.** Here an unusual time reference reinforces the tone.

**WHAT:** An upROARious cavalcade of silly and mostly pointless entertainment courtesy of Lionsford's best!

✷ **Write a brief, catchy summary.** A pun on Lionsford ('upROARious') reinforces the tone.

**WHERE:** 42 Strikear Avenue, Lionsford

✷ **Give the address.**

**WHEN:** Sat. 1st to Sun. 9th August 2015
8pm nightly; 2pm Sat. matinees

✷ **Give the season information (days, dates and times for the show).** A simple layout makes the basic show details clear for the viewer. This approach is clear and specific, and contains abbreviations that make the details easy to read and understand.

**HOW MUCH:** $18 adult
$12 concession
$10 kids under 12
$50 family of 4

✷ **List ticket types and prices.**

**BOOKINGS & MORE INFO:** www.lionsfordcph/bookings
Ph. 1800 454 545

✷ **Provide contact details.**

# PERSUASIVE TEXT

## Playbill

**WRITING YOUR OWN SAMPLE**

Plan your sample on the lines provided.

- **Write a brief teaser before giving the name of the play.** The teaser does not have to be silly or funny. It may simply be *Coming soon …* or something similar. A teaser is not necessarily an element of every playbill.
- **Include an appropriate image from or related to the show.** This image must help establish a tone for the show.
- **State the name of the play and present it in an appropriate and eye-catching typeface.** The typeface should establish a tone that suits the style of the performance being advertised and gives audience members an idea of what to expect at the show.
- **Name the venue.**
- **Write a brief, catchy summary.**
- **Give the address.** Remember to make the details as clear and simple as possible. Separate the parts of the address on different lines to make them easy to read. The address may be presented as part of the season information.
- **Give the season information (days, dates and times for the show).**
- **List ticket types and prices.** These should reflect the type of patron expected to attend and whether this is a professional (expensive) or amateur show. People will be more likely to attend if there is a group or family discount. Like the venue details, the ticket details should appear separated on a series of lines.
- **Provide contact details.** Include a phone number, website and/or email address, where people can get further information about the show and book tickets.

# UNIT 8 PERSUASIVE TEXT

## Open letter

**READING WORK**

## On-screen smoking

Why Smoking Kills
244 Warning Ave
North Bondi NSW 2062
whysmokingkills.org

17 April 2016

Attn: Philippa Morg
Executive Content Advisor
Screen V
20 Rattley Rd
Paddington NSW 2021

**On-screen Smoking**

Dear Ms Morg,

I am writing to you on behalf of Why Smoking Kills, a non-profit organisation that educates young Australians about the risks associated with smoking tobacco. This is an open letter intended for distribution on social media and in film industry publications.

Why Smoking Kills is of the opinion that there has been a dangerous resurgence of cigarette smoking on both local and international film screens. I attribute this to complacency among regulatory bodies such as the Department of Health, because there is a misconception of tobacco's movie image as a 'problem solved'.

Happily, smoking has lost some of its glamour over the past twenty years but it remains a major threat to public health. While there is little that Why Smoking Kills can do to stymie the flow of silver screen smokers still pouring out from Hollywood, we can address this issue locally and urge bodies like yours, Screen V, to regulate the content of independent films, short films and web series eligible for State and Federal funding.

According to the *Tobacco Advertising Prohibition Act 1992* (TAP Act), a smoking advertisement is defined as a moving picture that 'gives publicity to, promotes or intends to promote: smoking, the purchase of tobacco products, a particular brand of tobacco product, a specific tobacco manufacturer or any words or images closely associated with a tobacco product'. You will note that the issue does not centre on selling a product; the act of smoking alone is enough to promote it.

Why Smoking Kills simply requests that any moving image produced in Australia be subject to the restrictions of the TAP Act. Is that not reasonable?

The good news is that the 2013 National Drug Strategy Household Survey (NDSHS) found a recent decline—or at least a delay—in youth smoking. The age for 14- to 24-year-olds trying their first cigarette increased from 15.4 years of age in 2010 to 15.9 years in 2013. Indeed, a positive step. Excitingly, the NDSHS also indicated that, in 2013, the number of 12- to 17-year-olds who had never smoked was very high, at 95 per cent.

Let's hasten this decline in youth smoking! Why Smoking Kills is identifying relevant cases of arts funding to build on these positive trends. Please know that we are also reaching out to other Australian arts councils on this matter.

Why Smoking Kills staunchly advocates freedom of expression but when independent Australian filmmakers receive taxpayer-dollar production funding we are morally obligated to question how those funds are utilised.

As such, we must insist that Screen V publicly respond with an explanation of the group's stance on this issue.

Yours sincerely,

*J Pufflet*

Jeffrey Pufflet
Chief Media Liaison, Why Smoking Kills

- The **sender's name and address** precede those of the recipient. The choice of how to lay out a letter should consider the readability and purpose of the letter. Prior to the advent of computers the sender's address was usually written on the right-hand side of the page. Computers and the need to minimise keystrokes introduced the convention of having everything start on the left-hand side of the page. Of course, if an official letterhead is used, the sender's address and contact details can appear wherever the designer of the letterhead has placed it—this is often at the top of the page but can be elsewhere.
- The **date** on which the letter was written follows.
- The **recipient's name and address** appear next. If a company is the recipient, an appropriate contact person or representative is also named.
- The letter is given a **heading** that indicates the subject.
- A **formal salutation** (greeting) opens the letter.
- The writer raises the **issue** immediately.
- The writer makes it plain that this letter will be **shared with the public**.
- 'Silver screen' is a **colloquial term** for the big-budget film industry.
- The **diction** (word choice) conjures images of smoke 'pouring out' from Hollywood.
- **Factual details**, including pieces of legislation, terminology and statistics, are cited to add to the authority of the letter.
- A single sentence **sums up** the request of Why Smoking Kills and shows that it is a reasonable one. It is followed by a rhetorical question that cements this idea.
- The writer **appeals** to the recipient—and all readers of the letter—from a positive standpoint.
- The letter closes with a **polite demand**. The writer is giving the recipient a specific way to respond to the issues raised in the letter. Now the onus is on her organisation (Screen V).
- The **sender's signature** precedes his full name and position in the organisation behind this letter.

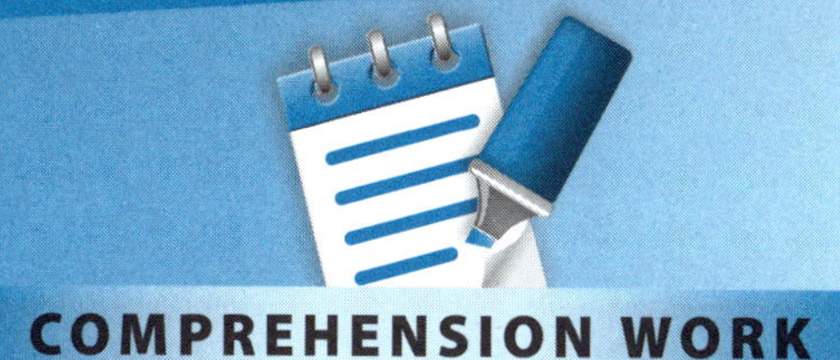

# PERSUASIVE TEXT

## *Open letter*

COMPREHENSION WORK

### Literal questions

*Hint: Read the text carefully to locate specific facts and details.*

**1** Who is the composer of the letter?

**a** Jeffrey Pufflet **b** Philippa Morg **c** Why Smoking Kills

**2** What does the composer find exciting about the NDSHS findings in 2013?

______________________________

**3** What right does Why Smoking Kills advocate (actively support)? ______________________________

______________________________

### Interpretive questions

*Hint: These questions require you to combine facts and details to synthesise the meaning.*

**4** Complete this statement based on the language features used in the text.

In the first sentence of the third paragraph, the composer uses

**a** 'oh' assonance to suggest a moaning sound. **b** sibilance ('s' sounds) to create an evil image of a snake.

**c** the phrase 'pouring out' and the word 'flow' to evoke a smoke image.

**5** What is the function of the sentence beginning 'You will note …' on line 30?

**a** It defines a section of the TAP Act. **b** It interprets a section of the TAP Act.

**c** It contradicts a section of the TAP Act.

**6** Why Smoking Kills is 'also reaching out to other Australian arts councils on this matter'. Why?

______________________________

**7** Why has the composer chosen a formal letter structure to raise this issue?

______________________________

**8** Which abstract noun in the second paragraph (lines 17–20) is the reason given for 'complacency among regulatory bodies'?

**a** 'resurgence' **b** 'screens' **c** 'misconception'

**9** What is the role of 'bodies like Screen V'?

**a** They help independent filmmakers get funding. **b** They create legislation like the TAP Act.

**c** They promote tobacco products.

**10** What evidence is there for 'a recent decline—or at least a delay—in youth smoking'?

______________________________

### Applied questions

*Hint: These questions require you to understand a text's implications to infer meaning from the text.*

**11** Why has the 'Executive Content Advisor' of Screen V been chosen to receive this letter?

______________________________

**12** Why might 'regulatory bodies' see the on-screen smoking issue as 'a problem solved'?

**a** They think it is the responsibility of film bodies like Screen V to comply with the TAP Act's restrictions.

**b** Smoking's image is not as glamorous now as it was in the past. **c** both **a** and **b**

# PERSUASIVE TEXT

Open letter

SPELLING WORK

## List Words

All of the words in the box below appear in the text 'On-screen smoking'.

| | | | | |
|---|---|---|---|---|
| executive | advisor | behalf | organisation | associated |
| eligible | complacency | recent | centre | excitingly |
| manufacturer | identifying | hasten | staunchly | utilised |

**1** One word in each sentence has been misspelt. Write the correct word on the line provided.
*Hint: List words are used in each sentence, but not all are misspelt. Some are used correctly.*

**a** This independent filmmaker will be elgible for funding. ____________

**b** Smoking is directly assocciated with lung cancer. ____________

**c** Excitingly, the goverment has announced more funding for short films. ____________

**d** Researchers are idenifying links between movies and youth smoking. ____________

**e** On be-half of Why Smoking Kills, I wish to challenge your complacency. ____________

**f** We must protest stanchly if we are to fix this problem. ____________

**2** Many words can be found inside other words. Make a list word that

**a** begins with a present tense form of *have*. ____________

**b** ends with a currency-related word. ____________

**c** begins with a synonym for *gent*. ____________

**d** ends with a sun-hat. ____________

**e** begins with another name for a *donkey*. ____________

**f** ends with an adjective for a prickling sensation. ____________

**3** Form complete words from the list words and the text 'On-screen smoking' by adding letters before or after the portions given. *Hint: You need to look for the word portions in both the text 'On-screen smoking' and among the list words.*

| | | |
|---|---|---|
| **a** ____________ payer | **b** ____________ acco | **c** ____________ bject |
| **d** film ____________ | **e** uti ____________ | **f** dang ____________ |
| **g** ____________ gible | **h** ____________ half | **i** ____________ nation |

**4** One word in each set is not a real word. Cross it out. *Hint: Each set is derived from a list word.*

| | | | | | |
|---|---|---|---|---|---|
| **a** eligibility | eligibleness | ineligible | **b** executor | executing | executar |
| **c** utilising | utilisationer | utilitarian | **d** manufactured | manufacture | manufracture |

**5** Split the letter chains below to make list words. Write the words on the lines provided.
*Hint: Gaps have been placed in irregular places in the chains to make this task more challenging.*

**a** elig ibleexec utivesta unchly ____________

**b** cen trecom placen cyutili sed ____________

**c** be hal fex citi nglyid entif ying ____________

**6** The letter groups below are pairs of nested words—that is, one word inside another. Separate the words and write them on the lines provided.

**a** assocomplacencyciated ____________

**b** uteligibleilised ____________

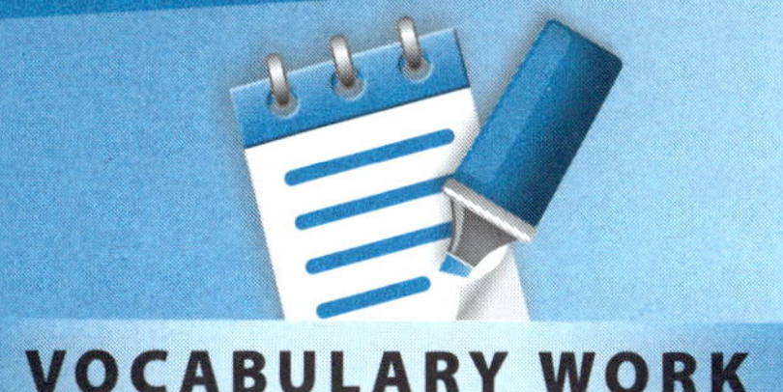

# PERSUASIVE TEXT

## Open letter

## VOCABULARY WORK

**1** Each sentence below contains a pair of correctly spelt words, but one doesn't work in the context. Circle it.
*Hint: The correct words are not necessarily list words.*

**a** The students' parents arranged to make car payments on her behalf / half.

**b** Our non-profit organiser / organisation sends open letters to companies like yours.

**c** We must decide how your skills can best be used / utilised.

**d** Because of his good credit record, Sav was legible / eligible for the loan.

**e** The park was an ideal meeting place due to its centre / central location.

**f** Computer complacency / competency will serve you well when applying for a job.

Many **word roots** (parts of words) and entire words in the English language have their origins in the language of Latin. We can improve our vocabulary by becoming familiar with these roots and words.

**2** **a** The issue of advertising tobacco products—inadvertently or on purpose—is raised in the text 'On-screen smoking'. The word *advertising* has its roots in the Latin word *advertere*, which means 'turn towards'. Write other words that belong to the same word family by completing the blanks.

ad ______________ er (noun) ad ______________ nt (noun) ad ______________ d (verb)

**b** In the text 'On-screen smoking', we read about the principles that Why Smoking Kills 'advocates'. This word comes from the Latin *advocare*, which describes the act of asking for help. Write other words that belong to the same word family by completing the blanks.

ad ______________ te (noun) ad ______________ cy (noun) ad ______________ d (verb)

**3** Complete the word families below. The first word in each family comes from the list words.

| | | |
|---|---|---|
| **a** executive | ex ______________ te | ex ______________ or |
| **b** advisor | ______________ sed | ______________ ory |
| **c** excitingly | ______________ te | ______________ dly |

**4** Based on their use in the context of the letter, write *true* or *false* for each word meaning provided.
*Hint: These words all appear in the open letter but are not list words.*

| Word | Meaning | True or False? |
|---|---|---|
| **a** morally | based on what is right | ______________ |
| **b** councils | small businesses | ______________ |
| **c** series | sets of texts | ______________ |
| **d** purchase | hunt down | ______________ |
| **e** stymie | slow or stop | ______________ |

**5** These words appear in the annotations on the open letter. Based on their contextual meanings, match these words with synonyms by drawing lines. There are two sets, with four word pairs in each set.

| Set 1 | |
|---|---|
| **a** conjures | expensive |
| **b** big-budget | generates |
| **c** responsible | obligated |
| **d** appeals | pleads |

| Set 2 | |
|---|---|
| **a** standpoint | addressee |
| **b** recipient | position |
| **c** colloquial | obvious |
| **d** plain | informal |

### Noun revision

**Nouns** are **names** of things. They can be **concrete** (that is, they can be perceived by one or more of the five senses) or **abstract** (that is, they can't be perceived by any of the senses, such as emotions and ideas). Some nouns can be either, depending on their use. Here are the main types of nouns:

- common nouns (names of things, such as *cloud* and *basket*)
- proper nouns (capitalised names, such as *Mr Wilson* and *Japan*)
- compound nouns (names consisting of more than one word, such as *pickpocket* and *water bottle*)
- mass nouns (names of things that can't be counted, such as *music* or *food*)
- collective nouns (names of groups of things, such as *class* and *choir*)
- gerunds (nouns derived from verbs and ending in *ing*, such as *swimming* and *thinking*).

The words in Questions 1 to 3 have all been taken from the text 'On-screen smoking'.

**1** Circle the nouns in this group of words. *Hint: Not all nouns are objects.*

years bodies series never councils positive tobacco
step promote locally decline reaching eligible increased

**2** Circle the gerunds in this group of words. *Hint: Not all of the words in the group are nouns.*

smoking funding excitingly moving morally pouring writing

**Abstract nouns** may be the opposite of concrete nouns, but they are not always easy to spot. For example, the nouns *work* and *war* can be abstract or concrete, depending on the context in which they are used.

**3** All these nouns are possible abstract nouns but some are always abstract nouns. Write them in the correct column below.

risks consideration threat health misconception
parenthood belief glamour opinion

| Possible abstract noun | Always an abstract noun |
|---|---|
| | |
| | |
| | |
| | |
| | |

**4** Circle the type of noun highlighted in each sentence.

**a** Throw out that **bunch** of old ticket stubs. collective / abstract / common / proper
**b** I like to go to the movies with my **family**. collective / abstract / common / proper
**c** Smoking in films goes against the **TAP Act**. collective / abstract / common / proper
**d** The **argument** against smoking is not a new one. collective / abstract / common / proper
**e** We need to tell the **truth** about smoking's effects. collective / abstract / common / proper

**5** Identify the noun types used in each sentence. *Hint: Any of the types listed above may have been used.*

**a** Let's stop teenagers from taking up smoking. Type of noun: ____________________
**b** Movie viewing is a common pastime in our town. Type of noun: ____________________
**c** The audience of kids brought pocket money for snacks. Type of noun: ____________________

# PERSUASIVE TEXT

*Open letter*

PUNCTUATION WORK

## Apostrophes

The chief enemy of many English students, the **apostrophe** can confound writers and make a mess of a text if used incorrectly. Here is a reminder of the two basic functions of this problematic punctuation mark.

- An apostrophe can show possession (ownership). For example, *the dog's collar*.
- An apostrophe can indicate that one or more letters have been removed from words to form a contraction. For example, *doesn't (does not)*.

Apostrophes are not used:

- in possessive adjectives (such as *yours*, *theirs* and *its*)
- to form plurals of nouns (such as *videos*, *potatoes* and *Americans*) or abbreviations (such as *PhDs*)
- to form plurals of numbers (such as *20s to 30s*) and dates (such as *the 1990s*). In some of these instances, apostrophes aren't strictly incorrect but they are unnecessary.

**1** Brush up on your skills by writing in the blanks to complete these statements about apostrophes.

**a** tobacco's movie image — The apostrophe shows that the owner of the ______________ is tobacco.

**b** Let's hasten this decline — The letter ___ is missing, as indicated by the apostrophe.

**c** the group's stance — The apostrophe shows that the ______________ has a ______________.

**2** We read 'problem solved' in the text 'On-screen smoking'. Why is this **not** an example of apostrophe use?

______________________________________________

**3** Identify how apostrophes have been used below by writing *possession*, *contraction* or *error* in the spaces.

**a** The group Why Smoking Kills has voiced it's opinion. ______________

**b** Jeffrey Pufflet's signature closes the letter. ______________

**c** Philippa Morg is Screen V's representative. ______________

**d** Teenagers and those in their early 20's are at risk. ______________

**e** You're opinion is valued by our organisation. ______________

**4** Circle any incorrect uses of apostrophes below. *Hint: This includes incorrectly omitted apostrophes.*

**a** Mr Pufflet raise's questions in his letter that mustn't be ignored by the film industry.

**b** My doctors advice is to give up smoking immediately.

**c** Filmmaker's often dont give much thought to the influence of film star's on-screen actions.

**5** The passage below is related to the information in the text 'On-screen smoking'. Read it carefully then insert all punctuation marks where they are missing. *Hint: You will need to use at least three apostrophes.*

A smoking advertisement according to the TAP Act is defined as a moving picture that 'gives publicity to, promotes or intends to promote smoking. If this is the case how can we continue to allow filmmaking bodies like screen v to plaster images of smokers all over australian and international screens as though its no big deal

The government doesnt seem to think that smoking on-screen is its problem but if laws like the TAP act arent being adhered to theyd better start thinking about doing something

# PERSUASIVE TEXT

## Open letter

WRITING WORK 1

### Open letters

An **open letter**, as the name suggests, is the opposite of a closed (or private) letter. This type of letter:

- is a persuasive text published in a forum where the public can read it, in order to bring attention to the issues it raises—sometimes an open letter is distributed in more than one forum or context
- offers the writer wider exposure than a private letter offers
- is a non-violent form of protest.

### Open letter recipients

Irrespective of who the **recipient** is, the writer wishes to speak to them in a **public forum**. An open letter's recipient may be:

- one person (such as the President of a nation)
- a company (often represented by one person, as we see in the text 'On-screen smoking')
- a large group of people (such as retirees or golfers)
- the general public—the writer might not have any particular recipient in mind but may simply be airing a viewpoint, as we see in an editorial, blog or social media post.

### Open letter writers

Just as there is not always a single addressee, there may not be a single writer, but a **group of writers**. In this case, an open letter can function as a small petition.

**1** Based on the context, define or give synonyms for these words from the information you've just read.

| Word | Definition or Synonym? | Word | Definition or Synonym? |
|---|---|---|---|
| **a** forum | ____________ | **b** format | ____________ |
| **c** airing | ____________ | **d** blog | ____________ |
| **e** addressee | ____________ | **f** petition | ____________ |

### The main features of an open letter

The basic **structure** and **features** of an **open letter** are:

- a clear introduction where the topic or issue is identified and an opinion or stance given
- points clearly divided into sections
- supporting evidence (such as a quote from the TAP Act)
- complex sentences linked by connectives (for example, *As such*)
- a brief conclusion and/or request made to the recipient.

Common language features of an open letter include:

- strong adjectives (such as *major* threat) and adverbs (such as *staunchly* advocates)
- emotive language (for example, *dangerous resurgence*)
- rhetorical questions (for example, *Is that not reasonable?*)
- appeals (for example, *Let's hasten this decline in youth smoking!*).

**2** Why are the features described above—particularly the language features—used by open letter writers?

______________________________________________

______________________________________________

______________________________________________

# PERSUASIVE TEXT

## Open letter

WRITING WORK 2

### What makes an open letter effective?

To ensure that an **open letter** is **effective** in persuading readers about an issue, the composer of the text must:

* address the letter to a target audience (using appropriate diction) and publish it in a relevant context.
* state the issue clearly at the beginning.
* support claims and opinions with relevant, authoritative evidence.

Open letters are also commonly given titles so the public will get an idea of the issue immediately.

**3** What are some other things, including language features, that can be included in an open letter to make it more persuasive? *Hint: Look through the annotations on the letter for ideas.*

______________________________

**4** **a** What is the composer of the text 'On-screen smoking' trying to persuade readers to understand or realise about the issue of on-screen smoking?

______________________________

**b** What is the composer trying to persuade the specific recipient of the letter to do?

______________________________

**5** In the text 'On-screen smoking' we read that the letter is 'intended for distribution on social media and in film industry publications'. Complete the table to show features that could be added to or changed in the letter to maximise its impact in these settings. Also note the purpose of each feature. Two examples have been provided as a guide but you still need to write at least one idea of your own for each setting.

| Setting | Feature or features to add or change | Purpose |
|---|---|---|
| **a** *ScreenNow*, a movie magazine | brief interview with a major film director who is opposed to on-screen smoking | to support Why Smoking Kills' argument |
| **b** *Screen Share*, a newsletter for independent filmmakers | | |
| **c** *Shorts*, an e-zine about short films | an embedded video montage of on-screen smoking | to show how prevalent it is |
| **d** Facebook | | |

The composer of the text 'On-screen smoking' wants to convey some **important messages** regarding the dangers of smoking. Some are overt, while others are implied. Some are based in fact; others in opinion.

**6** Match the messages below with relevant excerpts from the text by writing **a** to **e** in the correct spaces.

| | |
|---|---|
| **a** smoking is creeping back into popularity | ____ 'Let's hasten this decline in youth smoking!' |
| **b** teenagers are influenced by movies | ____ 'there has been a dangerous resurgence' |
| **c** Screen V can't solve the smoking issue alone | ____ 'also reaching out to other Australian arts councils' |
| **d** Why Smoking Kills has pure motives | ____ 'the act of smoking alone is enough to promote it ' |
| **e** cigarettes are advertised in subtle ways | ____ 'we are morally obligated' |

# PERSUASIVE TEXT

## WRITING SAMPLE

Here is a sample text showing you how to structure and write an open letter.

Concerned and Outraged Mothers of America (COMA)
32 West Pleasance Ave
Bridgewater, Connecticut 06752

**Write your name and address.** Traditionally, the sender's name and address are positioned on the right in British and Australian formal letters and on the left in American letters.

Mr Jack Leonard Warner
Movie Mogul, Warner Bros. Studios
3400 West Riverside Drive
Burbank, California 91522

**Write the recipient's name and address on the left.** You may also wish to show the sender's name on the left. This sample letter is dated 1953, so it is in the traditional format.

Monday April 27, 1953

**Write the date on which the letter is written.**

***House of Wax* Deception**

**Give an appropriate title to the letter.**

Dear Mr Warner,

**Write a formal salutation (greeting).**

I write to you exasperated, scandalised and deeply disillusioned with the so-called 'entertainment industry'. I am compelled to frame my complaint as an open letter, in the hope that I and other cinema patrons might urge your studio to take greater care in its advertising methods. My complaint is well founded, as evidenced below.

**State the issue in the first sentence.** The writer insists that the movie studio 'take greater care in its advertising methods'.

It is a long-standing tradition in the Mansfield family home that Clive (my husband), Clive Jr (our son, first born), Dotty (daughter, second) and I visit the Bridgewater Picture Palace in our noble home state of Connecticut each Sunday evening. I cannot emphasise strongly enough the importance of this weekly family ritual.

**Frame the issue with some background information.** Here the writer explains her 'family ritual' of going to the movies each week. The writer uses emotive language such as 'our noble home state' to imply that Mr Warner and his studio are 'sullying' that image.

For the past nine days, a Warner Bros. Studios advertisement for your latest picture, *House of Wax,* has been plastered across Litchfield County's central billboard. Being devoted to both romantic cinema and the timeless art of wax modelling, I was immediately entranced. So yesterday evening the Mansfield Family succumbed to your billboard's urgings and attended the 6:10 pm screening of *House of Wax* in Bridgewater's Cinema 2.

**Include specific details like dates and statistics to give weight to the complaint.** The writer provides the number of days that the advertisement has appeared in town. The writer sets herself up as a kind of victim who has apparently been duped by the movie studio. Precise screening details are given in the hope of supporting the writer's case.

Mr Warner, you can only imagine my horror when *House of Wax* turned into, well, *a horror*! Now, I can stomach a little gratuitous flesh-melting as well as the next moviegoer, but I WILL NOT TOLERATE it when it is accompanied by bare shoulders and low-cut necklines on the usually dignified silver screen. Both were in abundance in this picture. Worse, on leaving, we were refused a refund (despite our loyal patronage to the Bridgewater Picture Palace).

**Use a key word in an impactful way.** The writer makes use of the word 'horror' for impact, referring to both the unexpected genre of the film House of Wax and the shock suffered by Mrs Mansfield. Capital letters give the impression that the writer is feeling outraged and practically shouting. Two main complaints are made: the film featured too much flesh and no refund was given.

As a result of this ordeal, my children are now skittish and of a sickly pallor. My husband is despondent; our marriage has suffered dreadfully. The blame rests with you, Mr Warner, and your studio's deceptive marketing department. This was NOT a harmless romance! This was NOT a celebration of wax modelling! You have aided and abetted in the sullying of a family tradition. Worse, you have taken the shine off our sweet Dotty's love of candle making.

**Enhance the persuasive power of the letter by giving examples of the personal and social impact of the issue being discussed.** The writer alleges that family problems have resulted from this movie experience. The writer elaborates on her complaint about the film, claiming that the billboard was misleading. An additional, rather outrageous claim is made about the negative impact of the film.

I demand a full apology, written by you and signed by every member of *House of Wax*'s cast and crew. I will not beg of you a reimbursement of the $1.80 we spent on our four tickets, although I do believe that to be well within my rights.

**Make a specific request or demand of the recipient and/or the larger organisation.** The writer makes a rather outrageous demand—a written apology signed by the movie's cast and crew—and mentions another possible demand to imply that she is being generous by not making it.

Yours in most sincere outrage,

**Write a sign-off line.** The writer uses this as an opportunity to make a final jab.

*D. M. Mansfield*
Dorothy Mansfield
Caretaker Chairwoman, COMA

**Write a signature and full name to close the letter.** The writer has added her position in the organisation COMA (Concerned and Outraged Mothers of America).

# PERSUASIVE TEXT

## Open letter

Plan your sample on the lines provided.

- **Write your name and address.** Or adopt a role and make them up. Position these details on the right or left side of the letter.
- **Write the recipient's name and address on the left.** If a company or group is the recipient, also name an appropriate contact person or representative.
- **Write the date on which the letter is written.** If you wish, make up an appropriate date to match the issue.
- **Give an appropriate title to the letter.** This title should sum up the issue being raised.
- **Write a formal salutation (greeting).**
- **State the issue in the first sentence.** Make a general request or demand of the recipient.
- **Frame the issue with some background information.** Use emotive language to appeal to the morals or loyalty of the recipient.
- **Include specific details like dates and statistics to give weight to the complaint.** Explain your position and the impact of the issue on you and/or a group you represent. Provide additional evidence to support your case.
- **Use a key word in an impactful way.** Use capital letters to indicate the strength of your feelings. Make or elaborate on your main complaint.
- **Enhance the persuasive power of the letter by giving examples of the personal and social impact of the issue being discussed.** Elaborate on your complaint further by providing more details or supporting evidence.
- **Make a specific request or demand of the recipient and/or the larger organisation.**
- **Write a sign-off line.**
- **Write a signature and full name to close the letter.** For this exercise, your name can be either real or made up.

# UNIT 9 NARRATIVE TEXT

## Journal

**READING WORK**

## Scott's journal

*British explorer Captain Robert Scott (better known as 'Scott of the Antarctic') led an expedition to the South Pole in November 1911. His team made it but they also made the devastating discovery that a Norwegian team had beaten them there by a month. On the return journey, the men slowly ran out of supplies and succumbed to frostbite and exhaustion. Their frozen bodies were found many months later. Scott's expedition journal, published in 1913, offers sad but fascinating insights into the tragedy. Below are the final six entries. Some have been abridged (cut down) using ellipses (…), while others are shown in full.*

**Wednesday, January 17**

Camp 69. T. –22 degrees at start. Night –21 degrees. The Pole. Yes, but under very different circumstances from those expected. We have had a horrible day—add to our disappointment a headwind 4 to 5, with a temperature –22 degrees, and companions labouring on with cold feet and hands.

… the wind is blowing hard, T. –21 degrees, and there is that curious damp, cold feeling in the air which chills one to the bone in no time. We have been descending again, I think, but there looks to be a rise ahead; otherwise there is very little that is different from the awful monotony of past days. Great God! This is an awful place and terrible enough for us to have laboured to it without the reward of priority. Well, it is something to have got here, and the wind may be our friend to-morrow ... Now for the run home and a desperate struggle. I wonder if we can do it.

**Thursday morning, January 18**

… we have just arrived at this tent, 2 miles from our camp, therefore about 1½ miles from the Pole. In the tent we find a record of five Norwegians having been here... We carried the Union Jack about ¾ of a mile north with us and left it on a piece of stick as near as we could fix it... Well, we have turned our back now on the goal of our ambition and must face our 800 miles of solid dragging—and good-bye to most of the day-dreams!

**Friday, March 16 or Saturday 17**

Lost track of dates, but think the last correct. Tragedy all along the line. At lunch, the day before yesterday, poor Titus Oates said he couldn't go on …

… We can testify to his bravery. He has borne intense suffering for weeks without complaint, and to the very last was able and willing to discuss outside subjects. He did not—would not—give up hope till the very end. He was a brave soul. This was the end. He slept through the night before last, hoping not to wake; but he woke in the morning—yesterday. It was blowing a blizzard. He said, 'I am just going outside and may be some time.' He went out into the blizzard and we have not seen him since.

**Thursday, March 22**

Blizzard bad as ever—Wilson and Bowers unable to start—to-morrow last chance—no fuel and only one or two of food left—must be near the end. Have decided it shall be natural—we shall march for the depot with or without our effects and die in our tracks.

**Thursday, March 29**

Since the 21st we have had a continuous gale from W.S.W. and S.W. We had fuel to make two cups of tea apiece and bare food for two days on the 20th. Every day we have been ready to start for our depot 11 miles away, but outside the door of the tent it remains a scene of whirling drift. I do not think we can hope for any better things now. We shall stick it out to the end, but we are getting weaker, of course, and the end cannot be far. It seems a pity, but I do not think I can write more.

R. Scott

***[Final entry; probably written the day Scott died]***

For God's sake look after our people.

- Each entry begins with the **day and date**.
- Highly **economical language** is used.
- Candid, **opinion-based expressions** are given.
- The open and **informal style** allows for strong exclamations and expressions of desperation.
- **Emotive adjectives** are used.
- This is an **idiom** meaning *the return journey*.
- This is an **idiom** for the British flag.
- The **tone** is becoming more pessimistic.
- Several **omitted words** and a reference to confusion over dates indicate Scott's growing despair.
- This is a **euphemism** for *he was about to die*.
- Straightforward, **understated description** conveys the horror and sadness of the situation.
- A series of **truncated expressions** use language economically and imitate Scott's thought process.
- **Abbreviations, measurements, dates** and **details** throughout the text add to its authenticity.
- An **absence of contractions** indicates the time period.
- A **sign-off** (the author's name) is given.
- A type of **coda**, in a different style to the rest of the journal, directly addresses an unnamed person or group at home in England.

# NARRATIVE TEXT
*Journal*

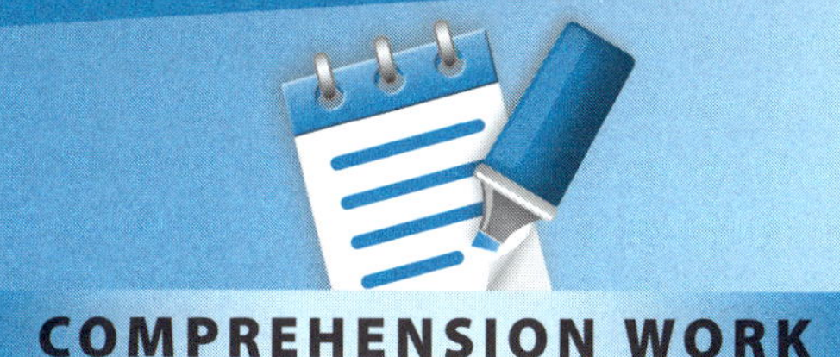

**COMPREHENSION WORK**

## Literal questions
*Hint: Read the text carefully to locate specific facts and details.*

**1** Apart from Scott, find three surnames (last names) of members of the British team.

______________________ ______________________ ______________________

**2** Who went out into the blizzard and didn't return? ______________________

**3** When Scott and his team arrived at the tent on 18 January, what did they find inside?

**a** a record **b** five Norwegians **c** a Union Jack

## Interpretive questions
*Hint: These questions require you to combine facts and details to synthesise the meaning.*

**4** Which of the following is an example of personification?

**a** the air which chills one to the bone in no time

**b** Great God! This is an awful place

**c** the wind may be our friend to-morrow

**5** 'We are getting weaker, of course …' Which of these factors is the main reason for this problem?

**a** lack of money **b** lack of hope **c** lack of food

**6** What does Scott mean when he says that they reached their destination 'without the reward of priority'?
*Hint: Re-read the introductory information above the text for help.*

______________________

**7** What is meant by 'whirling drift' in Scott's entry on 29 March? ______________________

**8** Regarding Oates, why can Scott and his team 'testify to his bravery'? Give three reasons from the text.

______________________

______________________

______________________

**9** What is meant by 'tracks' in the context of the phrase 'die in our tracks'?

**a** railway line **b** path **c** snowshoes

**10** Which of the following best explains why Scott says 'to-morrow last chance' on 22 March?

**a** no fuel and only one or two of food left

**b** blizzard bad as ever

**c** Wilson and Bowers unable to start

## Applied questions
*Hint: These questions require you to understand a text's implications to infer meaning from the text.*

**11** Why did Scott's team carry a Union Jack (British flag)?

______________________

**12** When Scott says 'Have decided it shall be natural', to what is he referring?

**a** marching **b** food **c** death

# NARRATIVE TEXT

## *Journal*

**SPELLING WORK**

### List Words

All of the words in the box below appear in the text 'Scott's journal'.

| | | | | |
|---|---|---|---|---|
| whirling | effects | priority | descending | circumstances |
| apiece | temperature | headwind | borne | depot |
| continuous | tragedy | ambition | monotony | disappointment |

**1** The passage below contains ten list words. Some of them are incorrectly spelt. Find the words and write them correctly in order on the lines provided. *Hint: Some homophones (words with the same sound) and other similar forms of list words have been used to trick you, so read the passage carefully to find incorrectly spelt words based on their use here.*

Extreme cold affects the temprature and functioning of the human body in ways that can result not only in frustration, but in tradegy. The monotony of a state of continual cold cannot be born by a person for more than a week or so, as Scott and his team discovered when they battled a continuous wirling headwind on their attempted march to their South Pole deppo and their circumstances took them from disappointment to death.

__________ __________ __________ __________ __________

__________ __________ __________ __________ __________

**2** Unscramble the following sets of letters to make list words.

**a** fecstef __________ **b** epecia __________

**c** yorritip __________ **d** gyrated __________

**3** Transform list words into other words based on the instructions given below.

**a** Change a ten-letter word into an adverb by adding *ly*. __________

**b** Change a word in the third column into a verb. __________

**c** Remove a prefix to make a word that means 'meeting'. __________

**d** Replace an *e* with an *a* to make a word that means 'impacts'. __________

**4** Each sentence below contains a word from the text 'Scott's journal' and a homophone. Circle the correct word based on the meaning of the sentence.
*Hint: Although individual words in this question appear in the text, the full sentences do not.*

**a** 'If you'd been here / hear, we wouldn't have this problem,' said Wilson.

**b** The weather's more unpredictable than it's ever been / bean.

**c** We came across a scene / seen of utter destruction.

**d** In Antarctica, you may be expected to bear / bare the pain of surgery without anaesthetic.

**e** The storm was so loud that the dog sled team past / passed without us noticing.

**f** It is only threw / through suffering that some people learn to appreciate the value of life.

**5** The words below contain more pairs of words that are homophone spelling traps. Write each pair on the lines provided. *Hint: One word in each pair appears in the text.*

| | | | | | |
|---|---|---|---|---|---|
| time | witch | daze | which | course | thyme |
| dye | coarse | find | die | fined | days |

______ / ______ ______ / ______ ______ / ______

______ / ______ ______ / ______ ______ / ______

# NARRATIVE TEXT

## *Journal*

## VOCABULARY WORK

### Twin adjectives: *continuous* and *continual*

The word 'continuous' is used by Scott to describe the unrelenting polar wind that ravaged him and his team. This word is commonly confused with *continual.* Like many other **adjective pairs** with very **similar meanings**, the two words are not interchangeable. They both describe the duration of an event but *continuous* does not allow for interruption. For example, *The continuous lurching of the ship during the storm made him seasick.* The word *continual* indicates something happening over a period of time, but not incessantly (without ceasing); it may stop and start. For example, *The continual domestic tension and arguments wore her down.*

**1** Show your understanding by circling the correct word to complete each sentence below.
*Hint: The twin adjectives have been transformed into adverbs for two of the sentences.*

- **a** Hugh told Ben that boarding school was a place of continuous / continual torture.
- **b** 'Our continuous / continual goal is social justice,' said the Committee President.
- **c** The baby screamed continuously / continually for two minutes until Aunty Suki picked her up.
- **d** It drizzles continuously / continually in Seattle, especially during winter.

**2** Select the best synonym for *continuous* or *continual* in the context of these sentences.

| | |
|---|---|
| **a** From afar, the complex dot painting just looked like one **continuous** line. | infinite / unbroken |
| **b** A working circuit depends on a **continuous** current. | uninterrupted / repeated |
| **c** London's skyline is known for its **continual** cloud cover. | occasional / frequent |
| **d** This is the largest **continuous** bamboo forest in China. | single / consistent |
| **e** The burglar endured forty-five seconds of the **continuous** alarm, then fled. | incessant / lasting |
| **f** There was a **continual** struggle for money in our family. | ongoing / everlasting |

**3** What do the following idioms mean in the context of the text 'Scott's journal'?

- **a** 'effects' ____________________
- **b** 'depot' ____________________
- **c** 'Union Jack' ____________________
- **d** 'to the very last' ____________________

**4** The following word pairs consist of a word that has been used in the text 'Scott's journal' and a near-homophone for that word. From each pair, circle the word that actually appears in the text.
*Hint: Homophones are words sharing an exact sound; near-homophones sound similar (but not identical).*

| | | |
|---|---|---|
| **a** vary / very | **b** wonder / wander | **c** reward / reword |
| **d** disparate / desperate | **e** face / phase | **f** sold / solid |

**5** Each sentence below contains one list word and a word with which it is easily confused. Circle the most appropriate word based on the sentence's meaning. *Hint: The correct word is not necessarily the list word.*

- **a** The tiny spiders were born / borne on the wind to far-off places.
- **b** The affects / effects of severe poverty are terrible.
- **c** Climbers are often surprised to find that descending / ascending Everest is harder than going up.
- **d** He grabbed a piece / apiece of bread and hurled it angrily at the ducks.
- **e** 'It's vital that a continuous / consistent level of pressure be applied to this wound,' said the doctor.
- **f** Stamped URGENT, this was clearly a prior / priority document.
- **g** The teacher's monotone / monotony voice lulled us to sleep.

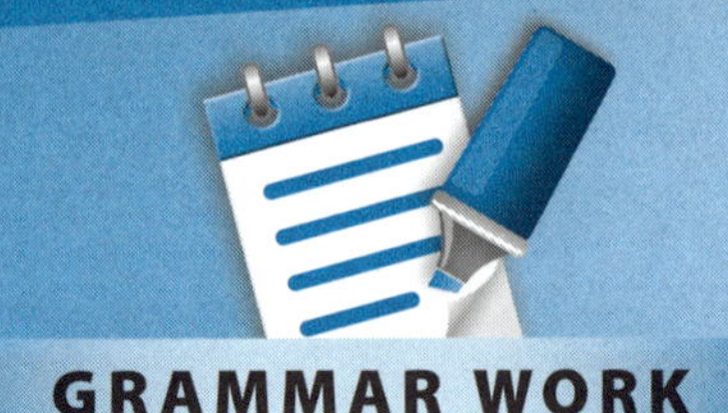

# NARRATIVE TEXT

*Journal*

GRAMMAR WORK

## Contractions

A **contraction** is a word derived from **two separate words**. When words are contracted (squeezed together), at least one letter is removed and replaced with an **apostrophe**. For example, *don't*, *I'll*, *you're*. A contraction:

- is generally a mark of informal (colloquial) expression, as it mimics everyday, conversational speech
- saves writing time, space and reading time.

**1** Transform these word pairs from the text into contractions. *Hint: Remember to use apostrophes correctly.*

**a** we have ____________ **b** there is ____________

**c** that is ____________ **d** we are ____________

**e** he has ____________ **f** did not ____________

**g** would not ____________ **h** I am ____________

**i** have not ____________ **j** we shall ____________

**2** These word pairs do not appear in the text. Make a contraction from each pair.

**a** I did ____________ **b** what would ____________

**c** she had ____________ **d** that will ____________

One feature of **idioms** and **vernacular** is the presence or absence of contractions. Scott wrote his journal at a time when contractions were not commonly used in written English. As a result, the whole text has an old-fashioned feel.

**3** In the excerpt from his journal, Scott has used only one contraction.

**a** What is it? ____________ **b** From which two words is it made? ____________

**Abbreviations** save a lot of time in journal writing, and since a journal writer is also his or her own main target audience, the assumption can be made that the reader knows what the abbreviations mean!

**4** Robert Scott uses some abbreviations in his journal. From the options below, circle each full word or phrase that he has abbreviated. *Hint: Find each abbreviation in the text and define it according to its use in the context.*

**a** T. temperature / Thursday / Titus

**b** W.S.W. New South Wales / west-southwest / west-south wind

**c** S.W. Scott and Wilson / southwest / strong wind

**d** R. Robert / Royal / regiment

**5** Define these common abbreviations that do not appear in the text. *Hint: Using a full stop (.) is optional here.*

**a** ASAP ____________ **b** ETA ____________

**c** DIY ____________ **d** VIP ____________

**6** Use all four abbreviations from Question 5 in a single sentence. ____________

____________

____________

____________

# NARRATIVE TEXT

## Journal

**PUNCTUATION WORK**

### Hyphens and dashes

It can be confusing telling the difference between **hyphens** and **dashes**, and knowing their different functions. There are actually at least five different types of punctuation mark in this category but the most useful information about hyphens and dashes appears below. Note that these are not rules, but conventions; the conventions described below are those applied throughout this book but be aware that different writers have different opinions about how these conventions should be applied.

The hyphen:

- is a short horizontal stroke (-)
- should never have spaces placed around it
- divides compound words (this is more common in early twentieth-century usage, like that seen in the text)
- is generally used in compound proper nouns or proper adjectives (for example, *mid-June*; *French-speaking*)
- is an optional extra in words with a prefix ending in a vowel and whose root word starts with the same letter (for example *no-one*; *co-ordinate*)
- can be used for clarity at various times at the discretion of the writer.

There are two main types of dash in everyday use: the en dash (or en rule, –) and the em dash (or em rule, —).

The en dash:

- is a horizontal stroke longer than the hyphen, so-called because it is about the width of a capital *N* (–)
- functions as a minus sign, as in the text 'Scott's journal' (for example, 'temperature –22 degrees')
- is the best choice for showing a range between two numbers (for example, *I saw 50–60 birds that day*.)
- can be used instead of an em dash, in which case it should have spaces around it.

The em dash:

- is a horizontal stroke longer than the en rule, so-called because it is about the width of a capital *M* (—)
- does not require spaces around it
- can be used in a pair like parentheses (for example, *She sang way out of tune—she was five years old—but with such gusto!*)
- divides ideas or sections in an informally written sentence (for example 'Blizzard bad as ever—Wilson and Bowers unable to start—to-morrow last chance')
- shows an afterthought or additional detail (for example, *Failing wasn't an option right now—not today)*.

Read this sentence from the text: 'Blizzard bad as ever—Wilson and Bowers unable to start—to-morrow last chance—no fuel and only one or two of food left—must be near the end.' The use of a hyphen and four dashes makes this sentence look strange.

**1** What is the function of the hyphen in that sentence?

**a** It indicates a conjunction.
**b** It indicates a compound word.
**c** It indicates an abbreviation.
**d** It creates a pause.

**2** What is the function of the dashes in that sentence?

**a** They separate a series of related details.
**b** They create pauses.
**c** They indicate compound words.
**d** They are used as minus signs.

In the same way as idioms belong to a certain place, group or time, some uses of punctuation are peculiar to a certain time period. Various **compound words containing hyphens** belong in this category.

**3** Three hyphenated compound words have been used by Scott that we no longer write in this way. List them.

____________ ____________ ____________

# NARRATIVE TEXT
## *Journal*

WRITING WORK 1

### Journals

In the days before Twitter and Facebook, people kept **journals** (personal diaries) to record their experiences and thoughts. In most cases, a journal is a very private text and a place of introspection. Sometimes, however, a journal is of interest to historians or the general public (for example, *The Diary of Anne Frank*, which records the experiences of a teenage girl and her family during World War II). Journals of this kind are generally published after the death of the author. Here are some of the main features of journal writing.

- Opening statements describe the context and indicate the purpose of the journal.
- A series of chronological entries records events over a period of time.
- Entries are written at regular or irregular intervals, depending on the composer and the circumstances.
- A date, day and/or time of day is given at the beginning of each entry.
- Optional salutations (for example, *Dear Diary*) and sign-offs (usually the author's name) are used.
- Entries will switch between descriptions of events and personal reflections while outlining thoughts, emotions and evaluations.
- A consistent narrative voice generates a sense of the author's identity and assists the reader in getting to know the author intimately by the end of the journal.
- Diction (word choice) reveals the author's historical context, personal background, values and attitudes.
- Idiom, colloquial expressions and allusions also reflect historical and personal context.
- A range of tenses is used between and sometimes inside entries.
- Reflections are made on recent events and future ones are anticipated.
- Various conjunctions and connectives are used for different purposes; for example, temporal (*then, suddenly, while*), causal (*because, although, since*) and opinionated (*fortunately, sadly, obviously*).
- Journal writers commonly limit their use of figurative language.
- Personal opinions, judgements and emotions are expressed directly.
- The whole journal is concerned with a particular theme, issue or set of circumstances. This is the case in the text 'Scott's journal', which is actually a series of diaries covering various episodes in Scott's Antarctic adventures. The text we are considering is obviously the last in this series.

**1** Circle the connective in each of these lines from the text. *Hint: The answer may be a word or a phrase.*

a 'Now for the run home'

b 'We have been descending again, I think'

c 'Since the 21st we have had a continuous gale'

d 'we are getting weaker, of course'

**2** Change these first-person statements from the text into the third person. An example has been done for you. *Hints: Focus on pronouns. For example, the original narrator ('I') is a man, so look for places to use 'he' instead.*

a Every day we have been ready to start — Every day they have been ready to start.

b we have been descending again, I think ____

c the wind may be our friend to-morrow ____

d I wonder if we can do it ____

e We can testify to his bravery ____

f I do not think I can write more ____

**3** Why do you think that figurative language is limited in most journal writing?

____

**4** Give two examples of Scott's directly expressed personal opinion or judgement from the text.

____

# NARRATIVE TEXT
## *Journal*

WRITING WORK 2

### Other types and functions of journals

Journal texts come in many **forms** and have even more **functions**. This is because they are highly personal texts created for a particular set of circumstances. The text 'Scott's journal' is the last in a series of expedition records and reflections kept by one of Britain's great adventurers. The student text on the following page is a travel diary that also functions as a keepsake of an emotional and inspirational encounter with people on the other side of the world.

**5** Complete this table to explore seven different types of journal. *Hint: Use the completed cells as a guide.*

| Journal type | Purpose | Examples of contents |
|---|---|---|
| Event planner | a | appointments and records of meetings<br>prices, quotes and receipts |
| Fitness log | b | measurements and times<br>personal goals |
| Reading record | to document and reflect on personal reading | c |
| Process diary | to track the development of a project | plans, diagrams, designs, preliminary sketches<br>inspiration from other composers |
| Creative scrapbook | d | a diverse range of stimulus materials<br>amusing or inspiring images and brief texts |
| Family chronicle | e | family tree (names, details and/or pictures)<br>dates of births, deaths and other key events |
| Botany portfolio | to record and sample plants, especially in an environment unfamiliar to the botanist | f |

There are many alternative words for *journal*. Seven were given in the table in Question 5.

**6** On the line below write the alternative words for *journal* used in the table, separated by commas.

______________________________

**7** List some other terms that can be used interchangeably with *journal* and/or other journal types not yet mentioned in this chapter.

______________________________

# NARRATIVE TEXT

## *Journal*

**WRITING SAMPLE**

Here is a sample text showing you how to structure and write a journal.

### Tanzania journal

✷ **Give the journal a literal and straightforward title.** It is not designed to be entertaining, as the primary audience of the text is the author herself. The title simply names the subject.

**Day 2, 7 January 2013**

I met my translator this morning—Elizabeth. She came with me to my sponsor child's house and translated the conversation between his parents and myself. On the walk to their house I began to prepare myself for what I might see, what I'm already seeing. I'm in a completely different world. One that I didn't believe existed outside of the ads on television late at night when I'm sitting in the safety of my home and comfort of my nice warm bed. It was like I was suddenly living inside the ad. The walk there took us past what I would describe as many broken-down, boarded-up, doorless, dusty rooms, not houses. It took us past bountiful numbers of small toothless children pointing at the 'mzungu', white person, they saw, and past a barn full of smelly, noisy, diseased pigs. What disturbed me the most was that Erick's house was next to this barn. Although the house was one bedroom, although there were no mattresses for this family to sleep on, although there were no lights, the nearest tap kilometres away, and a pig barn next door, I've never felt more at home. These people and this family have become my family, and this bedroom my home.

✷ **Write the first of two entries.** Look at the features of the Day 2 entry. Formatting and dating of entries is left to the discretion of the author (for example, 'Day 2, 7 January 2013'). Words from another language and their definitions are used seamlessly in sentences (for example, 'children pointing at the "mzungu", white person, they saw'). Commas may be used unconventionally, to convey emotions and thought processes; this is evident in the line 'what I might see, what I'm already seeing'. Truncation and fragments are used for emotional emphasis; we read, for instance, 'I'm in a completely different world. One that I didn't believe existed'. Repetition of 'although' is also used for emphasis. Little attention is paid to consistent tense or correct syntax; for example, we read, 'One that I didn't believe existed outside of the ads on television late at night when I'm sitting in the safety of my home'.

**Day 5, 10 January 2013**

I knew today was going to be hard. Last day with the kids at the project and I was absolutely dreading saying goodbye to my sponsor child. Arrived at the project and all the children were out the front of the centre waiting for us with their infectious smiles. I went and spoke to one of the teachers when we arrived and mid-conversation I felt a little pair of arms wrap around my legs. Erick came and found me and we went and played with bubbles and soccer balls. Before I knew it, the day was over and it was time for the kids to go home. Saying goodbye to Erick was the hardest goodbye I've ever had to say. I didn't think it was possible to love another human this much, especially a four-year-old living on the other side of the world to me. I told him 'nakupenda', I love you in Swahili, hopped on the bus and drove away from the place I will now and forever call home.

✷ **Write the second of two entries.** Look at the features of the Day 5 entry. For economy of expression, words are often omitted at the beginning of a sentence; this is seen in the sentences beginning 'Last day with the kids' and 'Arrived at the project'. Because the style is conversational and spontaneous, individual words—especially verbs—do not necessarily need to be unusual or exciting; for example, in the sentence 'I **went** and **spoke** to one of the teachers … and … Erick **came** and **found** me', the highlighted words are verbs. Punctuation is omitted when it is not deemed necessary by the composer; for example, quote marks are used only once in the line 'I told him "nakupenda", I love you in Swahili'. The use of contractions in journals is based on their function each time; we see a contraction omitted in the statement 'the place I will now and forever call home'—this statement is emphatic and sincere, and the absence of a contraction highlights this.

# NARRATIVE TEXT

## *Journal*

## WRITING YOUR OWN SAMPLE

Plan your sample on the lines provided.

- **Give the journal a literal and straightforward title.** Don't try to make it entertaining, as the primary audience of the text is you. The title simply names the subject or circumstances.

- **Write the first of two entries.** Begin the first entry with a date; ideally, this should be Day 1 of the journal, but you may use a date that falls in the middle of the events of the journal if you like. Use jargon and/or words from another language and their definitions in at least one sentence. Don't be too concerned with the correct use of commas; instead, use them to convey emotions and thought processes. Use truncation and sentence fragments for emotional emphasis. Repeat one word or phrase at least three times in one sentence for emphasis. Vary syntax (sentence structure) and/or tense without worrying about correct structure.

- **Write the second of two entries.** For economy of expression, write at least two sentences that are missing a word or phrase at the beginning. Use straightforward, literal verbs; because the style is conversational and spontaneous, verbs do not necessarily need to be unusual or exciting. Omit punctuation if you do not think it is necessary, and/or if it interrupts the flow of a sentence. Use a contraction in at least one sentence and omit a contraction in at least one sentence—remember: the use of contractions in journals is based on their function each time.

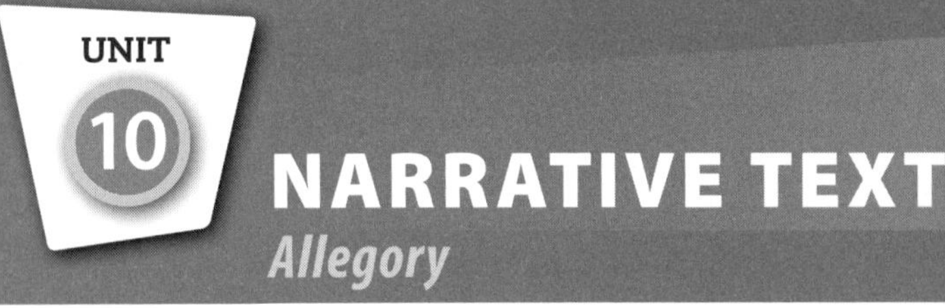

UNIT 10

# NARRATIVE TEXT

## *Allegory*

READING WORK

## The Wizard of Oz

### From Chapter 15: 'The Discovery of Oz, the Terrible'

*Dorothy, her dog Toto, and her friends the Scarecrow, the Tin Man and the Cowardly Lion, have returned to see the Wizard of Oz after fulfilling his demand of destroying the Wicked Witch of the West. They hope to be granted their various requests as a reward, but when they accidentally expose Oz as a fraud, they are shocked and disappointed that he is just a scared little man with a few impressive tricks.*

'Really,' said the Scarecrow, 'you ought to be ashamed of yourself for being such a humbug.'

'I am—I certainly am,' answered the little man sorrowfully; 'but it was the only thing I could do. Sit down, please, there are plenty of chairs; and I will tell you my story.'

So they sat down and listened while he told the following tale.

'I was born in Omaha—'

'Why, that isn't very far from Kansas!' cried Dorothy.

'No, but it's farther from here,' he said, shaking his head at her sadly. 'When I grew up I became a ventriloquist, and at that I was very well trained by a great master. I can imitate any kind of a bird or beast.' Here he mewed so like a kitten that Toto pricked up his ears and looked everywhere to see where she was. 'After a time,' continued Oz, 'I tired of that, and became a balloonist.'

'What is that?' asked Dorothy.

'A man who goes up in a balloon on circus day, so as to draw a crowd of people together and get them to pay to see the circus,' he explained.

'Oh,' she said, 'I know.'

'Well, one day I went up in a balloon and the ropes got twisted, so that I couldn't come down again. It went way up above the clouds, so far that a current of air struck it and carried it many, many miles away. For a day and a night I travelled through the air, and on the morning of the second day I awoke and found the balloon floating over a strange and beautiful country.

'It came down gradually, and I was not hurt a bit. But I found myself in the midst of a strange people, who, seeing me come from the clouds, thought I was a great Wizard. Of course I let them think so, because they were afraid of me, and promised to do anything I wished them to.

'Just to amuse myself, and keep the good people busy, I ordered them to build this City, and my Palace; and they did it all willingly and well. Then I thought, as the country was so green and beautiful, I would call it the Emerald City; and to make the name fit better I put green spectacles on all the people, so that everything they saw was green.'

'But isn't everything here green?' asked Dorothy.

'No more than in any other city,' replied Oz; 'but when you wear green spectacles, why of course everything you see looks green to you. The Emerald City was built a great many years ago, for I was a young man when the balloon brought me here, and I am a very old man now. But my people have worn green glasses on their eyes so long that most of them think it really is an Emerald City, and it certainly is a beautiful place, abounding in jewels and precious metals, and every good thing that is needed to make one happy. I have been good to the people, and they like me; but ever since this Palace was built, I have shut myself up and would not see any of them.

'One of my greatest fears was the Witches, for while I had no magical powers at all I soon found out that the Witches were really able to do wonderful things. There were four of them in this country, and they ruled the people who live in the North and South and East and West. Fortunately, the Witches of the North and South were good, and I knew they would do me no harm; but the Witches of the East and West were terribly wicked, and had they not thought I was more powerful than they themselves, they would surely have destroyed me. As it was, I lived in deadly fear of them for many years; so you can imagine how pleased I was when I heard your house had fallen on the Wicked Witch of the East. When you came to me, I was willing to promise anything if you would only do away with the other Witch; but, now that you have melted her, I am ashamed to say that I cannot keep my promises.'

'I think you are a very bad man,' said Dorothy.

'Oh, no, my dear; I'm really a very good man, but I'm a very bad Wizard, I must admit.'

- The **main characters** all function as both figures in the story and allegorical or symbolic figures. The most common interpretation of this symbolism is explained later in this chapter.
- **Alliteration**, particularly of the 'w' sound, is used frequently in the story because it is a sound device that appeals to the child reader. It also reminds the reader that the story is all about witches and wizards.
- This is a typical line of **direct speech** that has been broken into two parts.
- This section begins like a *once upon a time* story and explains the Wizard's past. This narrative technique is called **exposition**, because it *exposes* key information to both the other characters and the reader.
- The **dialogue directions** are specific and varied, to give the reader a break from the word '*said*'.
- This moment in the **flashback** explains how the Wizard came to be in his position of power.
- Dorothy asks many **questions** throughout the story. They are similar questions to what the reader is probably asking. We discover things when she does.
- This section of **direct speech** explains the key conflict between the Wizard and the Wicked Witches in the story. As you will find later in the chapter, this is also an important symbolic section pointing to issues in American politics at the time when Baum was writing.
- This is the same **conclusion** that the writer expects the reader to make. Dorothy simply says it for us.

## Literal questions

*Hint: Read the text carefully to locate specific facts and details.*

**1** According to the Wizard, what are two things that 'abound' in Oz?

**2** Why does the Scarecrow say the Wizard 'ought to be ashamed'?

**3** Why did the Wizard originally give the Emerald City that name?

**a** The city was made of emeralds. **b** He found many emeralds there.

**c** The country was green and beautiful.

## Interpretive questions

*Hint: These questions require you to combine facts and details to synthesise the meaning.*

**4** Which option below lists the Wizard's occupations in their correct order?

**a** ventriloquist, impersonator, balloonist **b** balloonist, impersonator, Wizard

**c** ventriloquist, Wizard, balloonist

**5** Which of these factors did *not* lead to the Wizard coming to the land of Oz?

**a** clouds **b** twisted ropes **c** a current of air

**6** Why do you think the composer has told most of this section of the story using direct speech?

**7** What is the most likely reason for Dorothy thinking that everything in the Emerald City is green?

**8** What is the effect of alliteration in the line 'the Witches were really able to do wonderful things'?

**9** Why were the citizens afraid of the Wizard of Oz when he first arrived in their land?

**a** They were strange. **b** He came from the clouds. **c** He was a Wizard.

**10** What has cured the Wizard's 'deadly fear' of the Wicked Witch of the East?

**a** melting **b** Dorothy's house **c** the good Witch of the North

## Applied questions

*Hint: These questions require you to understand a text's implications to infer meaning from the text.*

**11** Why does Dorothy think the Wizard is 'a very bad man'? Give three reasons from the text.

**12** The detail in the text which best explains why Oz can 'imitate any kind of a bird or beast' is that he:

**a** 'became a ventriloquist'. **b** 'mewed … like a kitten'. **c** 'was very well trained by a great master'.

# NARRATIVE TEXT

## Allegory

**SPELLING WORK**

### List Words

All of the words in the box below appear in the text 'The Wizard of Oz'.

| | | | | |
|---|---|---|---|---|
| sorrowfully | ventriloquist | midst | abounding | emerald |
| fortunately | scarecrow | willingly | answered | gradually |
| certainly | ought | imitate | spectacles | jewels |

**1** Each sentence below contains two list words. One has incorrect spelling. Write it correctly on the line.
*Hint: When checking the spelling of a word in the list, isolate it using your finger or a piece of paper.*

**a** The Wizard demanded that the scarcrow return his jewels. ____________________

**b** Being an impersonator, the Wizard would willingly immitate anyone. ____________________

**c** Dorothy said, 'You haven't apologised yet, but you certainly ough to.' ____________________

**d** Oz was a land abounding in precious joules. ____________________

**e** The citizens were certainly unaware that they had a dreadful liar in their mist. ____________________

With just one or two small changes, a word can be **transformed into a new part of speech or a different tense.**

**2** The following words are list words in a slightly different form. Write the original list word beside each one.

**a** jewellery ____________________ **b** imitation ____________________

**c** abounded ____________________ **d** fortune ____________________

**3** The following passage has been taken from the text, but it contains spelling errors. Circle them.
*Hint: There are more than ten errors.*

'Well, one day I went up in a baloon and the ropes got twirsted, so that I coulldn't come down aggain. It whent way up above the clowds, so far that a curent of air stuck it and caried it many, many miles away. For a day and a knight I travelled threw the air, and on the mourning of the second day I awoke and found the balloon floting over a stranged and beutiful country.'

**4** Using the letters in these list words, make three new three-letter words and two new four-letter or five-letter words. When making a new word, you may only use each letter in the list word once.

| List word | New three-letter words | New four- or five-letter words |
|---|---|---|
| imitate | | |
| emerald | | |
| spectacles | | |

**5** Make an **anagram** (a new word using all of its letters once) from the word 'ought': ____________________

**6** Choose four words (with at least four letters each) from the text and make anagrams from them.

| Word from the text | Anagram | Word from the text | Anagram |
|---|---|---|---|
| | | | |
| | | | |

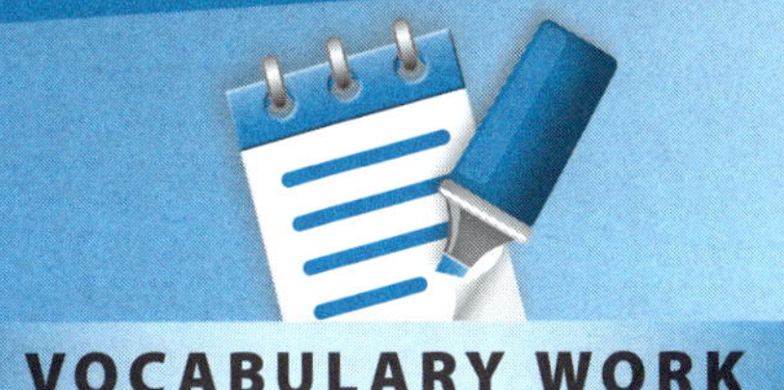

# NARRATIVE TEXT

## Allegory

## VOCABULARY WORK

In the late 1800s, when L Frank Baum was writing *The Wizard of Oz,* many interesting **idioms** were used that we are far less likely to hear today. You will find some of these in the story excerpt.

**1** Find each idiom in the story and use its context to choose and circle the closest meaning.

| Word | Meaning | | |
|---|---|---|---|
| **a** humbug | beetle | pretender | blanket |
| **b** spectacles | lenses | fireworks | eyes |
| **c** the good people | citizens | saints | politicians |
| **d** a great many | amazing | prime number | countless |

These idioms are harder to spot because they consist of single or paired words commonly used today.

**2** The highlighted words below function as idioms when used in certain phrases. Read each phrase in its context in the text then circle the closest meaning of the word or words in bold from the options given.

| Word | Meaning | | |
|---|---|---|---|
| **a** **Why**, that isn't very far from Kansas! | I mean … | wow! | what? |
| **b** to make **one** happy | a person | a happy | a number |
| **c** he mewed **so like** a kitten | so and so | like much | so similarly to |
| **d** **for** I was a young man | because | four | to |

A word with an opposite meaning to another word is an **antonym**. Knowing antonyms expands our vocabulary. The antonyms you need to find below are also adverbs, meaning that they describe or expand on an action. Like most adverbs they end in *ly* because they describe how something is done, said or thought.

**3** The following adverbs all have an antonym in the list words. Write these on the lines.

| Adverb | Antonym | Adverb | Antonym |
|---|---|---|---|
| **a** joyfully | ____________ | **b** uncooperatively | ____________ |
| **c** suddenly | ____________ | **d** dubiously | ____________ |
| **e** jubilantly | ____________ | **f** unluckily | ____________ |

A **word stem** is a small word or group of letters found inside a word. The stem's meaning never changes, despite the meaning of the word in which it appears. For example, *bio* (meaning 'life') is a Greek word stem used in many English words, such as *biology, autobiography, bionic* and *biodegradable.* We create **word families** using word stems.

**4** Each of these words contains a word stem found in a list word. Write each stem on the first line, then give a new word with the same stem on the second line. Don't simply use a slightly altered word from the list, such as *amidst* or *jewellery*. The first one has been done for you.

| Word | Word stem | New word with the same stem |
|---|---|---|
| **a** middle | mid | midriff |
| **b** boundless | ____________ | ____________ |
| **c** inspect | ____________ | ____________ |
| **d** gradient | ____________ | ____________ |
| **e** will | ____________ | ____________ |

# NARRATIVE TEXT

## Allegory

GRAMMAR WORK

### Adverbs

In any narrative text, **adverbs** bring the action and description to life by adding detail. Many adverbs have been used in the text 'The Wizard of Oz'. Among other things, these adverbs tell the reader:

- the particular way in which an action is performed
- the emotions or thoughts of a character
- how words are spoken by a character
- how quickly or slowly something happens.

**1** Which of the following words from the story excerpt are adverbs? Write them on the lines beneath.
*Hints: Don't confuse verbs with adverbs. Not all adverbs end in* ly. *Use every answer space provided.*

| | | | | | | |
|---|---|---|---|---|---|---|
| many | sorrowfully | little | well | seeing | willingly | every |
| all | floating | fortunately | plenty | surely | gradually | certainly |

_______________ _______________ _______________ _______________

_______________ _______________ _______________

### Adverb placement

Here is an important grammar rule regarding adverbs: in a sentence, **an adverb should not be positioned between the verb it is modifying and the direct object**. The best place for an adverb in a sentence is right next to the verb it describes. Look at the placement of the adverb carefully in the sentences below.

| Sentence | Correct or Incorrect? |
|---|---|
| Dorothy placed **carefully** the green glasses on her face. | Incorrect: the adverb is next to the verb but it is between the verb (*placed*) and the object (*glasses*). |
| Dorothy placed the green glasses on her face **carefully**. | Better |
| **Carefully**, Dorothy placed the green glasses on her face. | Better |
| Dorothy **carefully** placed the green glasses on her face. | Correct—the best version of the sentence. The adverb is beside the verb; the verb and the object are together. |

**2** Only some of these sentences contain correctly placed adverbs. Circle *correct* or *incorrect* for each one.
*Hint: The placement may be incorrect for reasons other than the grammar rule above.*

**a** Dorothy threw quickly the water on the Witch of the West. Correct Incorrect

**b** Loudly Toto barked at the Wizard. Correct Incorrect

**c** 'I have no heart,' Tin Man said sadly. Correct Incorrect

**3** Rewrite these sentences to show improved adverb placement. Remember to use correct punctuation.

**a** Dorothy gleefully skipped through the gates of the Emerald City.

_______________________________________________

**b** 'The Witch in a flash melted!' excitedly exclaimed Tin Man.

_______________________________________________

**4** Make single sentences using only the words in each group and without using any commas.

**a** excitedly Toto dog loudly was and barking Dorothy's

_______________________________________________

**b** breathlessly how Dorothy her house explained in so arrived had fast Oz

_______________________________________________

# NARRATIVE TEXT

## PUNCTUATION WORK

### Punctuating direct speech

When showing that words are directly spoken by a character in a story, we use **quotation marks** ('…'). You will have noticed that the text 'The Wizard of Oz' has been written almost entirely in direct speech. We only hear from the narrator occasionally. Here are some features and rules of speech marks.

- Quotation marks are also called inverted commas or speech marks.
- Quotation marks are always used in pairs. The first set begins the quote and the second set closes it.
- They are used to separate the direct speech or quote from the rest of the sentence.
- All punctuation marks related to the direct speech must be shown inside the quotation marks. For example, *Joe called out, 'I'll be stopping by the shop. Need anything?'*
- A capital letter must begin a line of direct speech, no matter where it starts in a sentence.
- Where a line of direct speech is in two or more parts, the first part should end in a comma unless it is an exclamation or a question. If the sentence within the direct speech continues, the second part of the line begins with a lower-case letter. For example, *'That's right,' said Kit, 'you really should go.'*
- You can use either double or single quotation marks ("…" or '…') but you must use them consistently throughout the text. Whichever you choose to use, when you have a quotation within the speech marks, enclose the quote-within-a-quote with the other form. For example, 'He told me to "get lost",' she said indignantly.

**1** Circle whether the use of quotation marks in each of these sentences is *correct* or *incorrect*.

| | | | |
|---|---|---|---|
| **a** | 'I'll get you, my pretty'! Shrieked the Wicked Witch of the West. | Correct | Incorrect |
| **b** | Tin Man cried, 'Run!' And they did. | Correct | Incorrect |
| **c** | Glinda explained to the Munchkins who 'Dorothy' was. | Correct | Incorrect |
| **d** | After a pathetic roar, the Cowardly Lion simply said, 'Sorry.' | Correct | Incorrect |

**2** The following passage contains no punctuation marks. Punctuate it correctly so that it makes sense and shows the direct speech of Dorothy. The passage does not come directly from the text. (For the purposes of this exercise, there is no need to use a new line for the direct speech.)

dorothy took off her old leather shoes and tried on the silver ones which fitted her as well as if they had been made for her finally she picked up her basket come along toto she said we will go to the emerald city and ask the wizard of oz how to get back to kansas again she closed the door locked it and put the key in her pocket

**3** Why do you think quotation marks are also called inverted commas? ______________________

______________________________________________

### Capital letters with special purposes

In *The Wizard of Oz,* L Frank Baum has turned some **common nouns** into **proper nouns** by using **capital letters**. You will note in the excerpt that he has done this with particular words for particular reasons:

- Wizard (to denote his leadership position)
- City (short for the Emerald City)
- Palace (to denote that it is the centre of the City)
- Witch (to denote power and to show that the word comes from a longer title, such as the Good Witch of the North).

**4** Circle all of the incorrect uses of capital letters in the short passage below.
*Hint: Remember that the capitalised words listed above have been used on purpose in Baum's story.*

with the witch dead, Dorothy enjoyed a hearty Supper. The richest Munchkin, named boq, was her waiter.

# NARRATIVE TEXT

## *Allegory*



### Decoding *The Wizard of Oz*

In the nineteen years between the release of *The Wizard of Oz* and his death author L Frank Baum refused to directly label the book as allegorical, but since that time most scholars have agreed that it can easily be read as an allegory that explores issues of finance and politics in America in the late 1800s. To understand this view, and to decode the story's meaning, you need to be aware of some key symbols in the text.

- **The Wizard of Oz**: Thought to represent William Jennings Bryan, a Populist politician (that is, one who appeals to popular interests and concerns), Congressman and two-time presidential candidate. He was depicted as a lion in the media due to his 'roaring' but empty political speeches, so it's likely that the Cowardly Lion, another character in the story, also symbolises Bryan. *Lion* is a homophone (word with the same sound) for *lyin'*. The lion has good intentions but very little courage. The Wizard is all talk and can't keep his promises. These are all common complaints against politicians.
- **Dorothy**: The everyman/everywoman of America, particularly its agricultural heartland, Kansas. Her quest becomes focused on the idea of home, which symbolises 'the great American dream' of owning one's own home. 'There's no place like home,' she says with increasing conviction in the story. Ironically, she wakes to find that her whole quest has actually been a dream. Perhaps Baum is urging ordinary Americans to 'wake up' and stop fantasising about financial security and home ownership.
- **Kansas and Nebraska, USA**: Dorothy is from Kansas and the Wizard is from Omaha, Nebraska, which borders Kansas. Being state neighbours, Dorothy (farming Americans) expects the Wizard (politicians like Bryan) to help her.
- **Hot air balloon**: Oz has allowed himself to be carried away by his own 'hot air' (a colloquial term for political spin and rhetoric), to the point where he can't go back to thinking and speaking like an ordinary person.
- **The Emerald City**: America is often said to revolve around money (colloquially called 'the Greenback' due to the colour of US paper notes). In the capital, Washington DC/the Emerald City, everything is seen through green spectacles/the lens of money.
- **The Wicked Witch of the East**: Wall Street bankers and the industries they funded, which enslaved the 'little people' of America (symbolised by the Munchkins). The sister of the similarly evil and silver-loving Witch of the West, she wears silver shoes (ruby slippers in the movie) that pass to Dorothy.
- **The Wicked Witch of the West**: Natural and manmade trials and oppressions suffered by ordinary Americans. Drought devastated the Mid-West farmlands—especially in Kansas—in the late 1800s (remember that this witch is destroyed by water, or rain), and silver and gold markets were controlled by powerful businessmen (the witch is no longer a threat when she melts and becomes *liquid,* which is a financial term meaning free-flowing wealth that can be quickly bought or sold). She summons her enslaved workers with a silver whistle. *Oz* is the abbreviation for *ounce,* the unit of measurement for silver and gold. Baum has linked her power in the land with her control of these precious metals.
- **The Good Witches of the North and South**: Bryan's supporters in the Upper Mid-West, North and South of the USA, who, like Bryan, had high ideals but no real way to achieve them. All 'good witches and wizards' (politicians and political activists) in the story have little or no power.

# NARRATIVE TEXT
## *Allegory*

WRITING WORK 2

### Allegories

An **allegory** is a text which appears to tell a story about one thing but is also telling a **hidden story**. The main purpose of this textual form is to explore issues. As such, they can be very important and valuable texts. Often, the composer clearly takes one side and protests against a person or group, but sometimes, as in the case of *The Wizard of Oz,* the allegory does not give a direct judgement about issues. Some allegories, like William Golding's *Lord of the Flies,* are even more general, and simply explore society and human behaviour.

### Main features of an allegory

- A complete plot with an orientation, complication, sequence of events, climax and resolution
- A surface story and a concealed story
- Symbolic characters, objects, places, names and events used consistently throughout the story
- Personification of objects, events, systems or issues into characters
- At least one moral or life lesson

**1** Match these allegorical messages with quotes from the text by writing *a* to *e* in the appropriate spaces.
*Hints: Make sure you have carefully read the information about allegories and symbols in the text before you answer. Look back at the story excerpt to see the quotes in context as you complete the task.*

| | |
|---|---|
| **a** People are intimidated by politicians. | ____ 'I'm really a very good man, but I'm a very bad Wizard.' |
| **b** People think wealth is all they need. | ____ 'the Witches were really able to do wonderful things.' |
| **c** Greed clouds our perspective. | ____ 'when you wear green spectacles, why of course everything you see looks green to you.' |
| **d** Banks and industry have great power. | ____ 'every good thing that is needed to make one happy.' |
| **e** Bad politicians aren't necessarily bad people. | ____ 'they were afraid of me' |

**2** How is an allegory different from a symbol?

________________________________________

**3** Why might L Frank Baum have disguised a discussion of political issues in a children's story?

________________________________________

The title of the chapter from which the excerpt comes is 'The Discovery of Oz, the Terrible'. In the 1800s and earlier, *terrible* could mean 'powerful' or 'terrifying', and was sometimes added to the titles of tyrannical leaders (such as the Russian tsar Ivan the Terrible). Baum uses the word with this connotation, because until this point in the story Oz seems very powerful, *and* to mean that in reality he is a terrible, hopeless Wizard.

**4** There are other words and phrases with double meanings in the excerpt. Three are listed below. Look back at their use in the text then suggest two meanings of each example. *Hint: The first meaning is literal.*

**a** this country ________________ ________________

**b** green ________________ ________________

**c** circus ________________ ________________

**5** Find two questions in the text. Write them below and note their effects.

________________________________________

________________________________________

________________________________________

# NARRATIVE TEXT
## *Allegory*

**WRITING SAMPLE**

Here is a sample text showing you how to write an allegory.

*Johnny Lykette is a teenage boy who has become obsessed with social media. One day he is stunned to find what look like feathers growing from his arms. This is an excerpt so the story is already under way at this point.*

### Excerpt from *Birds of a Feather*

**Create a title for the story that is symbolic and/or includes an allusion.** The title alludes to the proverb 'Birds of a feather flock together', which means that like-minded people tend to be friends. It also foreshadows that Johnny will literally transform into a vulture. The saying is a moral from one of Aesop's fables, which is like a short allegory.

Johnny ran his clammy, worried fingers down his arm, trying to make sense of the tiny stumps of coarse white … what were they? It was impossible, but they seemed to be getting longer—and somehow softer—by the moment.

**Introduce the main character and give him or her a symbolic name.** *Johnny Lykette* is a symbolic name. *Johnny* is a common first name, suggesting that this could be anyone. *Lykette* (pronounced *like it*) refers to Johnny's obsession with social media and receiving 'Likes' from his friends.

Just then, a familiar *blip* interrupted his thoughts. Immediately, he forgot his concerns and rushed to his laptop. Three more Likes! This took him to a record eighty-three in one day for one pic! Johnny screeched with pride and delight. Sure, the record was thanks to a snap of a guy falling out of his wheelchair, but it was all in a good cause, right? He didn't know the guy, so no harm done. And the look on his face … man! You couldn't help but laugh. Besides, if someone like that couldn't have a bit of sense of humour, he wouldn't get along too well in life. Johnny was just helping him toughen up a bit.

**Write a sequence of events that build on a complication.** The transitional phrase 'Just then' signals a change of direction or break in the plot events. The writer has used onomatopoeia ('*blip*') to distract Johnny and make us wait to find out more about the mysterious hairs. Johnny's 'screech' foreshadows his transformation into a carnivorous bird. This builds on the earlier feather clue. Johnny is speaking or thinking to himself; this is called internal monologue. He is trying to convince himself that he hasn't done anything wrong.

Another *blip*. This time it was a comment. Even better! Eagerly, Johnny moused over the icon and opened the comment on a new page. But he was dismayed when he saw a familiar face in the mini DP beside it. Wheelchair guy!

**Write the next plot event, building on previous ones but including a change or development.** This event is similar to the previous one but with a surprising outcome. Johnny's 'prey' has seen the picture of himself online and is about to respond. The use of computer and internet jargon ('icon', 'moused' and 'DP') add to the credibility of this scene.

'Dear Johnny', the lengthy comment began politely, 'You don't know me, but it's only taken me a few minutes to get to know you and what you are. I've been looking at your profile, your friends and your interest groups. While I was very angry and hurt at first to see your cruel photo of me during my accident, I'm beginning to pity you instead. YOU are the one with disabilities, Johnny. That is, you lack important abilities. You have no ability to feel compassion. You have no ability to value anything but quick popularity grabs. I fear that, soon, you will have no ability to behave or think like a human being at all. You and your so-called friends are a flock of flesh-ripping vultures. Vultures feast on the misfortunes of others. Their ravenous squawks shatter the peace and drown out the final, feeble cries of their prey. One more thing: vultures may flock together for a while, but they will peck out each other's eyes for the sake of their next meal. You don't know what you've made friends with—or what you are becoming yourself. I just hope you can understand this in time.'

**Continue telling the story and incorporate some additional narrative and language features.** The composer has interrupted the narrative with a form shift to direct speech in the first person (monologue). This section is the key to the reader understanding the symbolic events of the story so far and those that are yet to happen. The symbol of a vulture is explored in detail by this character to explain to the reader how it works. This, along with the teenage protagonist, suggests that the story is targeted at teenage readers. The composer has used a paradox: a person without any apparent disabilities can be disabled in other, more important ways. Johnny has become disabled from thinking and behaving like a decent person. Harsh 'f' alliteration links the key words 'flock', 'flesh', 'feast' and 'friends', and contrasts them with 'final' and 'feeble'. The phrase 'flock together' is a reference back to the title, showing the reader that the title—and the full proverb from which it has been taken—is being explained in this section of the story.

'What a psycho!' Johnny cackled loudly. Why had he even wasted one and a half precious minutes of his life reading that! DELETE. Shut up, loser.

**Continue to build the main character arc (development or transformation) of the protagonist by describing the next brief plot event.** Johnny's reaction suggests that the character arc is almost complete: he seems too far gone to change and is quickly transforming into a vulture. A second birdlike sound ('cackled') is used here to emphasise this.

But the comment had messed with his fun and he was distracted now. Time for a snack. He stamped out to the kitchen, and caught a flash of his profile in the hallway mirror on the way. Wait. Did his nose always look that pointy?

**Move the character to a different location and write another plot event.** 'But' marks another plot transition, allowing the composer to move the character to a different place and to use two devices —action and a question—to show the next step in Johnny's decline: his nose is becoming a bird's beak.

# NARRATIVE TEXT

## Allegory



Plan your sample excerpt on the lines provided.

- **Create a title for the story that is symbolic and/or includes an allusion.** If possible, the title should also foreshadow what will happen by the end of the story.

- **Introduce the main character and give him or her a symbolic name.** Describe the main character performing an action. Remember: the story is already underway by this point so don't describe everything.

- **Write a sequence of events that build on a complication.** Try using a transitional phrase to signal a change of direction or break in the plot events. Use some language features, such as onomatopoeia. Include a moment of foreshadowing in the action that points to something that will happen later in the story. Interrupt the regular narration with some internal monologue; internal monologue does not require speech marks.

- **Write the next plot event, building on previous ones but including a change or development.** Use some appropriate slang or jargon to add to the credibility of the scene.

- **Continue telling the story and incorporate some additional narrative and language features.** Interrupt the story with a form shift. For example, change from third person narration to direct speech in the first person (monologue) by another character. You may use this section to help the reader understand the symbolic events of the story so far and those that are yet to happen. Use alliteration. Refer back to the title in some way to build on its meaning.

- **Continue to build the main character arc (development or transformation) of the protagonist by describing the next brief plot event.**

- **Move the character to a different location and write another plot event.** Remember: the plot does not need to conclude or resolve here because this is only an excerpt from what would be a larger story.

UNIT 11

# NARRATIVE TEXT

## *Satirical script*

READING WORK

### Lady Darlingcot

*At rise, LADY DARLINGCOT is seated in her small but fashionable Victorian parlour, writing carefully in her diary. There is an enthusiastic rapping at the door. She rises purposefully and opens the door to LADY IDLEFORD, an overdressed and boisterously affectionate lady.*

LADY IDLEFORD *(Ecstatically)* DARLING! *(Air kisses)*

LADY DARLINGCOT *(Coldly)* Cot. Lady Darlingcot.

LADY IDLEFORD *(Laughs in an irritatingly high tone)* What a clever play on words!

LADY DARLINGCOT How are you, Lady Idleford?

LADY IDLEFORD Sublime! And you?

LADY DARLINGCOT Very well; quite … robust. Do come in.

LADY IDLEFORD Thank you kindly. *(Takes off her coat)* The weather continues charming!

LADY DARLINGCOT *(Uninterested)* Undoubtedly. *(Suddenly inspired)* Did you see the superb sunset last night? It was almost as though the sky was filled with blood.

LADY IDLEFORD *(Laughs)* What a dazzling metaphor!

LADY DARLINGCOT Simile. *(A beat)* Tea?

LADY IDLEFORD Please. Black with two sugars.

LADY DARLINGCOT Excellent. Dark and bittersweet, like death.

LADY IDLEFORD *(Laughs)* Oh, you! *(Suddenly noticing a red-toned painting on the wall)* My, what a striking painting! And a charming palette! What is your muse?

LADY DARLINGCOT Well, last week the milkman delivered camembert instead of brie. So I sliced off his arms and used his blood as paint. I suppose *he* was my muse. Briefly.

LADY IDLEFORD Ooh how witty!

LADY DARLINGCOT How about *we* paint a picture?

LADY IDLEFORD Oh I'm all thumbs when it comes to art, I'm afraid. So, where is Harold? Out fishing again, I suppose.

LADY DARLINGCOT Yes. In fact, *sleeping* with the fishes. *(Picks up a teaspoon and admires it)*

LADY IDLEFORD You are such a tease!

LADY DARLINGCOT Yes … *(Pause)* I had better go and sharpen this spoon. *(Walks off)*

LADY IDLEFORD *(Oblivious to that bizarre statement)* Righto!

*LADY IDLEFORD amuses herself for a few moments by pottering around the room. She picks up and inspects the following items, finding nothing alarming about them whatsoever: a smashed framed photograph of a fisherman (presumably Harold), a voodoo doll full of pins, a pair of blood-spattered kitchen gloves and a small handsaw. LADY DARLINGCOT suddenly emerges in the doorway and approaches LADY IDLEFORD menacingly.*

LADY DARLINGCOT *(Brandishing the teaspoon)* You don't understand, do you? Harold is dead. I killed him. Just like the milkman.

LADY IDLEFORD *(Laughing)* Darling! Next thing, you will be telling me that you killed my Mamma!

LADY DARLINGCOT I did. She was just as annoying as you. If it is of comfort, she died quickly.

*She starts jabbing LADY IDLEFORD with the spoon and continues to do so until the curtain falls.*

LADY IDLEFORD Whatever are you doing, dear?

LADY DARLINGCOT I am trying to kill you.

LADY IDLEFORD With a teaspoon? *(Laughs)*

LADY DARLINGCOT Undeniably.

LADY IDLEFORD Ooh that tickles! *(Pause)* Hm, a little to the left. *(Pause)* Gracious, how unladylike! *(Pause)* Oh, now that is starting to hurt a little.

LADY DARLINGCOT That is my intention.

LADY IDLEFORD You must have exceptional patience to kill someone in this fashion.

LADY DARLINGCOT You have no idea.

*CURTAIN*

- 'At rise' refers to **when the play begins** (that is, when the curtain rises).
- Character **names are usually capitalised** in scripts. Italics are also used when names are included in stage directions.
- The names have **connotations** that match aspects of each character's behaviour. These are addressed elsewhere in this chapter.
- This is a **line** from Oscar Wilde's *The Importance of Being Earnest*, a play after which this script is styled.
- This common stage direction indicates a **very brief pause** between or inside lines, often for comic effect.
- **Stage directions are shown in parentheses.** They either give details about the look of the stage or direct actors to speak or move in a certain way.
- This **exclamation**, like 'DARLING!' at the start, indicates both characterisation and an exaggerated acting style.
- 'Sleeping with the fishes' is a **euphemism** for death.
- These are elements of **farce**: an absurd action and an equally absurd reaction.
- Lady Idleford **explores the space** on behalf of the audience to reveal the truth about Lady Darlingcot. Ironically, she fails to understand what she is seeing.
- **Rapid-fire dialogue** speeds the action and heightens the comedy.
- This is a **comical progression** of action.
- *'CURTAIN'* denotes that **the play is over**. If there is an actual curtain across the stage, this is the point where it comes down.

### Literal questions

*Hint: Read the text carefully to locate specific facts and details.*

**1** What is the style of décor in Lady Darlingcot's parlour?

______________________________________________

**2** What happened to the milkman?

**a** He was Lady Darlingcot's muse. **b** He delivered camembert. **c** He had his arms sliced off.

**3** According to Lady Darlingcot, what does Lady Idleford's tea have in common with death?

______________________________________________

### Interpretive questions

*Hint: These questions require you to combine facts and details to synthesise the meaning.*

**4** The first line—'DARLING!'—is all in capital letters. What does this convey?

**a** the intended volume and tone of the speaker **b** that the character is a real 'darling' **c** emphasis

**5** What does Lady Idleford call the red palette Lady Darlingcot has used in her painting?
*Hint: The palette of an artwork is the colour scheme or collection of colours used by the artist.*

**a** charming **b** bloody **c** striking

**6** Why is Lady Darlingcot 'suddenly inspired'?

______________________________________________

**7** What does Lady Darlingcot really have in mind when she asks Lady Idleford to paint a picture with her?

______________________________________________

______________________________________________

**8** How many people do we know Lady Darlingcot has killed by the end of the skit?
*Hint: A skit is a very short, one-act play; usually comical. The text 'Lady Darlingcot' can be called a skit.*

______________________________________________

______________________________________________

**9** What does Lady Idleford's name suggest about her?

**a** She keeps idols. **b** She is not very productive. **c** She drives a Ford.

**10** What is the probable reason for Harold's framed photograph being broken?

**a** Lady Idleford dropped it. **b** Lady Darlingcot smashed it. **c** Harold left it as a clue.

### Applied questions

*Hint: These questions require you to understand a text's implications to infer meaning from the text.*

**11** What is this script satirising? Hint: A text that satirises something mocks it, often to make a point.

**a** milkmen **b** paintings **c** the upper classes

**12** Why do you think Lady Darlingcot has become a murderer?

______________________________________________

______________________________________________

# NARRATIVE TEXT

## Satirical script

**SPELLING WORK**

### List Words

All of the words in the box below appear in the text 'Lady Darlingcot'.

| | | | | |
|---|---|---|---|---|
| robust | palette | parlour | menacingly | whatsoever |
| boisterously | bittersweet | presumably | patience | exceptional |
| purposefully | camembert | overdressed | muse | simile |

**1** Organise the list words into columns according to the number of **syllables** in each word. Write them in alphabetical order and divide the syllables using slashes. Two words have been placed in the table for you.
*Hint: A syllable must contain one vowel sound. Say the list words aloud to split them.*

| One-syllable words | Two-syllable words | Three-syllable words | Four-syllable words |
|---|---|---|---|
| | | | |
| | | | ex–cep–tion–al |
| | | | |
| | | sim–i–le | |
| | | | |
| | | | |

**2** Answer the questions below with list words.

**a** Which word, minus a vowel, describes a facial expression? ______

**b** Which word is a homophone for a dentistry term? ______

**c** Which word is both a noun and a verb? ______

**d** Which word has a prefix meaning 'utterly' or 'completely'? ______

**3** Using the list words as a guide, circle the correctly spelt word in each pair below.

**a** pourposeful purposeful **b** exceptionally exceptionly

**c** patient paitient **d** menice menace

**4** This passage is a mess of spelling mistakes. Write the corrected words in the spaces provided underneath.
*Hint: Some List Words have been used with both correct and incorrect spelling.*

The Franklins came bouncing boisterously into the kitchen, weilding camembear cheese and a bottle of something they'de unearthed from their foetid bassment. Without needing any excuse whatsohever, and certanly without an invitation, theese highly annoying people could turn a peacefull afternoon into an ordeel.

______ ______
______ ______
______ ______
______ ______
______ ______

**5** Add consonants or vowels to the words below to make list words.
*Hint: You may need to add three or more consonants and vowels to each word in various positions.*

**a** smile ______ **b** use ______

**c** pour ______ **d** rust ______

**e** member ______ **f** pence ______

# NARRATIVE TEXT
## *Satirical script*

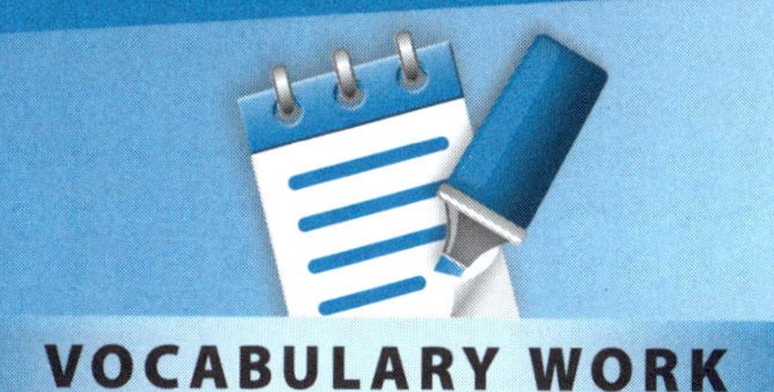

**VOCABULARY WORK**

### Adding interest with adverbs

As you may already know, a verb is the name of an action of some kind, and an **adverb** can describe how the action of a verb is carried out. Adverbs contribute detail, **interest** and levels of meaning in any narrative text but they are particularly useful in scripts. This is because stage directions, particularly those that direct actors to speak, look or move in a particular way, usually include—or simply are—adverbs.

**1** What do these adverbs from the script mean? Give their meanings, based on their context in the script.

**a** carefully ______________________

**b** ecstatically ______________________

**c** coldly ______________________

In the text 'Lady Darlingcot', we can infer a lot about the murderous protagonist simply from reading that she 'purposefully' answers the door. Consider what some of the other adverbs in the script tell us about her.

**2** Each adverb below describes an action of Lady Darlingcot in the text. Other actions of hers match this adverb and aid our understanding of the character. Which action doesn't necessarily match it? Cross it out.

| | | | |
|---|---|---|---|
| **a** carefully | ordering brie over camembert | committing murder very slowly | opening the door |
| **b** coldly | slicing off people's arms | sharpening teaspoons | joking about death |
| **c** menacingly | painting with blood | associating sunset colours with blood | keeping voodoo dolls |

**3** Answer these questions with list words to show that you understand their meaning.

**a** Which adverb means 'with intent'? ______________________

**b** Which adjective can be used to describe mixed emotions? ______________________

**c** Which word has the same meaning as the phrase *at all*? ______________________

**d** Which compound word describes Lady Idleford's appearance? ______________________

**e** Which noun is a positive quality of Lady Darlingcot's? ______________________

Lady Idleford uses words and phrases which tell us that she is a very enthusiastic socialite. Some of her gushy and highly emotional expressions are **idioms** that belong in the Victorian era; others are more timeless. In any case, they are ridiculously exaggerated and should not be taken literally in their context.

**4** Find and explain four such expressions used by Lady Idleford in the script. The first has been done for you as a guide. *Hint: The expressions may be single words, phrases, short sentences or questions.*

**a** 'dazzling' ______ so bright and/or beautiful that the viewer is blinded

**b** ______ ______________________

**c** ______ ______________________

**d** ______ ______________________

**e** ______ ______________________

**5** Fill in the blanks to complete three idioms from the text 'Lady Darlingcot'.

**a** I'm al____________s **b** I'm a____________d **c** You have no i____________

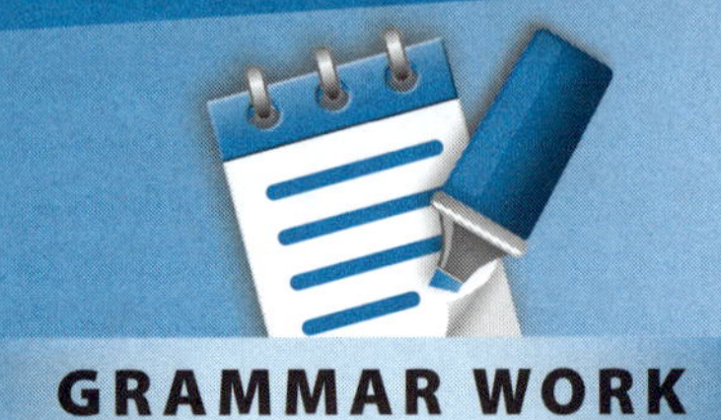

# NARRATIVE TEXT

## Satirical script

**GRAMMAR WORK**

**1** Transform these adverbs into verbs. *Hint: Some adverbs do not end in* ly. *These are called irregular adverbs.*

| Adverb | Verb |
|---|---|
| a annoyingly | ______________ |
| b enviously | ______________ |
| c tiredly | ______________ |
| d straight | ______________ |
| e wrong | ______________ |

**2** Change these verbs into adverbs. They do not appear in the list words.

| Verb | Adverb |
|---|---|
| a create | ______________ |
| b admire | ______________ |
| c sleep | ______________ |
| d mark | ______________ |
| e deceive | ______________ |

**3** Which two adverbs in the list words can be transformed into verbs? Write them and their verb form below.

| Adverb | Verb |
|---|---|
| a ______________ | ______________ |
| b ______________ | ______________ |

**4** Transform the four adverbs from the list words into nouns and write them in the spaces below.
*Hint: There are various types of noun, including abstract nouns, which describe concepts or emotions.*

| Adverb | Noun |
|---|---|
| a ______________ | ______________ |
| b ______________ | ______________ |
| c ______________ | ______________ |
| d ______________ | ______________ |

### Other functions of adverbs

**Adverbs** are very **special modifiers**, in that they can also be used to modify other adverbs and even adjectives. Look at this example: *We almost always travel during the school holidays.* The adverb *almost* modifies the adverb *always,* which modifies the verb *travel.* Now read this example: *That painting is quite expensive.* Here, the adverb *quite* is modifying the adjective *expensive.*

### Adverbs of frequency

**Adverbs of frequency** tell us how frequently (or often) something occurs. The first example above contains an adverb of frequency: *always.* There are many other categories of adverbs aside from this one.

**5** Write another six adverbs of frequency in the spaces below. Do not include 'always'.

______________ ______________ ______________

______________ ______________ ______________

# NARRATIVE TEXT

## Satirical script

**PUNCTUATION WORK**

### Italics

**Italics** are a special kind of **punctuation**, in that they are only really visible in typed text. They have quite a few different functions; in the text 'Lady Darlingcot' they are used in a number of these ways. Italics are used in these and other circumstances.

- They identify titles of texts or major works. For example, *My Fair Lady.* While this is a theatrical piece, it is not contained in a book of plays, so it is a standalone title. When identifying texts inside a collection, such as an album or anthology, only the compilation title is italicised. The individual text names are shown in speech marks. 'Lady Darlingcot', a skit, is in this category.
- They indicate stage directions. When they appear amid lines of dialogue, stage directions are also enclosed in parentheses. For example '(*Laughs*)'
- They emphasise particular words and phrases. For example, 'You named your son *Space-Cadet*?!' It is important in this kind of usage to not over-italicise, or the italics will lose their impact.
- They identify letters, partial words and whole words in a certain context. For example, 'Lady Darlingcot puts the *mad* in madam.'
- They identify examples of parts of speech and other linguistic features. For example, 'Three of the most commonly used prepositions are *of*, *in* and *to*.'
- They are used for words and terms from other languages, such as '*El Encierro,* The Running of the Bulls'.

**1** Based on the information in the list above, write the function of the italics in each of these examples.

**a** Well, what did you *think* would happen? ____________________

**b** *A sunny kitchen. Marion stands at the sink, crying.* ____________________

**c** The adverb *literally* is horribly overused. ____________________

**d** It's Fletcher-*Brown,* not Fletcher-*Brawn.* ____________________

**e** Let us consider the *zeitgeist* of 1960s America. ____________________

**f** And the Oscar goes to … *Jaws.* ____________________

**2** The following lines from the text 'Lady Darlingcot' contain italics. What is at least one effect of the italics in each case? *Hint: Read back over these lines in the script before answering.*

**a** Yes, *sleeping* with the fishes. ____________________

**b** I suppose *he* was my muse. ____________________

**c** How about *we* paint a picture? ____________________

**3** The following passage is (mostly) incorrectly punctuated. Punctuate it correctly so that it makes sense. The passage does not come from the text; it is about the main character, Lady Darlingcot.

lady darling-Cot took great pride in her victorian Parlour which despite being small was, very fashionable. The re-clusive woman didnt often receive callers so it was always quite an occasion when she did she ensured that the larder was fully-stocked with the essentials, camembert smoked-herrings, crispbread and of course arsenic. At the Darling-Cots an afternoons entertaining could reach a marvellously, murderous conclusion by six o-clock.

**4** Along with other punctuation, exclamation marks can be used in dialogue to create a particular tone. Match these lines from the script with the tone created by the exclamation mark.

| | | | |
|---|---|---|---|
| **a** | Gracious, how unladylike! | ____ | enthusiasm |
| **b** | My, what a striking painting! | ____ | amusement |
| **c** | You are such a tease! | ____ | understatement |
| **d** | Righto! | ____ | ignorance |

## Essential features of short scripts

A **short dramatic script** or **one-act play** consists of the following elements.

- The title is the name of the play, which can be eponymous (that is, the main character's name, such as Lady Darlingcot), literal, symbolic, cryptic, an allusion, a line from the play or a combination of some of these things.
- Dialogue, the lines spoken by characters, is structured down the page in a way that separates speakers and is easy to read.
- Characters' names are listed before the script itself and then positioned directly beside each line a character is to speak. They are usually printed in capital letters throughout the script.
- Stage directions describe the appearance of the stage, denote all main actions and direct actors to deliver lines in a certain way. Directions beginning and inside lines are shown in parentheses.
- A note about what is seen '*At rise*' describes everything the audience sees and hears when the curtain rises (not always literally) at the beginning of the play.
- Some notes on sound and lighting effects.
- The end of the play is denoted by '*CURTAIN*' or '*THE END*'.

## Creating emphasis in scripts

In the Punctuation Work section on page 106, we explored the ways in which italics can be used to create emphasis and identify special words in scripts and other narrative texts. **Emphasis** can also be created in **scripts** by these features:

- capital letters
- ellipses
- truncated sentences (very short, simple lines)
- repetition
- asides (words that only the audience can hear)
- beats (very brief pauses between or inside lines), pauses and silences
- exclamations and fillers (more on these below).

**1** Find an example of these two script elements in the text 'Lady Darlingcot' and state their functions.

**a** Beat ______________________________

______________________________

**b** Pause ______________________________

______________________________

## Exclamations and fillers

In any narrative text with dialogue, including scripts like 'Lady Darlingcot', **exclamations** (such as *goodness me!* and *aha!*) and **fillers** (such as *um* and *ah*) are used:

- to create naturalistic speech patterns and to show uncertainty, fear or deceit in a character
- as a sudden and impactful outburst
- as a feature of a character's personality, attitude and speech
- to create suspense, tension or awkwardness
- for a variation in vocal tone or mood.

**2** Find three exclamations and three fillers in the text 'Lady Darlingcot' and write them on the lines provided.

a Exclamations ______ ______ ______

b Fillers ______ ______ ______

As we have seen in the text 'Lady Darlingcot', italics, exclamation marks and other features of structure and punctuation can help create a particular **tone** in a script's dialogue.

**3** Complete the table to show where and how language features create a certain tone in the text 'Lady Darlingcot'. *Hint: You may wish to take some of the answers for the 'Tone created' column from the script's stage directions.*

| Language feature | Example from the script | Tone created |
|---|---|---|
| a unexpected or omitted punctuation marks | | |
| b fully capitalised words | | |
| c truncated sentences | | |
| d ellipsis (…) | | |

### Features of a satirical script

A text that **satirises** something mocks it, often to make a point or deliver a message. In the text 'Lady Darlingcot', upper-class society is being satirised. There is no direct message, but the composer makes fun of the characters to explore relationships and people's destructive and malicious behaviour.

A **satirical script** features the following **language and literary elements**:

- understatement and its opposite, hyperbole
- farce and/or unlikely situations and unusual people
- stereotypical or caricatured characters
- irony and double meanings
- parody and mockery.

As you can see, parody can be a part of a satirical text, or a text in its own right, but it is not another term for satire. A parody imitates a certain text, composer or style, with exaggeration for comic effect.

## Test your understanding

**4** What makes the text 'Lady Darlingcot' a satire and not a parody?

______

**Farce** is a type of humour that is both verbal and physical. It involves the deliberate exaggeration of a character's voice and movements by the actor. Elements of farce are not always featured in satirical scripts, but they can be used to complement mockery and caricature (the exaggeration of particular features of a person) in satire. This is the case in the text 'Lady Darlingcot'.

**5** Give four lines, actions or other features of the text 'Lady Darlingcot' that belong to the genre of farce. *Hint: Read back over the annotations on the script for one example, then find three others.*

______ ______

______ ______

# NARRATIVE TEXT

## *Satirical script*

WRITING SAMPLE

Here is a sample text showing you how to structure and write a satirical script.

### The PM

✱ **Come up with a title.** It identifies the eponymous character (the nameless PM).

*CS: lectern with a campaign poster for the PM (Prime Minister) attached. Another poster, protesting against the PM, lies on the ground. UR (known only by these initials), the PM's campaign consultant and voice of reason, wears glasses and a scarf and holds a tablet. UR can be male or female.*

✱ **Write initial stage directions that include a key prop, some other props and important details about at least one character.** The stage directions here include a key prop (a lectern) at CS (centre stage), other props (including a campaign poster) and important details about one character (UR). Optional details (such as the PM's costume) are omitted.

PM: And as such, in conclusion, ergo … cos sin theta … uh, to wrap up, the implementation of this salient nation-building legislation patently perpetuates a best and brightest zeitgeist and a fiscal feasibility that galvanises the expressive determination of a nation moving forward. *(Pause)* Um … Thank you.

*PM steps to the side, saluting his audience in huge, triumphant waves. SFX: A blend of polite applause and booing.*

✱ **Begin the action *in medias res* (in the middle of the action).** The PM's opening address immediately shows the script's genre of satire. The second set of stage directions prescribes actions for the main character to perform that cement his high status.

UR: Well, that was marvellous, sir. Thoroughly inspiring.
PM: Thanks, UR! Yah really think?
UR: I really do! *(Aside)* Except for the words.
PM: What?
UR: What? Nothing.
PM: How would you score it from one to one zero, zero, zero, zero, zero, zero, zero, zero?
UR: Uh, that's one hundred million.
PM: Yeah that.
UR: At about … a million?
PM: Wow, that's great; that's heaps!
UR: Yes it is.

✱ **Write an aside (a line spoken only to the audience) that reveals a character's attitude about another character and/or events.** It reveals UR's attitude about the PM and his speech. UR is the foil (contrasting character) to the dim-witted PM; UR's lines are juxtaposed with the PM's silly ones. The PM uses incongruous (ill-fitting) colloquial language to help develop his character. An ellipsis, a semi-colon and a comma are used to show actors exactly how to deliver the lines.

PM: *(Out of the side of his mouth)* To be honest, UR, I didn't understand a lot of the speech.
UR: *(Dismissively, with a 'whatever' wave of his hand)* Well …
PM: *(Quickly)* Any of it.
UR: No harm done. Now, please pay attention, sir. You have the charity luncheon at 12, a carbon trading convention at 2, and let's not forget your Japanese class at 7, seeing as the Opps already have the Chinese vote.
PM: *(Ignores UR and grabs the protest poster)* Hey, I like it! They even spelt my name right!
UR: Sir, that's a protest poster for APEC.
PM: Oh yeah, OPEC.
UR: Your campaign poster is here. *(Shows PM the poster on the lectern)*
PM: WHAT IS THIS? Who is this guy?
UR: It's you, sir.
PM: *(Squinting hard at the poster)* Ah, yes. Right you are. Ha! Right U.R! *(Laughs uproariously)* That's your name! UR! *(Laughs loudly again)* Wait, have I used that joke before?
UR: Yes, sir. *(Beat)* And it never gets old.

✱ **Reveal a shortcoming of a character to make fun of him or her and a wider group or occupation.** The PM's lack of intelligence is revealed to make fun of him and politicians in general. Details flesh out the scenario—here, the PM's busy schedule is outlined. Misunderstandings in the dialogue add to the mockery of the character. References to known events, such as the APEC Summit, add to the credibility of the scenario. Capital letters are used to show the shock and outrage of the character, and to indicate to the actor that the line should be shouted. A beat is included in UR's line to show sarcasm in the second half—without the beat, this line might sound sincere.

PM: *(Still chuckling)* Good times. Good times. *(Trails off)* Oh, that reminds me, UR, I want you to help me organise something.
UR: Certainly, sir. No problem.
PM: A war. I really want one! *(Pause)* And a ninja mask.
UR: Okay. Here's your mask. *(Takes off scarf and hands it to PM.)* But no war. Not today.
PM: It's not fair. Everyone gets to have a war but me. *(Throwing a tantrum)* Why can't I have a war?!
UR: Because they're not very nice things, sir. Generally speaking, people don't like wars.
PM: *(Pause, then triumphantly)* Let's have a war with Tasmania! *(Ties the scarf around his eyes like a ninja mask and tries to adopt a ninja stance).* YAAAA! *(Pause)* Wait, I can't see. *(Calling out)* UR? I can't see a thing in this. Come and fix it. UR?

✱ **Deal with an issue (like war) in a light-hearted way, but keep the underlying message serious.** The PM pauses because, like a child, he is thinking of an unreasonable request; repetition further emphasises the PM's childishness, features of the PM's characterisation. Understatement is used to emphasise the serious issue of war. The PM's absurd actions and words are elements of farce.

UR: *(Walking away shaking head)* You only do this job for the perks.

✱ **Have a character deliver a punchline.**

# NARRATIVE TEXT

## *Satirical script*

## WRITING YOUR OWN SAMPLE

Plan your sample on the lines provided.

- **Come up with a title.** It can be simple.
- **Write initial stage directions that include a key prop, some other props and important details about at least one character.** Optional details (such as characters' costumes) can be omitted.
- **Begin the action *in medias res* (in the middle of the action).** Write a line or two that immediately show the audience that the script is in the satire genre.
- **Write an aside (a line spoken only to the audience) that reveals a character's attitude about another character and/or events.** Use one character as the foil to another. Juxtapose this character's line with the lines of another character. Use incongruous language to reveal inconsistencies in a character. Use punctuation like ellipses and commas to show actors exactly how to deliver the lines.
- **Reveal a shortcoming of a character to make fun of him or her and a wider group or occupation.** Flesh out details of the scenario. Write misunderstandings into the dialogue to make fun of at least one character. Make references to known events to add to the scenario's credibility. Use capital letters to show emotions like shock and outrage, and to indicate to the actor that the line should be shouted. Include a beat in a line to show sarcasm or uncertainty in the second half of the line.
- **Deal with an issue (like war) in a light-hearted way, but keep the underlying message serious.** Include a pause and use repetition in a line spoken by one of the characters to emphasise features of characterisation. Use understatement to emphasise the serious issue or message, such as the futility of war. Write some absurd actions and words for a character as elements of farce.
- **Have a character deliver a punchline.**

# NARRATIVE TEXT

## Short story

**READING WORK**

### I told you

'Hey, boof-head.'

'Boof-face.'

'Hee hee hee!'

'Getcha boof on!'

'Hee hee hee hee hee!'

The usual after-school welcome home. It's Jordan and Jett, the evil Watson twins next door, laughing and taking it in turns to hurl really intelligent insults at me as I pass their house.

DOOF. Now they're hurling spitballs. A softball-sized mess of paper, glue, spit and who knows what diseases splats on the sidewalk right next to my foot. Ha. Lousy shots. I'm nearly at my gate and, thanks to the giant cabbage tree in our front yard, they can't see me from here. I'm home safe.

I bump open the broken gate with my bag. Dad still hasn't fixed it. He's been too busy. And, of course, we have no money. I can see that nobody is home. Looks like I'm on my own again. I'm getting used to this. Three years back, Dad went back to uni, meaning Mum went back to night shifts. Dad often has afternoon lectures, so until six or seven it's just me. In winter, it gets dark around five. I'm not scared of the dark but I always remember to lock the doors. Just in case.

Speaking of locked doors … I can't find my house key. I dive into the scummy recesses of my bag, but I already know it's not there. I can visualise it on top of the fridge, right where I left it as I grabbed my lunch this morning.

'You're kidding. Come *onnn*,' I groan to no-one.

There's no point trying to break in. Most of the windows in this ugly old shack are so stiff, they don't even open anymore. The ones that do have been carefully locked with track rods by my safety-conscious mother. You know, to stop anyone GETTING INSIDE. I shake my head at the irony.

I check my watch. It's four o'clock. Dad said he'll be home by seven. Just a few hours to kill. I wonder what I'll do till then. I suppose I can read my book on the verandah.

'Why are you reading books about war anyway?' Dad had asked a few days ago. He's a pacifist.

'For my History project,' I'd replied defensively.

'What project's that?'

*Continued*

- **Repetition** of 'boof' helps the dialogue to build in intensity and also shows the lack of originality in the twins' insults.
- 'Getcha' is a **slang** term written as it sounds. 'Sheesh' in line 46 is another one.
- This **builds** on the 'hurling' of words from the previous lines. Now actual projectiles are being hurled.
- The narrator has an **interior monologue**.
- **Contractions** are used consistently in this story to give Simon (the narrator) a clear voice.
- This is a **clue** to the family's lack of money. Others follow, including the need for Simon's mum to work night shifts, the stiff windows and the old, broken swing seat.
- This **foreshadows** the story's complication right before it happens.
- **Ellipsis** creates a natural tone as though Simon is speaking directly to the reader.
- A vivid **image** is created: a dirty schoolbag that might belong to a teenage boy.
- A **purposely misspelt word** ('onnn') conveys sound as well as thought.
- This is a **recurring action** in the story that helps to build tension.
- This **recurring subject** in the story relates to the tension between Simon and his dad and is the basis for the punchline at the end.

'I told you. My project about World War I.' I recall raising my voice just a little too much when I said that.

I sit in a toasty block of autumn afternoon sun reading, letting myself dissolve deeply into the blue and bloody landscape of Gallipoli. The sun takes its final bow, so I move closer to the front wall of the house and shelter beside our ancient, tattered swing seat. Death trap, that thing. You can't sit on it. Now I'm reading by the combined lights of a street lamp and the Watsons' house. But this book really has me engrossed, and suddenly it's five to seven. Awesome! Dad will be home any minute.

Sheesh, it's cold. I scan through the last few pages of the book and put it aside so I can hug my legs. Suddenly I'm hungry. Mugs of hot chocolate and cookies the size of saucers start swimming in my mind.

A car is coming. For a second I think it's Dad: it slows over the speed bump like he does, to save the suspension. But then it roars off up the avenue. Not Dad. It's all right. Any minute now.

An eternity later, I recheck my watch. It's six minutes past seven. My teeth are starting to yammer with the cold. Why is it so cold? Any minute now.

'Hurry up!' I say it aloud.

The stars are out. How did that happen so fast? Still, I love stargazing. I test myself on some of my favourite constellations, and before long, my mind wanders back to yesterday. Yesterday I did more than raise my voice at Dad. I really yelled at him. Didn't mean to, but I couldn't help it. I'd been cutting out pictures of soldiers from his *Time* magazines for my project poster. It was tricky, and I had to be careful not to snip off ears or noses. After an hour and a half of painstaking effort, a neat stack of soldiers sat on my History folder on the floor.

'Dad! Get off that!' He had accidentally stepped right on my work.

'What? Oh.' Dad looked down at the crumple of soldiers and bent folder under his feet. 'What's all this mess?'

'Mess? It's for my project,' I said, exasperated.

'What project?'

I couldn't believe it. He'd forgotten. 'I told you!' I spat angrily. 'At least twice! My World War I project!' I knew that was way too loud.

'Hey, Simon, there's no need to lose your temper, mate. You know, you should watch that.'

One cramped leg drops from the doorstep and jolts me awake. My neck is crinked up against a post. I must have drifted off to sleep.

*Continued*

- This is the **title** of the story. It increases in significance each time Simon talks with his dad and is implied as the next line that would follow the story's punchline.
- **Alliteration** and **contrasting colours** combine here to create strong connotations about a landscape of war. 'Blue' refers to both the ocean as well as bruises and injuries.
- This marks the beginning of a **sequence of events** that build in intensity while Simon waits for his dad.
- **Hyperbole** conveys Simon's concern.
- **Onomatopoeia** emphasises the cold.
- **Questions** become more frequent as Simon's worry increases.
- **Repetition** of 'yesterday' leads in to a flashback.
- A **reason** for Simon's frustration is given: his project is misunderstood and his work is not appreciated.
- We are told **indirectly** that Simon has yelled very loudly.
- This **action** brings us back to the present.

Now the night is at its inkiest and it is beyond freezing. I check my watch. Six past nine?! He isn't coming home. I shouldn't have shouted. I've upset him. It's after nine o'clock and he's died in a car crash. Or just gone away. Forever. And it's my fault. I'm being punished.

I rest my chin on my knees in an effort to keep my jaw still. My teeth are chattering like a chainsaw and I can't feel my fingers and toes.

Please God, don't let Dad be dead.

A skin-crawling growl suddenly comes from the azaleas, and I stop breathing. A stubby, rope-tailed possum trundles out from between the bushes. I inhale deeply and park my frozen hands in my armpits. I feel like crying; can't help it. I'm freezing and starving and my father has been killed in a car accident.

Another car comes up the road. It slows over the speed bump. Probably not … wait. Wait. I know that engine. My legs seem to hear it first: I pelt across the verandah, down four steps like they're one, vault the azaleas, nearly collect myself on the garden hose and hurtle headlong into a friendly yellow wash of headlights in the driveway.

Thankyouthankyouthankyou … I'm swallowing sobs as Dad parks and grabs his stuff from the car.

'Heya,' he says casually. 'You good? Why are you out here in the dark?'

I'm too relieved to speak. Dad's home. He's alive and he's home. A couple of shaky breaths and I manage, 'Forgot my key.'

'You been out here this whole time?' Dad laughs. 'Why didn't you just go next door? They would've given you something to eat.'

'Ugh. The Watsons?'

Dad laughs again and puts his hands on my shoulders, smiling and shaking his head affectionately.

'You said seven. Where were you?' I ask, but I consciously don't raise my voice.

'My lecture ran late, then I had a meeting,' Dad explains. 'I'm so sorry, mate. You must be cold.'

I follow him up the front steps. It doesn't matter how cold and hungry I am; Dad's alive. We're both okay. I scoop up my library book from the verandah.

'At least I read this book for my project before it got dark,' I tell him.

'Good job,' Dad says, unlocking the door. 'What project?'

- An **interrobang** shows Simon's shock and worry.
- A **single, isolated sentence** sums up Simon's unreasonable fears.
- This passage of **fast action** is told in a way that mimics Simon's speed.
- Dad's casual voice **contrasts** starkly with Simon's panic.
- **Dialogue directions** like 'manage' and 'laughs' give extra details not offered by words like say.
- **Understatement** emphasises the cold.
- The story has a punchline-style **twist**.

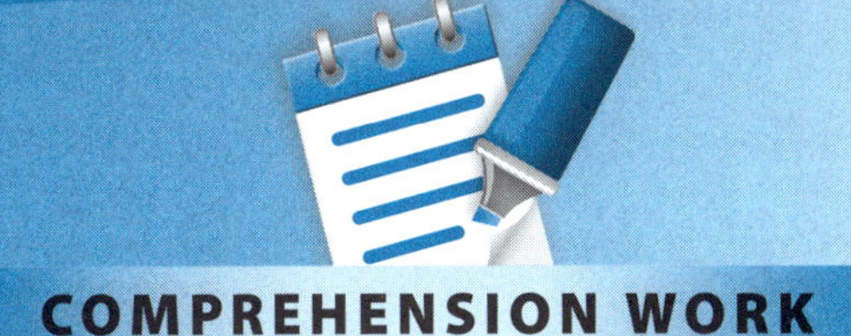

# NARRATIVE TEXT

## *Short story*

COMPREHENSION WORK

### Literal questions

*Hint: Read the text carefully to locate specific facts and details.*

**1** What, according to Simon (the story's narrator), probably contains diseases?

**2** Why does Simon not bother looking too hard for the house key?

**3** Describe two features of the night when the time is 9:06 pm.

### Interpretive questions

*Hint: These questions require you to combine facts and details to synthesise the meaning.*

**4** Which of the following explains why Simon stops breathing?

**a** 'I inhale deeply' **b** 'I feel like crying' **c** 'a skin-crawling growl'

**5** Which two things help Simon to identify his father's car?

**a** the speed bump and the engine's sound **b** the speed bump and the headlights

**c** the headlights and the suspension

**6** What kind of language technique is used in the phrase 'really intelligent insults'?

**7** Why do you think the writer has used the present tense to tell this story?

**8** Why do we assume that 'Thankyouthankyouthankyou' is directed towards God?

**9** Which of the following suggests the story's narrator is a teenager?

**a** He refers to school and his History project. **b** He refers to his parents as Mum and Dad.

**c** He gets cold and hungry after dark.

**10** Re-read line 33, ''Why are you reading books about war anyway?' Dad had asked a few days ago. He's a pacifist.' From the context, what is a pacifist?

**a** a person who enjoys war **b** a person who is opposed to books **c** a person who is opposed to war

### Applied questions

*Hint: These questions require you to understand a text's implications to infer meaning from the text.*

**11** How do capital letters show a relationship between these two sentences from the story?

'You know, to stop anyone GETTING INSIDE. I shake my head at the irony.'

**12** When Simon says, 'I consciously don't raise my voice', what can we assume?

**a** that he doesn't want to be heard by the neighbours **b** that he is learning to control his temper

**c** that he unconsciously raises his voice

# NARRATIVE TEXT
## Short story

SPELLING WORK

### List Words

All of the words in the box below appear in the text 'I told you'.

| | | | | |
|---|---|---|---|---|
| recesses | visualise | pacifist | verandah | defensively |
| engrossed | dissolve | constellations | painstaking | exasperated |
| stargazing | inkiest | azaleas | casually | headlong |

**1** Each sentence below contains one spelling error. Find each error and write the word out correctly. *Hint: All the errors have been made in the list words, so be careful when more than one list word is used in a sentence.*

**a** Simon enjoys stargrazing, which involves looking for constellations. ________________

**b** When the night is at its inkest, it is also at its coldest. ________________

**c** Dad speaks causally, setting me at ease. ________________

**d** The azaeleas make a pretty hedge. ________________

**e** Simon acts defensivelly when he gets exasperated. ________________

**f** Dad is an academic and a pacifest. ________________

**2** The following words contain tricky double letters. Using each list word below as a guide, circle the correct spelling of a different word that uses the same double letter.

| | | | |
|---|---|---|---|
| **a** constellations | allegations | aleggations | alleggations |
| **b** casually | natturally | naturaly | naturally |
| **c** recesses | necessary | necessarry | neccessary |
| **d** engrossed | embossed | emmbossed | embosed |
| **e** dissolve | disentt | dissent | dissentt |

**3** Unscramble the letters to form words from the list.

**a** lisivaule ________________ **b** pantsginaik ________________

**c** hanglode ________________ **d** dahranev ________________

When words feature the same main letter combination and are different forms of the same root word, we can group them into a **word family**. Word families are mainly used to distinguish between different parts of speech (for example, adjective and noun) and to devise superlatives.

**4** Complete the table below to show word families, using the list words in the first column.

| List word | Adjective | Noun |
|---|---|---|
| inkiest | | |
| dissolve | | |
| defensively | | |
| casually | | |

**5** Use slashes ( / ) to separate the following letter string into list words. *Hint: There are more than six words.*

stargazingpainstakingheadlongdissolveazaleasverandahconstellationsdefensively

# NARRATIVE TEXT

## Short story

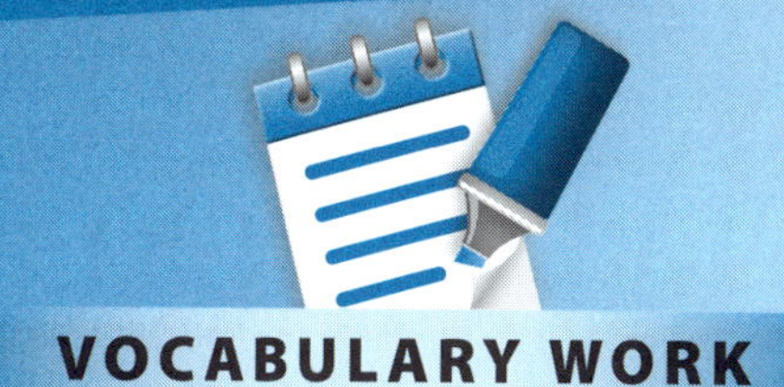

**VOCABULARY WORK**

### Synonyms

The English language can sometimes bamboozle us because it contains so many **synonyms** (words that share similar meanings). This is one reason why it is so important to develop a strong vocabulary and to be confident that we know what the words in our vocabulary really mean.

**1** Identify whether the definition of each list word below is correct by circling *true* or *false*.

| Word | Meaning | | |
|---|---|---|---|
| **a** engrossed | deeply interested | True | False |
| **b** painstaking | causing injury | True | False |
| **c** constellations | galaxies | True | False |
| **d** headlong | having a pointed head | True | False |

**2** Give a synonym for each word below based on the word's use in the context of the text.

| Word | Synonym | Word | Synonym |
|---|---|---|---|
| **a** recesses | ______________ | **b** safety-conscious | ______________ |
| **c** exasperated | ______________ | **d** landscape | ______________ |
| **e** verandah | ______________ | **f** ancient | ______________ |
| **g** inkiest | ______________ | **h** headlong | ______________ |
| **i** visualise | ______________ | **j** affectionately | ______________ |

Words can have qualities in common for various reasons. In the next exercise, each question features words that are related for different reasons. Can you figure out what they are?

**3** Each set of words below features only two related words. Circle the mismatching word in each trio.
*Hint: Look back at the words in their story context if you need help with their meanings.*

| | | | | | |
|---|---|---|---|---|---|
| **a** defensively | exasperated | painstaking | **b** tattered | broken | bump |
| **c** visualise | stargazing | constellation | **d** locked | safety | open |
| **e** azaleas | verandah | engrossed | **f** sobs | breaths | cold |

**4** For each word below, write a list word that is a synonym then give another synonym of your own.

| Word | Synonym from the list | Another synonym |
|---|---|---|
| **a** laborious | ______________ | ______________ |
| **b** enthralled | ______________ | ______________ |
| **c** melt | ______________ | ______________ |
| **d** offhandedly | ______________ | ______________ |

While the expressions of English speakers can vary widely from place to place, some expressions are used in more than one context wherever English is spoken. We call these **common** English language **idioms**.

**5** The phrases below are common English language idioms taken from the text 'I told you'. Test your vocabulary: match each phrase with its single-word meaning on the right by drawing connecting lines.

| | |
|---|---|
| **a** 'a few hours to kill' | bide |
| **b** 'can't help it' | imminently |
| **c** 'any minute' | uncontrollable |

# NARRATIVE TEXT

## Short story

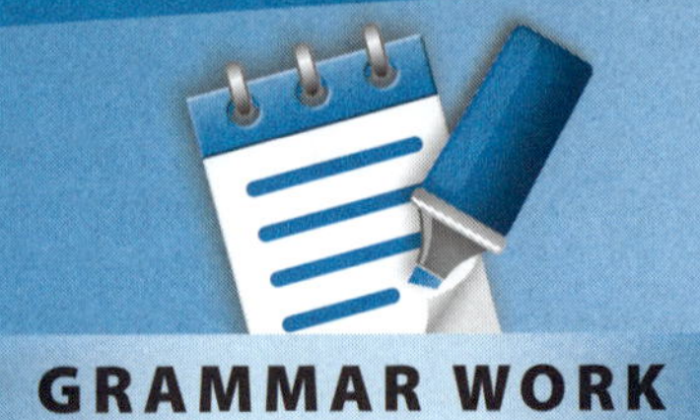

GRAMMAR WORK

### Adjectives

**Adjectives describe** nouns and pronouns. Here are some important things to know about them.

- They can be placed before or after what they describe.
- They can be used in strings of words, usually separated by commas (for example, *I just couldn't get comfortable in this cold, cramped, concrete-hard bed*), but not always (for example, *we're now living in a swanky new terrace house*).
- Adjectival phrases are groups of words that offer a more full description than a single adjective but don't use a string of adjectives. Often, they will be as effective as an adjective string because they involve an adverb (for example, *this jacket is surprisingly expensive*).

**1** Carefully re-read the following extract from the text 'I told you' and circle all of the single adjectives. *Hint: Remember that adjectives can come in strings, with or without separating commas.*

'I sit in a toasty block of autumn afternoon sun reading, letting myself dissolve deeply into the blue and bloody landscape of Gallipoli. The sun takes its final bow, so I move closer to the front wall of the house and shelter beside our ancient, tattered swing seat. Death trap, that thing. You can't sit on it. Now I'm reading by the combined lights of a street lamp and the Watsons' house. But this book really has me engrossed, and suddenly it's five to seven. Awesome! Dad will be home any minute.'

The **present tense** expresses actions in a way that suggests they are currently or continually happening. It is the main storytelling mode used in both of the sample short stories in this chapter.

**2** Re-read the following extracts from the text 'I told you' below, then change each one to be in either the past tense or the future tense as instructed. *Hint: Don't add or subtract any words unless the change of tense requires it.*

**a** 'An eternity later, I re-check my watch. It's six minutes past seven.' Change to the **past** tense:

________________________________________

**b** 'I feel like crying; can't help it.' Change to the **past** tense: ____________________

________________________________________

**c** 'I test myself on some of my favourite constellations, and before long, my mind wanders …' Change to the **future** tense: ____________________

________________________________________

**d** 'Dad laughs again and puts his hands on my shoulders.' Change to the **future** tense:

________________________________________

________________________________________

**Onomatopoeia** is the use of words that echo, suggest or directly imitate the sound they are describing. These words add a great deal of interest to a story and help create vivid imagery.

**3** Circle the examples of onomatopoeia in the words below. They are all used in the text.

| | | | | | | |
|---|---|---|---|---|---|---|
| yammering | chainsaw | DOOF | ugly | stargazing | crying | splats |
| hee hee hee | spitballs | fridge | ugh | laughing | roars | lousy |

# NARRATIVE TEXT

## Short story

**PUNCTUATION WORK**

### Truncated sentences

A **truncated sentence** is one that is very short and seems to have been shortened by being abruptly chopped off. Here are some important things to note about using this syntax technique.

- It is a common technique and is used in virtually every kind of written text.
- It has various functions in both written and spoken language.
- One of its main purposes is to echo everyday (colloquial) speech.
- It can also echo natural thought patterns.
- Truncation can be used in conjunction with repetition. An example from the text 'I told you' is 'Dad's home. He's alive and he's home'.
- Sometimes a truncated sentence will contain a partial or incomplete idea or thought. An example from the text is 'I couldn't believe it'. Couldn't believe what? We need to keep reading to find out.
- The other main purpose of truncation is to build momentum. Rhythm, tension, excitement and a sense that time is moving quickly are all effects of sets of truncated sentences.

**1** Circle the answer that best describes the effect of each truncation example provided.
*Hint: These examples have been taken from the text 'I told you'. Make sure you look back at each example in its context before you answer.*

| Example | Effect | |
|---|---|---|
| **a** 'Just in case.' | rhythm | incomplete idea |
| **b** 'Not Dad. It's all right.' | echoes natural thought patterns | excitement |
| **c** 'I knew that was way too loud.' | echoes natural thought patterns | builds momentum |
| **d** 'Or just gone away. Forever. And it's my fault.' | tension | excitement |

**2** Re-read the following truncated sentences in the text and note at least one effect of each.
*Hint: Be specific and try not to give the same effect for different sentences.*

**a** 'Death trap, that thing.' ______________________________

______________________________

**b** 'Any minute now.' ______________________________

______________________________

**c** 'I really yelled at him.' ______________________________

______________________________

**d** 'Wait.' ______________________________

______________________________

**3** The following passage contains no punctuation marks. Punctuate it correctly so that it makes sense when you read back over it. *Hint: The passage is based on the sample short story but not taken directly from it. You may still find it helpful to look back at the short story to check the punctuation of particular words or phrases.*

jordan and jett the evil twins next door think its so hilarious to call me names and use me for target practice every afternoon as i walk home from school you could say that passing the watsons house isnt the best part of my day its really getting beyond a joke but dad always says just laugh right back at them

# NARRATIVE TEXT
## *Short story*

### Short stories

A good **short story** should almost seem to be ending right at the start. What this means is that the story should begin *in medias res* (in the middle of things). There is no time in a short story (unlike in a novel) for a long, detailed orientation, where landscapes, characters and situations are described in detail. It needs to get moving immediately, and be densely written using key pieces of action and description.

### Main features of a short story

A short story typically contains:

- a plot
- one main setting
- one main character
- one main complication.

The plot ideally consists of:

- an orientation that very briefly introduces us to the world of the story
- a complication (problem or quest) that drives the story forward
- a series of key events that build upon the complication (these may unfold chronologically or using flashbacks)
- a climax that resolves the complication
- a resolution (which may contain or be followed by a twist or surprise) that occurs either simultaneously with the climax or immediately after it.

### Style and language features of a short story

To write an effective short story, we must:

- begin the story in the midst of the action
- focus on one main character
- create vivid descriptions of locations and action
- use meaningful dialogue
- maintain a clear narrative voice and viewpoint
- be consistent with our use of tense and punctuation
- employ figurative language (e.g. metaphor) to create imagery
- build on one main complication and resolve it at the climax
- end the story quickly by using a twist or punchline if it makes sense and is effective.

**1** Look back at the text 'I told you' and describe the following three parts of the plot.
*Hints: The orientation orients us to the world of the story by telling us who, what and where. The resolution resolves the complication. The twist surprises us by twisting what we expect to read at the end.*

Orientation: ______________________________

______________________________

Resolution: ______________________________

______________________________

Twist: ______________________________

**2** Apart from length, what are some ways in which a short story is different to a novel?

______________________________

**3** How would the text 'I told you' be different if the narrator was six years old?

______________________________

# NARRATIVE TEXT

## Short story

**WRITING WORK 2**

### Narrative and language features in short stories

Short story writers employ many types of features in their writing. Some are **narrative** and common to all short stories (for example, plot, characters and setting). Others are used to create interest for the reader. These **language features** are often called **aesthetic** features (concerned with the creation or appreciation of beauty) or **stylistic** features (concerned with the creation of a particular writing style).

**4** The text 'I told you' contains some narrative and language features that are commonly used by writers of short stories. Match each feature below with an example from the text. Write the number of the feature beside the quote that it matches.
*Hint: Use the annotations provided on the text 'I told you' as a guide as you answer this question.*

| Feature | | Example from the text |
|---|---|---|
| **a** simile | ______ | The sun takes its final bow |
| **b** onomatopoeia | ______ | Wait. I know that engine. |
| **c** antagonistic minor character(s) | ______ | Not Dad. It's all right. |
| **d** personification | ______ | My teeth are chattering like a chainsaw |
| **e** truncated sentences | ______ | What project? |
| **f** interior monologue | ______ | I stop breathing. |
| **g** tension | ______ | DOOF. |
| **h** repetition | ______ | the evil Watson twins |

**5** Four common language features are shown in the table below. In the text 'I told you', find two examples of each feature. Note the effect of each example in the third column.

| Language feature | Examples from the text | Effect in the text |
|---|---|---|
| **colloquial language**<br>everyday, informal expressions | **a** | |
| | **b** | |
| **adjectives**<br>words that modify or describe nouns | **c** | |
| | **d** | |
| **adverbs**<br>words that modify or describe verbs | **e** | |
| | **f** | |
| **questions** | **g** | |
| | **h** | |

# NARRATIVE TEXT

## *Short story*

WRITING SAMPLE

Here is a sample text showing you how to structure and write a short story.

### Lost in Athens

✹ **Give the story an interesting and appropriate title.** The title points to the result of the main complication.

The plane finally lands after many cramped, draining hours in the air.

'Ladies and gentlemen, welcome to the beautiful city of Athens!'

I disembark, relishing each flex of my legs, and start looking for my friends: Aria, Josh, Poh and Mitch. We find each other, then a shuttle bus, then, eventually, our youth hostel. We lug our bags up to the room, exhausted and jet-lagged.

✹ **Write a brief orientation that presents some basic details about the who and where of the story.** This story starts in the midst of the action and gives the narrator a clear voice. We read in this section that Alyssa (the narrator) has just arrived in Athens with her four friends.

Despite being completely new to the place, I decide to take a little walk in an effort to feel human again. I venture out alone and am immediately refreshed by the cool afternoon air.

✹ **Write the complication.** This problem or situation drives the whole story and will be solved in the climax and resolution.

'Yia sou,' an elderly Greek lady greets me with a smile. I punctuate my return smile with a feeble wave in an effort to cross the language barrier. This is nice. I do a slow 360 and make a conscious effort to take in the charming surrounds. I stroll past little delis waggling with chubby salamis, wagons with fruit and flowers spilling out like still-life fireworks and an austere sandstone library. After another block or so, I encounter a large green lake, and settle myself on a bench to admire the vista and get my bearings. I suddenly realise I haven't brought my handbag. Doofus. I won't bother returning for it now.

My thoughts drift to home, and with a wince I remember the fight I had with Dad. Him yelling at me saying I should stay home and finish my education, like he did. But I longed to explore the world, to experience different cultures, new religions, exotic foods, stunning architecture … everything!

'If you go gallivanting,' he'd started in familiar fashion—replacing a respectable word like 'travelling' with a frivolous one that made me look foolish—'you will not get anywhere in life, you will not have a full education to get a good job … and I will be very disappointed in you.' Inspiring parting words on the eve of my six-month Europe stint.

I rise and start walking in the same direction, still thinking ruefully about home. After a while, I wonder if maybe it was a bad idea coming overseas but I soon push it aside, taking in the marvellous sights, made even more glorious by the beckoning fingers of sunset.

A custard-yellow crescent of moon starts creeping into view and before I know it darkness is sweeping the streets. Time to head back. I turn up an alley, then another, then another. The shuttered shops are all starting to look the same, and they've decidedly lost their earlier charm. I can no longer see the lake at all, and even the main streets are looking narrow and strange. I turn down the millionth alley and find myself stumbling over a pile of rubbish. I hear a shuffle.

'H-hello?' No answer. That's all right: I think I'd prefer that. Walk faster.

This isn't good. I can't ask for directions: I don't speak the language. I can't call my friends: my phone is in my bag. Which is not here.

Again, my pace quickens. I glance left, then right: do I recognise these shop names? Not yet.

✹ **Write a sequence of key events in the story, including plenty of vivid description of places, action and feelings.** This large block of story contains the sequence of events. One of these events, Alyssa's conversation with her father before leaving for Athens, is told in flashback. The composer has used internal monologue (the main character speaking to himself or herself) instead of dialogue ('Doofus'). A list of the things Alyssa longs for gives the reader an insight into her character and why she is overseas: the use of ellipsis (…) suggests that this is only a partial list and that Alyssa is thrilled by the idea of travel. Because no minor characters are present in this scene, the composer has crafted some flashback dialogue between Alyssa and her father instead, offering an element of conflict in the story. The composer has included specific details about the setting that help draw the reader into the world of the story. There is also a building of intensity, emotion and suspense as the events unfold, leading up to the turning point, or climax. Figurative language techniques add colour to the descriptions—an example is the composer's use of personification in 'darkness is sweeping the streets'. The sound device of alliteration has been used in 'the shuttered shops.' The composer has kept the narrator's voice consistent, and introduced small conflicts (both situational and internal) to keep the story interesting. Truncated sentences and colons combine to speed up the action and heighten the tension.

The anxiety starts to kick in, then the adrenaline. Now I'm running. My thoughts are in a flurry … What if I can't find the hostel? I don't have a phone, money, passport … I don't have anything. How will I get home? What will my dad think? WHERE AM I? Wait, wasn't I just here? I don't know. My panicked heart thuds to the beat of my feet.

'A-ly-ssa!' A far-off voice wisps its way to me. I stop dead and listen, praying that I didn't imagine those three precious syllables.

'Alyssa! Alyssa!' I start galloping in the direction of that sound; the sound of my name. There's the lake! I'm almost able to make out some other familiar shapes when I run headlong into a sweaty Aria and three other scared-looking Aussies. Relief floods through me.

✹ **Write the climax and the resolution.** In this story they have been blended; the composer demonstrates that the climax and the resolution need to address and eliminate the complication. Capital letters ('WHERE AM I?') help us identify this section as the climax—this is the point at which the climax collides with the resolution ('… when I run headlong into a sweaty Aria'). Technically, the main resolution consists of only four words: 'Relief floods through me.'

# NARRATIVE TEXT

*Short story*

## WRITING YOUR OWN SAMPLE

Plan your sample on the lines provided.

- **Give the story an interesting and appropriate title.** It is easier to do this after you have finished writing the story.

- **Write a brief orientation that presents some basic details about the who and where of the story.** Start in the midst of the action and give your narrator a clear voice.

- **Write the complication.** This is a problem or situation that will drive the whole story and be addressed and solved in the climax and the resolution. It does not have to be a major crisis.

- **Write a sequence of key events in the story, including plenty of vivid description of places, action and feelings.** One or more of these events can optionally be told in flashback. The events should involve tension and build in intensity as the story unfolds, leading up to the turning point, or climax. Employ some figurative language techniques and sound devices to contribute to the setting and the mood, such as alliteration. Make sure that the narrator's voice remains consistent throughout this main body of the story, and introduce small conflicts (both situational and internal) to keep the story interesting. Use dialogue carefully and with purpose. If no minor characters are present, write some flashback dialogue or use internal monologue (the main character speaking to himself or herself) instead; internal monologue does not require speech marks.

- **Write the climax and the resolution.** The resolution can be blended with the climax or happen immediately after it. Remember that the climax and the resolution need to address and eliminate the complication.

- Optionally, **write a punchline, surprise or twist at the end if it makes sense and enhances the story.** The text 'I told you' contains a punchline. The student story, 'Lost in Athens', does not contain any kind of twist.

# TIPS FOR THE SAMPLE TESTS

STUDY TIPS

## Know what to expect

- Find out from your teacher what knowledge and skills will be assessed in the sample test.
- Find out what format is being used for the sample test.

## Revise and rehearse

- Revise the relevant knowledge and skills.
- Write some practice analysis paragraphs about sample texts.

## Read carefully

- Read all instructions on the test paper.
- Note the mark allocations. These indicate how much you should write and how much time you should spend on each answer.
- Read the questions before the texts so that when reading the texts you know what to look for.

## Make your answers count

- Use handwriting that is clear (not too large, too small or too cursive).
- Use all of the answer spaces provided.
- Be specific in your answers and don't use padding or repetition to make them look longer.

## Re-read and check

- Once you have completed a response, re-read it to make sure it actually answers the question. This will only take a few seconds.
- Edit quickly and clearly. If you need to, make corrections using single cross-out lines (not scribbles).

## Manage your time

- Write legibly but quickly.
- Ensure you are working through the test efficiently and not spending too much time on each question, or you may not finish the test.
- If you finish early, don't waste the leftover time. Spend that time checking, editing and possibly extending your answers.

## Be ready

- Always study English actively. This means using a pen and paper to make notes. It also involves recording grammar rules, language features and definitions of difficult terms.
- If you have prepared thoroughly for the test, you do not need to be nervous. Tests are not designed to trap you, but to give you an opportunity to show how much you know.

**Part A** Reading and comprehension

Read the following texts and answer the questions that follow on page 127.

### Text 1: Informative text—Product review

### Tech Review: Intel NUC 6i7KYK

Intel's super-compact NUC is what your IT friend means by *bare bone kit*. It's a semi-finished PC. But don't get bored yet. This pocket rocket computer is ready to perform, right out of the box. It has all the ports required for a keyboard, mouse and even up to three HD TVs. It offers instant connectivity and the double bonus of inbuilt wireless and Bluetooth.

The NUC range of PC kits may have had its debut a while back, but it's only now that they are being packaged with serious graphics processing power, largely to address rampant growth across online gaming, e-sports, digital content creation and video editing.

As a fully functioning, power-packed computer, the new NUC 6i7KYK has two exclusive attributes: maximum mobility and minimum visibility. It's tiny (a ludicrous 116 x 211 mm), yet by no means does this undermine its power. The NUC can breeze through most desktop applications, but it also has enough grunt to tackle some of the most popular titles in e-sports. In its earlier incarnation, the graphics processor wasn't up to a host of challenges, but this latest version boasts Iris Pro Graphics 580, which is not only exciting gamers and graphic content creators, but has massively ramped up NUC's allure in general.

Intel partners with resellers like MWave, Umart and JW Computers to complete the NUC with RAM, SSD and a Microsoft Windows OS. The true tech-head still enjoys the thrill of building a PC from the motherboard up, but really, you'd need to be pretty keen. The NUC offers similar build-appeal without you having to start from anywhere near scratch.

While its versatility gives widespread appeal, NUC's miniscule size allows resellers to pitch it directly to a range of otherwise unreachable customers for a plethora of new applications. Digital signage at POS (point of sale), office and home entertainment are all settings where the NUC really comes into its own. Its unobtrusive, space-saving body makes it ideal for rear-mounting on displays like menus, or for use in home theatre systems.

Due in large part to the superior graphics processing of this model, two other key product markets have emerged: entry-level mainstream gaming (with a focus on PC portable gamers) and digital content creators (meaning everyone from microbloggers to newsjackers).

A surprisingly powerful GPU and CPU make this machine the little engine that could. Check out Intel's family of resellers to buy the NUC either instore or online.

## Part A Reading and comprehension

### Text 2: Narrative text—Short story

**Lost in Athens**

The plane finally lands after many cramped, draining hours in the air.

'Ladies and gentlemen, welcome to the beautiful city of Athens!'

I disembark, relishing each flex of my legs, and start looking for my friends: Aria, Josh, Poh and Mitch. We find each other, then a shuttle bus, then, eventually, our youth hostel. We lug our bags up to the room, exhausted and jet-lagged.

Despite being completely new to the place, I decide to take a little walk in an effort to feel human again. I venture out alone and am immediately refreshed by the cool afternoon air.

'Yia sou,' an elderly Greek lady greets me with a smile. I punctuate my return smile with a feeble wave in an effort to cross the language barrier. This is nice. I do a slow 360 and make a conscious effort to take in the charming surrounds. I stroll past little delis waggling with chubby salamis, wagons with fruit and flowers spilling out like still-life fireworks and an austere sandstone library. After another block or so, I encounter a large green lake, and settle myself on a bench to admire the vista and get my bearings. I suddenly realise I haven't brought my handbag. Doofus. I won't bother returning for it now.

My thoughts drift to home, and with a wince I remember the fight I had with Dad. Him yelling at me saying I should stay home and finish my education, like he did. But I longed to explore the world, to experience different cultures, new religions, exotic foods, stunning architecture … everything!

'If you go gallivanting,' he'd started in familiar fashion—replacing a respectable word like 'travelling' with a frivolous one that made me look foolish—'you will not get anywhere in life, you will not have a full education to get a good job … and I will be very disappointed in you.' Inspiring parting words on the eve of my six-month Europe stint.

I rise and start walking in the same direction, still thinking ruefully about home. After a while, I wonder if maybe it was a bad idea coming overseas but I soon push it aside, taking in the marvellous sights, made even more glorious by the beckoning fingers of sunset.

A custard-yellow crescent of moon starts creeping into view and before I know it darkness is sweeping the streets. Time to head back. I turn up an alley, then another, then another. The shuttered shops are all starting to look the same, and they've decidedly lost their earlier charm. I can no longer see the lake at all, and even the main streets are looking narrow and strange. I turn down the millionth alley and find myself stumbling over a pile of rubbish. I hear a shuffle.

'H-hello?' No answer. That's all right: I think I'd prefer that. Walk faster.

This isn't good. I can't ask for directions: I don't speak the language. I can't call my friends: my phone is in my bag. Which is not here.

Again, my pace quickens. I glance left, then right: do I recognise these shop names? Not yet.

The anxiety starts to kick in, then the adrenaline. Now I'm running. My thoughts are in a flurry … What if I can't find the hostel? I don't have a phone, money, passport … I don't have anything. How will I get home? What will my dad think? WHERE AM I? Wait, wasn't I just here? I don't know. My panicked heart thuds to the beat of my feet.

'A-ly-ssa!' A far-off voice wisps its way to me. I stop dead and listen, praying that I didn't imagine those three precious syllables.

'Alyssa! Alyssa!' I start galloping in the direction of that sound; the sound of my name. There's the lake! I'm almost able to make out some other familiar shapes when I run headlong into a sweaty Aria and three other scared-looking Aussies. Relief floods through me.

## Part A Reading and comprehension

### Text 3: Persuasive text—Radio advertisement

**Campaign: Move Me Homes**

Project: 30 sec RC

Version: Draft 1

| SCENE | TIME | AUDIO |
|---|---|---|
| 000 | 1.5 secs<br>00:01.5 | *SFX: An auctioneer's voice taking bids and saying phrases associated with buying a home. Sound dissolves into Scene 001 and fades out by the end of the scene.* |
| 001 | 2 secs<br>00:03.5 | VO: When you're buying a new home, you're not just looking for a building … |
| 002 | 0.5 secs<br>00:04 | *SFX: Flourish of a harp to suggest a dream* |
| 003 | 1 sec<br>00:05 | VO: You're *building* a dream. |
| 004 | 6 secs<br>00:12 | VO: Don't trust your dream to just anyone. At Move Me Homes, we have the industry contacts and new home know-how to bring your dream to life. |
| 005 | 0.5 secs<br>00:12.5 | *SFX: Doorbell* |
| 006 | 3.5 secs<br>00:16 | VO: From securing the right finance to laying the welcome mat, Move Me Homes will guide you every step of the way. |
| 007 | 3 secs<br>00:19 | VO: We even offer testimonials from families in neighbourhoods of your choice. |
| 008 | 5 secs<br>00:24 | VO: Janine and the trusted team at Move Me Homes are waiting to take you on your new home journey. |
| 009 | 4.5 secs<br>00:29.5 | VO: Call 1300-MOVE-ME. That's 1300 66 83 63. Call now! Be moved … with Move Me Homes. |

# SAMPLE TESTS

## PAPER 1

### Part A Reading and comprehension

Answer the following questions:

#### Text 1

1 According to the writer of the review, what gives the NUC 'widespread appeal'? (1 mark)

2 What might a 'true tech-head' do with a motherboard? (1 mark)

3 Who are three companies in 'Intel's family of resellers'? (1 mark)

#### Text 2

4 What does the word 'lug' mean in the context of the story? (1 mark)

5 What is the effect or meaning of the capital letters in the question 'WHERE AM I?'? (1 mark)

6 The story's resolution is told in a single line. What is it? (1 mark)

#### Text 3

7 Two images refer to entering a house. One is based on sound and one on visuals. What are the images? (1 mark)

8 What alliterative phrase aims to persuade listeners to trust the Move Me Homes staff? (1 mark)

9 *You're*, *don't* and *that's* are all examples of what colloquial language feature beginning with *c*? (1 mark)

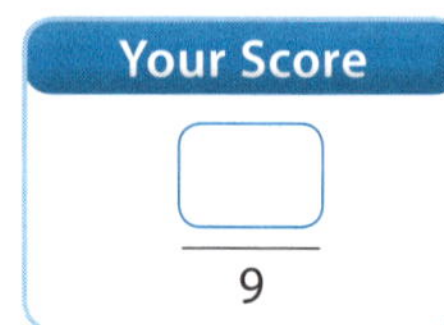

## Part B Language conventions

Answer the following questions:

### Text 1

1 This review is aimed at readers with a basic to intermediate knowledge of computers. Give two pieces of evidence that show this. (2 marks)

### Text 2

2 In Scene 003, why is the word *building* italicised? In your answer, refer to Scene 001. (2 marks)

### Text 3

3 Twice in the story, an ellipsis is used in a list of items given by Alyssa. What is the effect of each ellipsis? (2 marks)

Your Score

/6

## Part C Comparing texts

Answer the following questions:

Use the number of lines and the allocated marks as a guide to the length of your answer.

1 What do Texts 1 and 3 have in common? Answer with reference to purpose and audience. (2 marks)

2 Re-read and compare the endings of Text 2 and Text 3. How are they the same? How do they differ? (2 marks)

3 Each text has a unique structure. (4 marks)

a Briefly describe how each text is ordered.

Text 1: ______________________________

Text 2: ______________________________

Text 3: ______________________________

b Which structure do you find the most effective, based on purpose and audience? Why?

______________________________

Your Score

/ 8

## Part D Themes and meaning

Write a paragraph response to the question in the space provided. Use the number of lines and the allocated marks as a guide to the length of your answer.

1 Choose one of the three texts (1, 2 or 3) and write a paragraph about the messages explored by its composer. These messages do not need to be stated directly in the text—they can be implied as you read. (7 marks)

______________________________

______________________________

______________________________

______________________________

______________________________

______________________________

______________________________

Your Score

/ 7

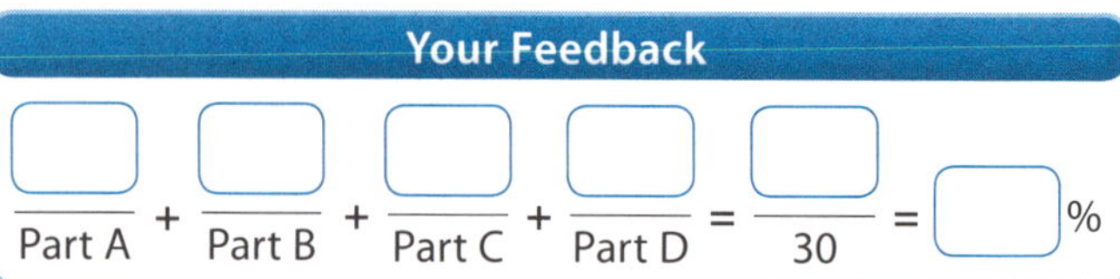

## Part A Reading and comprehension

Read the following texts and answer the questions that follow on page 133.

### Text 1: Informative text—Information report

### Deadly Australians

An island 'girt by sea', the mainland of Australia is geographically isolated and densely occupied by fauna. Some of the planet's most dangerous wildlife lives here, from tiny bugs to reptilian giants.

**Savage serpents**
There are around 172 snake species in Australia. Of these, 100 are venomous and 12 can inflict a fatal bite to humans. Typically, snakes only strike when hunting, or in self-defence.

- **Eastern brown snake:** This killer can survive—even thrive—in heavily populated areas. Although it feeds primarily on rodents and pests, it will strike any human seen as an intruder.
- **Common death adder:** Of Australia's many death adder species, this is the only one found in Sydney (the nation's most populous city). Unlike most snakes, this one waits for its prey to approach.
- **Coastal taipan:** Suspicious of nearby movement, this lethal snake can deliver a shot of deadly venom deep into human flesh.

**Wet 'n' wily**
Australia's coastal waters and river systems are quite literally overflowing with a proliferation of beautiful but deadly marine life.

- **Box jellyfish:** Also known as the sea wasp, the transparent tentacles of this venomous jellyfish can extend to 3 metres. Contact with these tentacles can lead to rapid cardiac arrest.
- **Saltwater crocodile (estuarine crocodile):** An Australian icon, the saltwater crocodile is an extraordinarily powerful predator found in rivers, swamps, creeks and estuaries.
- **Bull shark:** Found in river systems around Australia, the often aggressive bull shark is the only species capable of staying in fresh water for an extended period of time.

**Suspect insects**
While Australian insects and arachnids terrify many people, the good news is that few such creatures have the potential to kill us. The even better news is that antivenene is available for all of them.

- **Sydney funnel-web spider:** This fearsome spider thrives in urban areas and forests, but tales of their aggression are exaggerated. Only mature males can give fatal doses of venom.
- **Redback spider:** A close relative of the American black widow, the redback spider can live practically anywhere, although they are unlikely to attack unless a hand falls upon their web.
- **Honey bee:** Honey bees pose a deadly risk to anyone allergic to them. Statistically, they have claimed more lives than any spider.

**Staying safe**
To avoid becoming a victim of a deadly Australian, travellers and locals alike are urged to take precautions, read warning signs and, mainly, stay at a safe distance. But should you be bitten or stung, seek immediate medical attention.

## Part A Reading and comprehension

### Text 2: Narrative text—Satirical script

### The PM

*CS: lectern with a campaign poster for the PM (Prime Minister) attached. Another poster, protesting against the PM, lies on the ground. UR (known only by these initials), the PM's campaign consultant and voice of reason, wears glasses and a scarf and holds a tablet. UR can be male or female.*

PM: And as such, in conclusion, ergo … cos sin theta … uh, to wrap up, the implementation of this salient nation-building legislation patently perpetuates a best and brightest zeitgeist and a fiscal feasibility that galvanises the expressive determination of a nation moving forward. *(Pause)* Um … Thank you.

*PM steps to the side, saluting his audience in huge, triumphant waves. SFX: A blend of polite applause and booing.*

UR: Well, that was marvellous, sir. Thoroughly inspiring.

PM: Thanks, UR! Yah really think?

UR: I really do! *(Aside)* Except for the words.

PM: What?

UR: What? Nothing.

PM: How would you score it from one to one zero, zero, zero, zero, zero, zero, zero, zero?

UR: Uh, that's one hundred million.

PM: Yeah that.

UR: At about … a million?

PM: Wow, that's great; that's heaps!

UR: Yes it is.

PM: *(Out of the side of his mouth)* To be honest, UR, I didn't understand a lot of the speech.

UR: *(Dismissively, with a 'whatever' wave of his hand)* Well …

PM: *(Quickly)* Any of it.

UR: No harm done. Now, please pay attention, sir. You have the charity luncheon at 12, a carbon trading convention at 2, and let's not forget your Japanese class at 7, seeing as the Opps already have the Chinese vote.

PM: *(Ignores UR and grabs the protest poster)* Hey, I like it! They even spelt my name right!

UR: Sir, that's a protest poster for APEC.

PM: Oh yeah, OPEC.

UR: Your campaign poster is here. *(Shows PM the poster on the lectern)*

PM: WHAT IS THIS? Who is this guy?

UR: It's you, sir.

PM: *(Squinting hard at the poster)* Ah, yes. Right you are. Ha! Right U.R! *(Laughs uproariously)* That's your name! UR! *(Laughs loudly again)* Wait, have I used that joke before?

UR: Yes, sir. *(Beat)* And it never gets old.

PM: *(Still chuckling)* Good times. Good times. *(Trails off)* Oh, that reminds me, UR, I want you to help me organise something.

UR: Certainly, sir. No problem.

PM: A war. I really want one! *(Pause)* And a ninja mask.

UR: Okay. Here's your mask. *(Takes off scarf and hands it to PM.)* But no war. Not today.

PM: It's not fair. Everyone gets to have a war but me. *(Throwing a tantrum)* Why can't I have a war?!

UR: Because they're not very nice things, sir. Generally speaking, people don't like wars.

PM: *(Pause, then triumphantly)* Let's have a war with Tasmania! *(Ties the scarf around his eyes like a ninja mask and tries to adopt a ninja stance).* YAAAA! *(Pause)* Wait, I can't see. *(Calling out)* UR? I can't see a thing in this. Come and fix it. UR?

UR: *(Walking away shaking head)* You only do this job for the perks.

## Part A Reading and comprehension

### Text 3: Persuasive text—Speech

**Responsible pet ownership**

I would like to thank the RSPCA for hosting today's fundraiser, and for championing the cause of responsible animal ownership. We are here today to do the same. Many of you run veterinary practices, volunteer at local animal shelters or simply have a moral objection to the way in which this nation's pets are mistreated and discarded.

It is an old, yet increasingly pertinent truism: *A dog is not just for Christmas.* Each year the RSPCA rehomes 20 000 animals who have been abandoned by their owners. The biggest spike in abandonment occurs in January, as post-Christmas reality sets in, and cries like these go up all over the country:

'Change a litter tray? You must be joking!'

'I thought he'd *like* living in a high-rise!'

'She looked much cuter in the pet shop!'

In today's throwaway culture, pets are often considered accessories. A photogenic puppy makes great internet fodder (not to mention a nice handbag stuffer), but it is a dignified being and should be treated as such. We refuse to tolerate pet abandonment as 'another harsh reality of life'. This is something that we, as a society, can rein in through regulation. How, specifically?

Pet licenses. The State Government needs to introduce a system of formal permits for pet owners. This won't make all of our pet issues magically vanish, but it is a significant step up from the only current fix: rehoming. Pet licensing would serve two main purposes.

First, it would assist in educating potential pet owners about the practical responsibilities involved in domestic animal ownership. This needs to happen at point of purchase *and* beforehand. It's very simple: if you want a pet, you need to understand exactly what that means. Second, a pet permit would hold accountable those who have abandoned animals in the past, and those charged with acts of animal cruelty. It is clear that many people are unfit to provide shelter to animals and if we can create a national registry for pet ownership, we can stop at least some of them from doing so.

The Department of the Environment already requires permits for the keeping of certain exotic animals. This system is in place to protect our native wildlife and their habitats. Angling licences are required to preserve our fish stocks. But what about protecting our supposed best friends—our domestic pets? Frankly, at this point, nothing.

We have a petition here today. A petition that will put this issue onto the desks of the policymakers. Right now, only one thing is missing that could make that happen: your name.

Thank you.

# SAMPLE TESTS

## PAPER 2

## Part A Reading and comprehension

Answer the following questions:

### Text 1

1 What is meant by the noun 'proliferation'? (1 mark)

2 Why might the box jellyfish also be called the 'sea wasp'? (1 mark)

3 Why is the saltwater crocodile also called the 'estuarine crocodile'? (1 mark)

### Text 2

4 Who is UR? Be specific. (1 mark)

5 Why does the PM laugh uproariously? (1 mark)

6 Which two acronyms are confused by the PM? (1 mark)

### Text 3

7 According to the composer, why are pets often considered accessories today? (1 mark)

8 What is meant by the term 'internet fodder'? (1 mark)

9 What prevents the following line from being a rhetorical question? Look back at the text before answering. (1 mark)

But what about protecting our supposed best friends—our domestic pets?

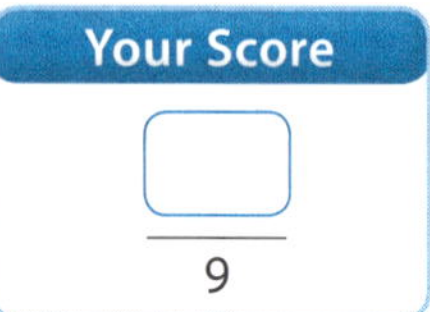

# SAMPLE TESTS

PAPER 2

## Part B Language conventions

Answer the following questions:

### Text 1

1 Two different sound techniques are used in the subheadings of the text. One is repeated; one is not. (2 marks)

a Technique 1: ______

Example of its use: ______

b Technique 2: ______

Example of its use: ______

### Text 2

2 Rhythm and pace are created in several ways in the script. Name two. Be specific in your answer. (2 marks)

______

______

### Text 3

3 Imagine that you were present when this speech was given. Based on what the speaker said (not on your own opinions), would you have signed the petition? Why or why not? (2 marks)

______

______

Your Score

/6

## Part C Comparing texts

Answer the following questions:

Use the number of lines and the allocated marks as a guide to the length of your answer.

1 We know that one purpose of Text 1 is to inform and one purpose of Text 2 is to create comedy. What is another purpose of each text? (2 marks)

Text 1: ______

Text 2: ______

2 Text 1 and Text 3 are both about animals. Based on this topic, compare the purposes of the texts. (2 marks)

a What is one reason or purpose that the texts have in common? Be specific.

______

b What is one reason or purpose that only applies to Text 3? Be specific.

______

**3** **a** Who is most likely to read Text 1? Give specific reasons. (2 marks)

**b** Texts 2 and 3 are likely to attract a similar type of audience. Describe these people. (2 marks)

Your Score

/8

## Part D Themes and meaning

Write a paragraph response to the question in the space provided. Use the number of lines and the allocated marks as a guide to the length of your answer.

**1** Choose one of the three texts (1, 2 or 3) and write a paragraph about at least two issues raised by its composer. Name the issues and give examples of where or how they are presented in the text. (7 marks)

Your Score

/7

Your Feedback

Part A + Part B + Part C + Part D = /30 = %

# ANSWERS

CHECK YOUR ANSWERS

## UNIT 1: ONLINE INFORMATION REPORT

INFORMATIVE TEXT
### Comprehension Work page 3

1 non-designated swimming areas
This is a **literal** question. It requires you to find key words from the question, such as 'fatal attacks' *(line 13)* and 'twenty years' *(line 14)* in the text. We read in the text that 'all of the fatal attacks in the past twenty years have occurred in non-designated swimming areas' *(line 14)*. Writing *The Northern Territory* as an answer is incorrect, as it already appears in the question.

2 **a** This is a **literal** question. Note the name of the website ('topendtourist.com') and read the opening statement 'In partnership with Northern Territory Wild Australia Administration (WANTA)' *(lines 3–4)*, and then find these two names in the options provided. Answer **b** is incorrect because one half of the answer, WILDWARY, is a slogan or idea. Answer **c** is incorrect because the Safety Team is a part of Northern Territory Wild Australia Administration.

3 ten
This is a **literal** question. Count the coloured, underlined hyperlinks in the report. Be careful not to count any items that could function as hyperlinks but are not phrases or names, as specified in the question. Only the underlined hyperlinks fit this description.

4 'Read the signs, use common sense and stay safe.'
This is an **interpretive** question. Locate the slogan 'WILDWARY' *(line 10)* and the 'Swimming' section of the report *(lines 12–24)*, then scan the whole section for a sentence that sums up the slogan. Only one sentence fully sums up what it means to be 'WILDWARY'.

5 **a** This is an **interpretive** question because it requires you to apply your knowledge of imperative questions to the text to find the answer. Answer **b** is incorrect because there is no evidence of a sarcastic tone anywhere in the report. Answer **c** is incorrect because there are no question marks to be found in the report. Also, the question states that you are looking for sentences.

6 **b** This is an **interpretive** question. The key to answering it is the Hint. It reminds you that this is an information report, and points you to the word 'informed' in Answer **b.** Even without using the hint, Answer **b** sums up the text's purpose. Answer **a** is incorrect because, while this is a message in the text, it is not the purpose of the text. Answer **c** is incorrect because it addresses only one part of the target audience of the text. Also, like Answer **a**, it does not describe a purpose.

7 Suggested answer: Each section of the bullet points refers to 'night' or 'after dark' and informs readers about safe behaviour at night in areas where crocodiles might be present. From this, we can infer that crocodiles are more active, and therefore more dangerous, at night.
This is an **interpretive** question. Find references to 'night' in the text and draw a conclusion about why they are repeated. The Hint points you towards this.

8 Sample answer: The target audience includes Northern Territory tourists and locals. We read references to these readers throughout the article. For example, 'Top End visitors' *(line 6)*, 'Territorian' *(line 7)*, 'locals' *(line 6)*, 'everyone visiting or living in the Top End' *(line 40)*.
This is an **interpretive** question. It requires an answer that includes evidence from the text. First, you need to decide who is being addressed by the writer.

9 **a** This is an **interpretive** question that can be answered by noting the close proximity of the phrase 'read the signs' with Answer **a**. When we read these excerpts in relation to each other, they clearly match. Answer **b** cannot be correct because it reminds us that in some places there are no signs to read. Answer **c** is incorrect because it mentions 'other signs', not why signs should be read at all.

10 **c** This is an **interpretive** question. It requires knowledge of the three language features listed as possible answers. In addition to this knowledge, you can refer back to the annotations in the text for clues. Answer **a** is incorrect because repetition of key words, phrases and ideas is used throughout the report. Answer **b** is incorrect because most of the report contains contractions and other features of colloquial language. If you noted that rhyme is not featured in the report, you would have found the answer immediately. There would be no need to check whether each language feature made the report 'clear and understandable'.

11 Suggested answers: Another crocodile safety sign used in the Northern Territory: this graphic would help readers identify these signs when they see them near waterways. A picture of a crocodile in the wild, preferably with its mouth open: this graphic would familiarise readers with what crocodiles look like and also show how dangerous they are.

# ANSWERS

This is an **applied** question. You need to understand the purpose of the report and the graphics already included, then apply this knowledge to select other appropriate graphics. Your answer must include two different graphics and an explanation of why you think they would enhance the report.

**12** **c** This is an **applied** question that asks you to consider the context in which the information report appears (a Northern Territory tourism website) and the probable reasons for its inclusion there. The report implies that having 'fun' on a Top End holiday can only happen if being 'safe' is a priority. The text 'Crocodile Safety' addresses these ideas from Answer **c.** You could also use the word 'information' in the question as a clue to finding the answer; Answer **c**, especially the word 'equip', is the only option that really fits with this key word. Further, Answer **a** is incorrect because the composer of the website wants people to visit the Top End. Answer **b** is incorrect because, while learning about crocodiles might appeal to a reader's sense of adventure, this is not the purpose of the information report.

## INFORMATIVE TEXT Spelling Work

page 4

**1** fasinating, directers, intrest, cartonish, Teríttory, vigillant, designatned, habitatts, harrass, personell, emplore, asume

**2** **a** assume **b** harass **c** retrieve **d** ensure **e** personnel **f** northern

**3** **a** berry **b** vigilant **c** fast **d** complacent **e** personnel **f** assume

**4** **a** independence **b** clearance **c** presence **d** proficient **e** defendant **f** sentence **g** pertinent **h** quadrant **i** magnificent **j** magnificence

**5** **a** commission **b** assume **c** commission **d** northern

## INFORMATIVE TEXT Vocabulary Work

page 5

**1** **a** WANTA, Wild Australia Northern Territory Administration
**b** NT, Northern Territory
**c** SWIMS, Safe Water Indicators, Markers and Signs

**2** **Set 1:** VIP—dignitary or guest, UN—an inter-nation committee, SETI—looking for alien life, ABC—a television network.

**Set 2:** ROM—a computer acronym, ASAP—denotes urgency, FBI—a law-enforcement agency, MS—a debilitating disease

**3** **a** territory **b** harass **c** vigilant **d** fascinating

## INFORMATIVE TEXT Grammar Work

page 6

**1** **a** synonyms **b** short **c** complete **d** participles

**2** **a** assume, assumption **b** fatal, fatality **c** quack, quay **d** altitude, altar **e** misery, misleading **f** burden, bureau **g** arch, architect **h** engage, engineer

**3** **a** about **b** pencil **c** occur **d** again **e** mountain **f** fisherman **g** president **h** supply **i** experienced **j** importance **k** amazement **l** syringe

**4** 'extremely' (the adjective it modifies is 'dangerous')

## INFORMATIVE TEXT Punctuation Work

page 7

**1** c

**2** a

**3** one-way street sign, aeroplane safety card, box of rat poison, can of hairspray, gas heater manual, medicine bottle

**4** Sample answer: Most email addresses and URLs do not include capitals.

**5** Corrected passage: The saltwater crocodile is an extremely dangerous creature common in Australia's Northern Territory. WANTA, or Wild Australia Northern Territory Administration, in conjunction with topendtourist.com, has published a report entitled 'Crocodile Safety' that explains to potential Top End tourists, along with locals, how to stay safe in crocodile habitats. Everyone in the Top End must ensure that their leisure activities only take place in designated swimming areas and certainly not where signs such as 'Warning: Crocodile Sighting' are posted.

## INFORMATIVE TEXT Writing Work

page 8

**1** Sample answer: An information report is similar in structure to an essay in that it contains a type of introduction, a series of body points or paragraphs, a single topic for each body section and a conclusion.

2 **a** related media and advertisements
**b** hyperlinks, graphics, embedded video
**c** header, bullet points, text boxes
**d** comments bar

3 to provide factual information, to inform people about an important issue

4 Sample answer: It is important to only use graphics and other visual elements that complement the information because ill-fitting visual elements may confuse, distract or mislead the reader.

5 economical language, second person, hyphenated words, explanatory parentheses

6 Sample answers:
**a** ' All of the fatal attacks in the past twenty years have occurred in non-designated swimming areas.'
**b** economical language usage and instructional tone
**c** 'crocs', 'Territorian'
**d** 'extremely dangerous', 'fatal'
**e** conveys the seriousness of the issue to the reader

## UNIT 2: REVIEW

### INFORMATIVE TEXT
### Comprehension Work

page 13

1 **b** This is a **literal** question. You simply need to check the options against the text and look for the correct number. Answer **a** is incorrect because it is the title of Adele's album. Answer **c** is incorrect because it is the number of vinyls sold by Taylor Swift that year.

2 a classic Beatles album (The word 'classic' is optional in the answer.)
This is a **literal** question. We read early in the text *(line 19)* that *Revolver* is one of 'fourteen classic albums' by the Beatles.

3 'If it's the … nostalgia factor that floats your yellow submarine.'
This is a **literal** question. You did not need to interpret any words to get the answer, only find them on the page. We read the key words 'absolutely cool attitude' directly after the answer in the text. *(line 37)* Your wording may have been slightly different to the answer here, but a correct answer must include the word 'nostalgia'.

4 **c** This is an **interpretive** question. We read all three options in the review, but only Answer **c** is correct. To choose it, you need to note that the words in **c** appear after the key phrase 'possibly more impressive' *(line 12)* in the text in a slightly different form. You also need to match 'beaten out by only two' in the text *(line 13)* with 'came close' in Answer **c.** Answers **a** and **b** are incorrect because both options appear in the text before 'possibly more impressive'.

5 **b** This is an **interpretive** question. We read the word 'sales' in two places near the word 'moved' in the text *(lines 12–14)*. You need to make the connection between these two words to find the answer. Answer **a** is incorrect because we can tell from the context that 'shifted' is not a relevant verb. Answer **c** is incorrect because we can tell from the context that emotions are irrelevant in this line.

6 Sample answer: An allusion is made to the song in the phrase 'if [that's] what floats your yellow submarine'. This phrase is a variation of the idiom *what floats your boat*. The original idiom has been altered to function as an allusion.
This is an **interpretive** question. Your wording may vary from this answer, but it is only correct if you have explained the language feature. Simply naming it is not sufficient.

7 **a** This is an **interpretive** question. You need to understand that the review has been composed in a personal manner, and that 'confessions of one serious fan' is a colloquial phrase applied to the review as a whole. We read some of the composer's 'confessions' earlier in the review, including the reference to 'eventually' accepting digital over analogue *(line 33)*. Answer **b** is incorrect because it has nothing to do with this review. Answer **c** is incorrect because we read towards the end of the review that the composer's refusal to persuade the reader to buy the album is 'not a cop-out' *(line 49)*. This (not a 'confession') is the context of that phrase.

8 Possible answers (three of the four are needed): 'go down this new road', 'stand at the crossing', 'look both ways', 'walk your own path'.
This is an **interpretive** question requiring knowledge of a language feature, a pun. With this knowledge, you simply need to locate three references to roads and crossing them in the text.

9 c This is an **interpretive** question. We read that any reader who is an 'analogue snob' is likely to have a 'digital prejudice' *(line 29)*. You need to make a link between the word 'prejudice' in the text and the word 'hate' in the question. Answer **a** is incorrect because it is the direct opposite of the answer given in the text. Answer **b** is incorrect because all readers of this text are likely to have a love of record player

# ANSWERS

CHECK YOUR ANSWERS

needles. If you saw other connotations in that word, they are irrelevant to this question.

**10** **a** This is an **interpretive** question. To answer it, you need to understand the meaning of the word 'roll' in context, which is 'a list of names'. Once that meaning is established, a process of elimination leads directly to the answer. Answer **b** is incorrect because 'remasters' and 'earlier editions' do not match the idea of a 'roll', as they do not mean 'collection' or 'group'. Answer **c** is incorrect because 'copies' does not match the idea of a 'roll' and 'royalties' are irrelevant to this question.

**11** Suggested answer: Only the band members' first names are used because the composer assumes that Beatles fans are reading this review and will therefore know the members' names. This technique also creates a familiarity between the composer and the reader that complements the informal style of the review.
This is an **applied** question. It requires you to make an assumption about the target reader of the review and recognise its informal composition style.

**12** **b** This is an **applied** question requiring you to choose, as the Hint indicates, the best answer. Answer **a** is close to being correct, because another term for 'vinyl' in the review is 'LP'. But the best answer is not 'vinyl' singular, because this is closer in meaning to a type of fabric, but *vinyl records* – that is, 'LPs'. Answer **c** is incorrect for partly the same reason (that is, 'vinyl' is singular). Also, it is clear from a quick re-read that the composer assumes that the reader is someone who 'loves' vinyl records, not someone who 'hates' them.

## INFORMATIVE TEXT Spelling Work page 14

**1** **a** eleven **b** sixty **c** eighty
**d** one hundred / hundred
**e** one hundred and forty-four
**f** two thousand and forty **g** half **h** eighth

**2** **a** guitar **b** chord **c** cello
**d** bass **e** rhythm **f** hymn

**3** **a** *kerching* **b** It is meant to signify money or earning money. The sound comes from an old-fashioned cash register, which made this sound when a transaction was completed and money changed hands.

**4** **a** clang **b** tish **c** buzz **d** tinkle
**e** warble **f** croon **g** oompah
**h** doof-doof **i** plunk **j** boom

**5** **a** iconic/genres/technology/lilts/fluid/guitar/vocals
**b** anthology/fourteen/album/bass/diehard/vinyl/literal
Remaining list word: discernible

## INFORMATIVE TEXT Vocabulary Work page 15

**1** **a** CP **b** H **c** CP **d** CP
**e** H **f** H **g** H **h** CP

**2** Jargon: LP, reissues, vinyl, remastered, bass line, masters
Idiom: swanky, rock 'n' roll, the order of the day, diehard, what's going on, the faithful

**3** **a** 252-page **b** fourteen-album
**c** long-retired **d** double-tracked

**4** **a** headphones **b** comeback **c** whoever **d** outfits

**5** able to be discerned

## INFORMATIVE TEXT Grammar Work page 16

**1** **a** phrase **b** phrase **c** clause
**d** clause **e** clause **f** phrase

**2** **a** now that you know the basics
**b** the listener can appreciate the way

**3** **a** if you're an analogue snob you will
**b** if it's primarily the nostalgia factor that floats

**4** adjective, adverb, conjunction, preposition, article

**5** Adjectives: nostalgia, yellow, cool, original Beatles
Adverbs: primarily, entirely

**6** **a** Nouns: Fab Four, inventory, it, vinyl. Verbs: remade, should (this is an auxiliary verb and is optional in this answer).
**b** Nouns: question, you, vinylphile, cop-out. Verb: answer.
**c** Nouns: crossing, ways, your (this is a possessive pronoun), path. Verbs: stand, look, walk.

## INFORMATIVE TEXT Punctuation Work page 17

**1** **a** correct **b** incorrect **c** correct **d** incorrect

**2** **a** the way it should be, which is on glorious vinyl
**b** put that hate aside and drop the needle **c** more impressive is that across all vinyl record sales

**3** the comma

# ANSWERS

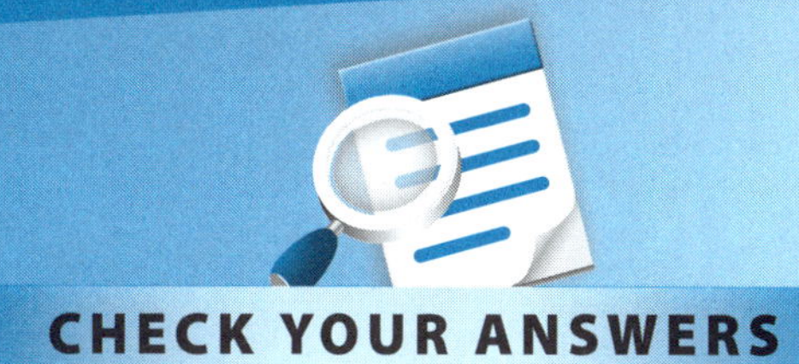

CHECK YOUR ANSWERS

**4** There's a new kid on the music industry block: the old bloke. The LP. It's been a very long time, but it was worth the wait: the best of The Beatles has been remastered. How? You guessed it: on vinyl. The box set includes the following: all fourteen Beatles' albums, static-resistant sleeves and a commemorative book.

**5** **a** none **b** none **c** none **d** because **e** and

INFORMATIVE TEXT

## Writing Work

page 18

**1** Answers will vary.

**2** The answer will be based on your personal experience, but to be correct your answer must include a specific reason for your choice.

**3** Suggested answer: Embedded videos, targeted ad placement on review pages and sponsored advertorials that seem to be informative but have been paid for by the company behind the item being reviewed.

**4** Suggested answer: Feature: strong casual tone Example: 'drop the needle on this baby'.

**5** Suggested answers:
- **a** I will not be listening to this album again.
- **b** While they have many fans, I'm not one.
- **c** I have very strong reasons for loving this band.
- **d** If you don't buy this box set, you are missing out.

**6** Suggested answers: Fans might be so insulted that they will turn against the writer and never read another review of theirs. The artist, company or industry might see the writer as lacking credibility, or may even sue the writer for libel if the review is particularly vicious and unfair.

**7**
- **a** you're very likely to love it
- **b** this new pressing may not be for you
- **c** Even if you've got *Abbey Road*

**8** Note: Answers to **a**, **e** and **g** may vary slightly; answers to **b**, **d**, **f** and **h** may vary widely.
- **a** you're, I'm, it's
- **b** casual, friendly tone
- **c** jargon
- **d** credibility, authority
- **e** album sales
- **f** evidence, interest, context
- **g** look both ways
- **h** interest and humour, reinforces readers' free choice

## UNIT 3: BIOGRAPHY

INFORMATIVE TEXT

### Comprehension Work

page 23

**1** **c** This is a **literal** question. A knowledge of the basic sentence components subject, verb and object helps here. We read the key phrase 'best known' at the beginning of the first sentence of the article *(line 3)* but we must read past the verbs to the end of the sentence to find its subject: 'Peter Rabbit'. So while Beatrix Potter is well known for Answers **a** and **b**, both are incorrect as answers to this particular question.

**2** Beatrix bought Hill Top Farm and married William Heelis (1913).
This is a **literal** question requiring you to find two or more important events occurring in one year. The only year in which this is the case is 1913 *(line 38)*. On reading this section of the article, you would have found the answer.

**3** This is a **literal** question that requires you to find and abbreviate dated incidents and other key events in the text. Presentation styles and wording will vary but the following events and dates should be included:

Born England 1866 *(line 5)*, began sketching as a child *(line 12)*, wrote about Peter Rabbit *(line 17)*, *The Tale of Peter Rabbit* published 1902 *(line 31)*, bought Hill Top Farm 1913 *(line 38)*, married William Heelis 1913 *(line 38)*, became a conservationist *(line 40)*, died 1943 *(line 43)*. You may have included additional events also.

**4** **c** This **interpretive** question requires scanning and elimination. We read that Peter Rabbit is 'naughty' *(line 25)*, 'daring' *(line 23)* and 'mischievous' *(line 19)* in his adventures in Mr McGregor's garden. Answer **a** is incorrect because, while he was 'published' in books, this word can't be used as a description in this context. Also, he is not 'rich'. Answer **b** is incorrect because all of these adjectives describe Beatrix Potter, not Peter. It is true that Peter may be 'strong-minded' and sometimes even 'unapologetic', but we have no proof that he is 'artistic'.

**5** **b** This is an **interpretive** question. To answer it, you need to note the inclusion of these items in the paragraph about Potter's stories and to have a basic knowledge of things that might be found in a rural landscape. Answer **a** can be eliminated because it is not realistic. While Answer **c** is partly correct, this is not the right answer, as lettuces and beans can be grown anywhere.

# ANSWERS

**6** Sample answer: Because she was an only child and may have been lonely.
This is an **interpretive** question requiring you to come to an informed conclusion based on what the article says about aspects of Beatrix's life (that is, she was an only child, she 'didn't belong' in society and she had imaginary animal friends, *line 12*). When we read the article, we can also infer that she was eccentric and enjoyed escaping everyday life and responsibility. You may have mentioned those ideas in your answer.

**7** thirty-six
This is a basic **interpretive** question that simply requires you to find dates and make a calculation: 1902 (when Potter was first published, *line 31*) minus 1866 (when she was born, *line 5*).

**8** This is an **interpretive** question, for which there are various possible answers. There are four likely reasons why Beatrix was elected President of a sheep breeding association. Answers can include any of them (and possibly others that are similar). These are: Potter was famous (and wealthy, *line 37*), she would be the first woman president of the association *(line 42)* (she had already broken ground in the male-dominated world of publishing), she had experience as a conservationist *(line 40)*, she was a landowner and farmer *(lines 38–39)*.

**9** **b** The key to answering this **interpretive** question is the phrase 'based on its use in the text'. To get the answer, you need to test the implication of 'well-connected' in the context of the first paragraph against the options given *(line 8)*. In the opinion of someone like Beatrix's mother, the most valuable type of family is one with power and influence in society *(line 8)*. Answer **a** is incorrect because more detail is needed to make it work. We don't know what the family is 'linked' to. Answer **c** is incorrect because it implies that the family is *inwardly* strong, which would be of little importance to Beatrix's mother.

**10** **a** This is an **interpretive** question requiring you to scan the whole text again and then use a process of elimination. Adjectives, common nouns and lists are all frequently used throughout the text to inform the reader about Beatrix Potter. Answer **b** is incorrect because only adverbs are used in the text, and not frequently. Answer **c** is incorrect because none of these features appear in the text.

**11** Suggested answer: It is likely that Beatrix didn't belong in society because she was more interested in nature and art than in money, fashion and gossip.
This is an **applied** question that requires you to piece together information from the article and then speculate about the subject (Beatrix) based on this information. You may have had a different answer, incorporating her individuality, the dominance of creativity in her personality, her upbringing as an only child, or other factors.

**12** **b** This is an **applied** question. The first task is to note the phrase 'best suit'. The text may be used in any of the contexts listed, but it is 'best suited' to Answer **b**. Beatrix Potter was a nature enthusiast, nature illustrator, farmer and sheep breeder. This makes her a figure of interest to the readers of a nature magazine. Answer **a** is incorrect because the article is not simple enough to be understood by young children and it is too long to fit onto a poster. Answer **c** is incorrect because it would need altering to work as a parliamentary speech and it is not suited to this setting in any case.

INFORMATIVE TEXT
## Spelling Work
page 24

**1** **a** Rabbit **b** bequeathed **c** anthropomorphic **d** unapologetic **e** probably **f** interested

**2** Crossed-out words: **a** anthropographer **b** enchantful **c** illustrationer **d** conservatious

**3** **a** picnicked **b** natural **c** daydreamer **d** characters **e** author **f** thirty **g** tenacious **h** sleeve **i** well-moneyed

**4** **a** unapologetically **b** disenchanted **c** conservationist **d** acreage **e** careering

**5** **a** countryside, lunchbox, freefall, birthday, weekend
**b** Sample answers: spaceship, skateboard, workplace

INFORMATIVE TEXT
## Vocabulary Work
page 25

**1** **a** delightful **b** countryside, acre, conservation **c** beloved, treasured **d** unapologetic **e** bequeathed

**2** **a** Z **b** Z **c** A **d** Z **e** A **f** A **g** Z

**3** **a** anthropology, philanthropy/philanthropic, morphing, metamorphosis
**b** automatic, automobile, biopic, biology

**4** Set 1: **a** past tense **b** full of **c** with the features of **d** verb form
Set 2: **a** without **b** with the qualities of **c** capable of **d** native of

# ANSWERS

CHECK YOUR ANSWERS

INFORMATIVE TEXT
## Grammar Work page 26

**1** **a** three **b** *ing* **c** The present perfect

**2** **a** enchant **b** delve **c** treasure **d** bequeath **e** begin **f** while

**3** Corrected passage (check any circled uses of tense against this): Dear Diary ... Now I wander over the hills again, and gaze with delight upon the endless array of greens that stretch from the McGregor farm to the horizon. It has been / is a constant source of inspiration to me, this landscape. I never tire of its wonders. Its tiny residents, while they aren't much troubled by me, show some interest in my presence and pop their dear little noses in and out of their holes as I pass.

**4** Corrected passage with unnecessary commas removed: After much effort and frustration, the work of this patient, tenacious woman was finally in print but practically everyone believed the book would mark both the beginning and the end of her writing career. As it turned out, however, she continued to write and would eventually make both herself and the Warne publishers very rich.

INFORMATIVE TEXT
## Punctuation Work page 27

**1** **a** Beatrix Potter was feisty, funny and fearless.
**b** Popular for many decades, the *Peter Rabbit* books are still bestsellers.
**c** Born in Kensington, England, Beatrix Potter showed artistic talent at an early age.
**d** 'Go back to your room, Beatrix,' insisted her mother, but the fearless young lady marched right past her.

**2** Beatrix Potter, one of Britain's most admired children's author-illustrators, inspired women of her day to pursue their career goals and she continues to do so today. She is celebrated not only for her talent but also for her tenacity and perseverance, making her a heroine for many girls with an interest in earning a living from art. Potter's creativity, childlike imagination and sparkling originality make her an enduringly popular composer.

**3** Circled words and phrases: william, victorian, castle cottage, hill top farm, national trust, tom kitten

**4** Circled words: **a** madge, Great (second use) **b** none **c** rabbit **d** potter, Countryside **e** Stories, co. **f** Buck Rabbit

INFORMATIVE TEXT
## Writing Work page 28

**1** **a** Beatrix Potter was best known for
**b** children have enjoyed (already in the present tense); children enjoy Or are enjoying
**c** the reader could find
**d** before Mr McGregor can grab him

**2** **a** Simple past **b** Past perfect
**c** 'she spent most of her time writing'
**d** She had been doodling
**e** 'We know from her diary'
**f** Present perfect continuous
**g** 'She has been lauded as one of the most successful author-illustrators'

**3** Sample answer: It is important to limit figurative and emotive language in order to keep the style of the article informative and objective.

**4** Suggested answers: the English countryside where Beatrix spent a lot of time, the original book cover of *The Tale of Peter Rabbit*, the wedding of Beatrix and William. Other possible answers: Hill Top Farm, Castle Cottage, Beatrix Potter's grave, other characters from her books.

**5** Suggested answer: Apart from a picture of Beatrix Potter, the most obvious choice of graphic with which to headline the article is an illustration of Potter's most well-known creation, Peter Rabbit.

**6** Suggested answers:
**a** Example: Born Helen Beatrix Potter on the 28 of July 1866. Effect/purpose: Authority and context.
**b** Example: 'patient', 'tenacious'. Effect/purpose: Fills out the subject's profile.
**c** Example: First woman elected as President of Hardwick Sheep Breeders Association. Effect/purpose: Reveals another side to the subject (apart from art and literature).
**d** Example: 'sketching animals—real and imagined—in their natural setting'. Effect/purpose: Detail through economical language use.

## UNIT 4: PROCEDURE

INFORMATIVE TEXT
## Comprehension Work page 33

**1** **c** This is a **literal** question. The key to answering it is the use of parentheses. 'Baking soda' is given as a synonym in parentheses directly next to 'bicarb soda' *(line 7)*. Answer **a** is incorrect because it is a

separate ingredient. Answer **b** is incorrect because, on its own, that word means 'carbonated water'.

**2** 100° C
This is a **literal** question. To answer it, you need to know that 'max.' is an abbreviation of *maximum,* and to connect the words 'just-warm' with the temperature in parentheses.

**3** Any variations on the following: Half an hour has passed, The shapes are white, The shapes have hardened.
This is a **literal** question. You could use the suggested answers in any order and with any phrasing.

**4** **c** This is an **interpretive** question. While 'shape' can be a noun or a verb, it is clearly a verb here because it is part of an instruction about using the clay. We can see that Answer **a** is incorrect because of the context, which suggests that something is being made. Answer **b** is incorrect because, if the word 'construction' is used in place of 'model' in the sentence, it makes no sense.

**5** **a** This is an **interpretive** question. It requires a basic knowledge of what a slash signifies when used between words in a sentence. It also requires you to use a process of elimination to determine that, in the context, Answers **b** and **c** do not work in the sentence.

**6** Suggested answer: The word 'recipe' is in speech marks in the introduction because this procedure is not literally a recipe. Normally a recipe results in an edible product but the product in this case is not edible.
This is an **interpretive** question. To answer it, you need to recognise that speech marks can be used to suggest that a word or phrase is being used in a non-literal way.

**7** 'gradually' and 'well'
This is an **interpretive** question requiring a knowledge of what adverbs look like and how they function. You also need to make a connection between the phrase 'ensure there are no lumps of flour' *(lines 11–12)* and the two adverbs.

**8** Any of the following answers are acceptable: 'Model clay into shapes as desired', 'Press decorative heatproof objects … into the clay', 'Paint and decorate', pierce the shapes, string the shapes, hang the shapes.
This is an **interpretive** question, requiring you to distinguish the aspects of the procedure that are not optional or based on personal ideas from those that are. The words 'Optional' and 'Hint' *(lines 21 and 27)* in the text would have helped you. Any combination or variation of the suggested answers (including paraphrasing) is acceptable.

**9** **a** This is an **interpretive** question. To answer it, you need to notice the word 'closest' in the question and look for a word with similar meaning to 'trinkets'. This means that you need to have an idea of what 'trinkets' may be. The two corresponding words have been placed close together in a sentence, which should have helped you. Answer **b** is incorrect because it is not a plural. A word which has 'the closest meaning' to the plural 'trinkets' should also be a plural. While Answer **c** can be read as singular or plural, it is too general a term to be the 'closest' match to 'accessories'. Like art, craft encompasses many things and many processes.

**10** **b** This is an **interpretive** question. Clues to the answer include the introductory statement, which lists 'trinkets' and 'accessories' as things that the reader can make using this procedure *(line 2)*, and the hint at the end, which mentions that the reader may 'hang [the] clay shapes' made. A process of elimination also helps with this answer, in combination with a focus on the word 'clay' in the question. Answer **a** is incorrect because 'paints' are not made from clay in this procedure. Answer **c** is incorrect because none of the items listed are made from clay. They are also impossible to make using this procedure.

**11** Possible answers include: An oven and a stovetop are involved in the procedure; The assumed knowledge of abbreviations and terminology (such as 'max. 100 °C'); Some of the vocabulary is not likely to be understood by children (for example, 'durable', 'nears', 'alarmed', 'pliable'); The tone appeals more to an adult reader (for example, 'Try this simple craft "recipe" and you might just be hooked!').
This is an **applied** question requiring you to synthesise information in the text and your own knowledge. You may have had other answers.

**12** **b** This is an **applied** question. It assumes your knowledge of the word 'link' in this context, and that you know this text is likely to be read by a person who knows what a link is and how to use it. It also requires you to imagine what the reader of this procedure would find the most helpful or interesting as a linked text or image. The most likely answer in this case is a link to a similar procedure that extends on the process outlined in this one. You also need to check the other options to eliminate the least appropriate ones. Answer **a** is incorrect because, while an oven is mentioned in the procedure, it is only one small aspect of it. The reader may have little or no interest in buying an

# ANSWERS

CHECK YOUR ANSWERS

oven. Answer **c** is incorrect because shells are only briefly mentioned as one possible item to include as a decoration in the procedure. Showing shells on a beach is not relevant.

INFORMATIVE TEXT
## Spelling Work
page 34

**1** Crossed-out words:
**a** accessorise **b** recipe **c** insure
**d** pierce **e** string **f** endurable

**2** **a** travelling **b** ailing **c** totalling
**d** modelling **e** rolling **f** fledgling

**3** **a** pierce **b** receive **c** thieves
**d** achievement **e** believe **f** chief
**g** ceiling **h** piece

**4** **a** ensure **b** dough **c** heatproof **d** pierce

**5** Crossed-out words:
**a** borrow **b** rouge **c** trough
**d** drought **e** flow **f** do

INFORMATIVE TEXT
## Vovabulary Work
page 35

**1** **a** heatproof **b** mashed **c** hardened
**d** white **e** smooth **f** alarmed
**g** pale **h** modelling **i** pliable

**2** Sample answers:
**a** sold at a high price **b** one-of-a-kind or special
**c** free from lumps and rough patches
**d** used for embellishment or attractiveness
**e** left to the individual's choice or discretion

**3** model, object, shape, cook, craft

**4** **a** accepts **b** cooking **c** plan
**d** consider **e** washable

**5** Sample answers:
**a** instructions, procedure, steps, guide
**b** tough, permanent **c** pot, skillet
**d** seldom, rarely, sometimes **e** guarantee, know

INFORMATIVE TEXT
## Grammar Work
page 36

**1** Sample answers:
**a** km/kilometre **b** Nov./November
**c** Tues./Tuesday **d** Dr/Doctor
**e** homie/home-boy (close friend)

**2** **a** centimetres **b** question **c** teaspoon
**d** as soon as possible **e** continued
**f** breakfast and lunch combined
**g** first **h** romantic comedy

**3** Answers should be very similar to:
**a** a maximum of one hundred degrees Celsius
**b** three-quarters of a cup of water
**c** approximately half an hour

**4** **a** in my opinion **b** I love you **c** thanks
**d** great **e** before **f** 'seeya' (see you soon)
**g** people **h** you only live once

INFORMATIVE TEXT
## Punctuation Work
page 37

**1** **a** for example **b** that is **c** around / approximately
**d** each year / annually **e** and so on

**2** **a** Once upon a time. There were three little foxes who lived in a burrow.
**b** In this procedure, the mixture must be re-heated. Not once. But twice.
**c** The prime minister both began and ended her speech by exclaiming. 'Freedom!'
**d** Rubbing her arms vigorously, she asked, 'Why is it so cold in here?'.
**e** For example. The colour blue represents calm

**3** **a** denotes a numbered step in the procedure
**b** abbreviation (for *approximately*)
**c** ends a sentence **d** abbreviation (for *maximum*)
**e** ends a sentence. Wording of these answers may vary.

INFORMATIVE TEXT
## Writing Work
page 38

**1** Sample answer: Combine ingredients to make a smooth mixture, cook mixture, cool and knead mixture, make shapes, air-dry and decorate shapes. This answer does not need to be expressed as a full sentence.

**2** Suggested answer: It is important to use language economically in a procedure because the main aim of the text is to clearly explain something. Entertaining the reader is not particularly important and may not happen at all. Students may give different and/or additional answers.

**3** Answers may include: An oven and a stovetop would either not be involved or would require adult supervision, not as much assumed knowledge of abbreviations and terminology (such as 'max. 100° C'), use of vocabulary that is more likely to

be understood by children (for example 'soft and squishy' instead of 'pliable'), a tone that appeals to young readers. Students may give different and/or additional answers to these.

4 **a** Suggested examples: 'mix', 'add', 'stirring', 'remove', 'paint' **b** simple present tense **c** procedural
**d** suggested examples: '100° C', '½ hour', 'approx.'
**e** Suggested effect: provides precise, factual detail; helps to ensure the success of the procedure
**f** Suggested examples: 'knead clay', 'remove shapes from oven'
**g** Suggested effect: Names the procedure's specific purpose and outcome.
**h** Suggested effect: Makes the procedure easy to follow and achievable. Students' answers may vary from suggested examples and effects.

## UNIT 5: SPEECH

PERSUASIVE TEXT
### Comprehension Work page 43

1 Many of Lance Armstrong's [millions of] fans.
Note: The phrase 'millions of' is optional in this answer. This is a **literal** question. We read in the first paragraph, which is about Lance Armstrong, that 'Many of his millions of fans could more accurately be called disciples' *(lines 12–13)*. You simply need to find this statement, which is partly quoted in the question, and answer using the beginning of the sentence.

2 A bunch of The Avengers hurling things about in downtown New York City.
Note: This exact wording from the text is optional; a paraphrase is also correct. This is a **literal** question. You need to find 'immediately sprang up' in the text *(line 33)*, note that it is preceded by the words 'the image' and then quote or paraphrase the image, which is described in the second half of the sentence.

3 **b** This is a **literal** question, once again requiring you to match up key words in the question and the text. We read the words 'increasingly popular archetype of the superhero' directly before the words 'So we're back to The Avengers again' *(line 43)*, which is the correct answer. Answer **a** is incorrect because Lance Armstrong is now the opposite of an archetypal superhero. Answer **c** is incorrect because people like 'your mum' are given as opposing examples of the archetype.

4 **a** This is an **interpretive** question. You need to find the key words in the text referring to being 'heartbroken' *(line 17)*, then look back a little in the text to see that Lance Armstrong's drug cheat status is what has specifically caused the heartbreak *(line 16)*. Answer **b** is incorrect because, while it is generally true, it is not specific enough to be the right option here. Answer **c** is incorrect because it describes one of the results of the heartbreak, not the cause of it.

5 changing a nappy
This is an **interpretive** question. You need to infer from the section about changing a nappy *(line 48)* that an 'everyday task' is being described and that the speaker associates such tasks with real heroism.

6 'drug cheats, thugs, casual crims and mischief-makers'
This is an **interpretive** question, requiring knowledge of alliteration. You simply need to find all of the lists in the text and check which one features two examples of alliteration in a row ('**c**asual **c**rims and **m**ischief-**m**akers', *line 18*).

7 **b** This is an **interpretive** question. You need to look for the key word 'height' and the key phrase 'determined by … the fans' in the text *(line 30)*. The ellipsis in the question suggests that the phrase may contain more words in the text, which you should have noted. Then you need to piece together the key phrases in the section 'the fall from grace as the height of the fall' *(line 29)* and match it to Answer **b**. Answer **a** is incorrect because nowhere is an athlete's physical height mentioned. Also, this cannot be 'determined by the fans'. Answer **b** is incorrect because the 'high' in 'drug high' has a different meaning from 'height'. Also, it cannot be 'determined by the fans'.

8 **b** This is an **interpretive** question. We read in the annotations that one effect of this line is 'humour'. A synonym for humour is 'comedy', which is part of one of the options in the question and matches the second part, 'surprise'. The preceding one-word line ('Nope.' *line 8*) which, as we read in the annotations, is 'offered as a full response to the topic', has these effects and ensures that the next line has them also. Answer **a** is incorrect because we can see that the speaker is not being sincere, and beginning a speech by ending it gives the opposite impression to 'authority'. Answer **b** is incorrect because, while this technique might be seen as ironic, it is not angry; nor does it create 'anger' in the listener. Rather, it has the opposite effect.

9 They can all be held up as heroes.
Note: The wording of this answer may be slightly different. This is an **interpretive** question. We read in

the last section of the speech that the speaker believes ordinary members of our families to have just as much right to be called heroes and idols as 'a brattish tennis ace or an overpaid soccer god' *(line 47)*, both of whom are mentioned in the question. This means that what 'your great-great aunty' has in common with these people is the potential to be seen as a hero.

**10** **a** This is an **interpretive** question, requiring an understanding of the word 'attitudes and' an ability to piece together key words and ideas in the question and the text. We read in the text that 'idealisation' gives way to (or is replaced by) 'disillusionment', which is followed by 'hatred' and 'contempt *(lines 27–28)*'. This means that Answer **a** is the correct answer. Answer **b** is incorrect because 'hatred' is not mentioned first, 'grace' has been taken out of context and 'idealisation' is not a part of the list, because it has been replaced. Answer **c** is incorrect simply because 'hatred' and 'disillusionment' are not in the right order.

**11** **a** This is an **applied** question. To answer it you first need to understand that the 'claim' the question asks about is made through the use of a rhetorical question ('Is that fair?', *line 37*); second, to see that sports stars are being called 'ordinary people' in this section *(line 36)*; and third, to note from re-reading that 'that kind of standard' in the text *(line 37)* and 'superhero standards' in the question are the same thing. Answer **b** is incorrect because the speaker is not claiming that 'having ordinary human failings' is unfair: everyone has them. The claim of unfairness applies to people holding athletes, who are in most ways just ordinary people, to an unrealistic standard. Answer **c** is incorrect because it is not about fairness. Many people, not just sports stars, struggle with tasks like 'changing a nappy'.

**12** Suggested answer: The made-up word 'AHH-sum' is intended to be pronounced as it is spelt (phonetically). It is meant to sound like *awesome* in an American accent. The purpose of this language feature is to mimic or caricature a broad American accent. It also carries connotations of a brash American sports star and his fans. This is an **applied** question. It requires you to understand the function of a neologism (made-up word) and its connotations.

## PERSUASIVE TEXT
## Spelling Work page 44

**1** **a** False **b** True **c** False **d** True **e** False **f** False

**2** **a** memos **b** tornados or tornadoes **c** potatoes **d** zeros or zeroes **e** halos or haloes **f** studios **g** photos **h** tattoos **i** tomatoes **j** yo-yos

**3** **a** shouldn't, pedestals, disappointed
**b** stars, becoming, disillusioned, use
**c** Athletes, achieve, amazing, arena, being
**d** celebrity, status, a, lot, anxiety, your

**4** **a** humanity **b** seem **c** achievement **d** myth **e** accuracy **f** original

**5** **a** superhero/achiever/celebrity/pedestal/heroes/humanitarian/archetype/accurately
Extra letters that should be crossed out:
c, d, l, o, l, y
**b** seemingly/increasingly/expectations/origins/disillusionment/overpaid/mythologising
Extra letters that should be crossed out:
a, o, r, g, a, s

## PERSUASIVE TEXT
## Vocabulary Work page 45

**1** register, language, colloquialism, idiom, jargon

**2** Idioms: off the hook, tennis ace, fair and square, for that matter
Abbreviations: crims, mum
General colloquialisms: being awesome; hey; here's a thought

**3** Weakest to strongest: might, can, should, will, must

**4** **a** medium **b** medium **c** low **d** high

**5** Suggested answers: 'we should stop', 'we can admire', 'we need to stop', 'let's see', 'are we really expecting', 'why are we all so heartbroken'

## PERSUASIVE TEXT
## Grammar Work page 46

**1** Suggested answers:
**a** 'Why the horror?' 'Which is one thing.' 'Even if they have razor-cut abs.'
**b** 'But it's another thing entirely … let them down.' 'And the height is determined by us, the fans.' 'So the problem is not so much the fall from grace as the height of the fall.'

**2** Suggested answers:
**a** Even if they have razor-cut abs.
**b** Enjoy your delusion!
**c** Hello, Marion Jones. **d** Nope. **e** A lot.

# ANSWERS

CHECK YOUR ANSWERS

**3** **a** see/sees **b** will see **c** strung
**d** will string **e** horrified Present: horrify/horrifies

**4** **a** participle **b** will **c** was
**d** present **e** are **f** has

PERSUASIVE TEXT
## Punctuation Work
page 47

**1** **a** Let us see a brattish tennis ace
**b** you are not off the hook
**c** If you have heard of any
**d** here is a thought
**e** it is another thing entirely
**f** Hey, they are more than happy
**g** we are back to The Avengers

**2** **a** the height's determined by us
**b** which's one thing
**c** there're so many drug cheats

**3** **a** one-time, best-ever, performance-enhancing
**b** mischief-makers

**4** In any order: overpaid, downtown, heartbroken, superhero, downfall

**5** **a** dash and capital letter
**b** capital letter and full stop
**c** capital letters, apostrophe and full stop
**d** capital letter and apostrophe
**e** apostrophe and hyphen

**6** ellipsis (…)

PERSUASIVE TEXT
## Writing Work
page 48

**1** oral

**2** **a** ethics, ethically, unethical
**b** pathetic, sympathy, pathological
**c** logical, logistics, illogically

**3** register

**4** static

**5** **a** formal **b** casual **c** intimate
**d** static **e** consultative **f** consultative

**6** 'But why are we all so heartbroken about it …?' 'But are we really expecting sports stars … to live up to that kind of standard?' 'Is that fair?' 'What about your mum?' 'Your dad?' 'Your great-great aunty?'

**7** Suggested answer: The effect of the rhetorical question is inclusion. The audience is invited to think about the issue, which applies to the speaker as well as society in general. The use of sarcasm has two main effects: it separates the speaker from the audience by making fun of them and it creates humour.

**8** Suggested answers:
**a** 'Maybe the most worthy heroes are closer to home than we think.'
**b** 'a bunch of The Avengers hurling things about in downtown New York City' 'Now everyone hates him.'

**9** Suggested answers:
**a** The composer seems to want the audience to know the truth about some major sports stars.
**b** The composer seems to want the audience to think more deeply about who they idolise.
**c** The composer seems to want the audience to find better heroes than sports stars. There are various other possible answers in each section.

**10** Suggested answers: A brief video montage of 'fallen' sports heroes. A sound grab or brief clip of Lance Armstrong's confessions about drug use.

**11** Suggested answer: An appropriate forum for this speech is an entertaining debate attended by an audience of the general public.

## UNIT 6: ADVERTISEMENT SCRIPT

PERSUASIVE TEXT
## Comprehension Work
page 53

**1** eight
This is a **literal** question. It requires you to find the word 'silhouette' in the advertisement table and simply add up the number of people shown in this manner. There are two in Scene 002 *(line 14)*, four in Scene 003 *(line 17)* and two in Scene 004 *(line 21)*.

**2** There are fifty locations.
This is a **literal** question. We read in Scene 009 that there are 'fifty convenient locations' of Castle in the Clouds funeral services *(lines 40–41)*. We read in the question that a specific answer is required. This means that the answer should include the number 'fifty'. A general statement such as *there are lots of them* or *they're everywhere* is not correct.

**3** **a** This is a **literal** question. We read in the 'AUDIO' column that music begins and ends the advertisement. Answer **b** is incorrect because it is simply an aspect of the advertisement's structure and not a technical element. Answer **c** is incorrect because the advertisement does not begin with a voiceover; it almost ends with one but the music actually comes last.

**4** **b** This is an **interpretive** question requiring you to link the words 'edited' and 'draft' and to draw basic conclusions about the script being edited. Answer **a** is incorrect because the script must have been edited once if this is 'Draft 2'. Once the first draft (Draft 1) was edited, it became Draft 2. Answer **c** is incorrect because a second edit will result in the script becoming Draft 3.

**5** Answers may include: montage of caring staff, cemetery footage, phrases describing special relationships, gentle music, phrases like 'as the fairytale ends'. At least two of these (or other appropriate features) must be given in the answer.
This is an **interpretive** question. It requires a re-reading of the text, knowledge of the meaning of the word 'emotive' and the ability to find examples of techniques in the table that are emotive.

**6** 'pain-free' and 'ever-after'
This is an **interpretive** question requiring knowledge of the terms 'connotations' and 'hyphenated compound words'. The Hint helps with the latter. To answer the question, you need to find the three relevant words in the advertisement ('leather-bound', 'pain-free' and 'ever-after'), then decide which two have the strongest 'connotations of peace'.

**7** **b** This is an **interpretive** question. It requires knowledge of the word 'complements'. The phrase 'as the fairytale ends' in Scene 009 *(line 43)* is best complemented by this technical effect, which offers a transition from the dream or fairytale world into reality. Answer **a** is incorrect because details about the company's locations do not complement the phrase. Answer **c** is incorrect because this option's footage ends in Scene 006.

**8** **c** This is an **interpretive** question requiring you to carefully read the table's prescriptions and to find the first mention of a transition. Answer **a** is incorrect because, while it is similar to a transition, nothing has happened yet. It denotes a fade-up from black at the beginning of the advertisement. Answer **b** is incorrect because a voiceover is not a transition.

**9** The time at the end of the scene.
This is an **interpretive** question. It can be answered in one of two ways: either by looking at the seconds and time stamp for Scene 000 and drawing a conclusion *(line 6)*, or by reading in the annotations that 'the time at the end of the scene (in minutes and seconds)' is shown after the seconds in the 'TIME' column. The wording of this answer may vary slightly from the wording given here.

**10** **a** This is an **interpretive** question requiring some knowledge of parts of speech, specifically adjectives and adverbs. We read all of the answer options in the text, but only Answer **a** correctly identifies both parts of speech. Answer **b** is incorrect because 'sadly' is an adverb and 'ending' is a noun and a gerund (that is, a verb plus *ing* used as a noun). Answer **c** is incorrect because, while 'difficult' is the right adjective, 'cope' is a verb.

**11** **a** This is an **applied** question. The Hint is a guide to understanding that the word 'commercial' is a good fit for the C in 'TVC'. The knowledge that the abbreviation *TV* stands for *television* completes the task of choosing Answer **a**. Answer **b** is incorrect because 'context' is not an appropriate word here. Answer **c** is incorrect because 'capture' is not the most appropriate word here. You need to draw a conclusion about what 'TVC' is most likely to stand for. While it could stand for the words in Answer **c**, the most logical answer is Answer **a**.

**12** Connotations of a 'castle in the clouds' include heaven, fairytales with happy endings, true love and being together forever. These ideas are pleasant things to associate with the difficult subject of death so they work well in an advertisement for a funeral services company.
This is an **applied** question that asks you to consider connotations and make links back to the aims of the text's composer.

PERSUASIVE TEXT
## Spelling Work
page 54

**1** **a** television **b** advertisement **c** footage **d** images **e** between **f** scenes **g** economically **h** context

**2** **a** commercials **b** persuasive **c** reach **d** audience **e** rhetorical **f** repeated **g** on-screen **h** emotive

**3** **a** True **b** False **c** True **d** False

**4** **a** advertising, business, survival
**b** everyone, reacts, grief, different
**c** cemetery, peaceful

**5** **a** and, might, unconventional, but **b** be

PERSUASIVE TEXT
## Vocabulary Work
page 55

**1** **a** bow **b** quay **c** tear **d** weigh **e** write **f** site

2 **a** implement for (or act of) hitting; flying marsupial
**b** snack or gift; behave towards
**c** stem of a plant; sneak or follow furtively

3 Answers must provide the same sounds as:
**a** BAYCE, BASS **b** TEER, TARE
**c** BOUGH, BOE **d** DEZZIT, DEZURT.
They do not need to have these particular spellings.

4 **a** False **b** False **c** True **d** False

5 **a** parchment **b** fade **c** illuminated
**d** footage **e** scene **f** dissolve
**g** track **h** montage

PERSUASIVE TEXT
## Grammar Work
page 56

1 **a** No **b** No **c** Yes **d** Yes

2 **a** You want a boat. **b** Where are you?
**c** You are going. **d** Take a chance.
**e** You laughed. **f** Go now!

3 sunny, leafy, illuminated, leather-bound, caring, ornate

4 **a** beautiful, beauteous, beautified **b** sad
**c** dead, deathly, deadly **d** friendly **e** flowery
**f** illuminated, illuminating **g** cloudy
**h** happy **i** fairy tale **j** funeral, funerary

5 **a** beautiful **b** loving **c** treasured
**d** gentle **e** pain-free **f** convenient

PERSUASIVE TEXT
## Punctuation Work
page 57

1 **a** incorrect **b** incorrect **c** correct **d** correct

2 **a** Castle in the Clouds Funerals offer compassion, peace of mind and dignity to grieving families.
**b** When you're at your lowest point, why trust your loved one's funeral to just anyone? Call us.
**c** Here's one of our customers, Tai Jackson: 'Castle in the Clouds is the best in the business.'
**d** A television advertisement script should include voiceovers, music and scene timings.

3 VO 2: Sadly, the reality of life is that all fairytales must eventually end. Make that ending as pain-free as possible with Castle in the Clouds Funerals. Our family team offers the most compassionate care at the most difficult time.

4 They separate minutes and seconds in the time stamp.

5 parentheses ( )

6 Suggested answer: Quotation marks, like those in 'misty "dream" dissolve', show that an image or mode of expression is being suggested.

PERSUASIVE TEXT
## Writing Work
page 58

1 Suggested answer: An advertisement for television is different from one for radio in that it can include footage, on-screen text and visual transitions.

2 An advertisement script is divided into rows to show different scenes.

3 A montage has been used in the advertisement for Castle in the Clouds Funerals to quickly and economically show some of the services offered by the company, along with their positive qualities.

4 All advertisement scripts need small time buffers at both ends to accommodate for fade-ins and fade-outs (of audio and/or visuals).

5 **a** convenient, compassionate
**b** family-run, loved, respectful

6 Sample answer: Visit one of our **luxurious** stores today to experience our **superior** service. Speak to our **professional** staff about our **miraculous** products. We offer **unbeatable** prices and **expert** advice. You will be **astounded** and **inspired** by what's on offer.

7 Sample answers: **a** Jen is short.
**b** He has passed on. **c** I lost your coat.

8 scene, audio, on-screen text, vision, footage, fade

9 Repetition is used to help viewers remember the company name, Castle in the Clouds Funerals, in the advertisement. The name, which is the most vital detail, is repeatedly mentioned during the advertisement and shown on-screen, along with contact details to help the audience remember it.

10 The contrasting images of fairytale pictures (including silhouettes and a castle in the clouds) and people involved in funeral-related activities emphasise the sad reality of death, but reduce the impact of this reality by offering peace and a 'happy ending'.

11 The composer is trying to manipulate the emotions of love, sadness and grief. This is done in various ways, including the use of a fairytale theme, which romanticises relationships, showing footage of funerals, cemeteries and grieving families, and setting the advertisement to gentle, emotive music.

**12** Suggested answer: The advertisement may be made more effective by the addition of a testimonial from a person or family who can attest to the superior services and compassion of Castle in the Clouds Funerals.

## Unit 7: Playbill

PERSUASIVE TEXT

### Comprehension Work

page 63

**1** **a** This is a **literal** question. To answer it, you need to read the final line of information on the playbill that mentions 'door sales' *(line 23)*. Answer **b** is incorrect because 7:30 pm is when the show starts. Answer **c** is incorrect because it only refers to online ticket purchases not door sales.

**2** Bedesville
This is a **literal** question. To answer it, you need to distinguish between the name of the college and the name of the suburb where it is located. The suburb's name follows the college's name *(line 13)*.

**3** Wednesday, 17th March
This is a **literal** question. The answer is easy to locate, as it is simply the first date when the show is scheduled to be performed *(line 15)*.

**4** **a** This is an **interpretive** question, requiring you to combine details in the playbill ('School Chapel: raised amphitheatre seating', *line 14*) and in the question ('temporary amphitheatre'). Together, these details indicate that the show will be staged 'inside the chapel'. Answer **b** is incorrect because, if the amphitheatre were *outside* the chapel, the playbill would mention it and there would be no colon after 'Chapel'. Answer **c** is incorrect because the playbill specifically mentions 'raised amphitheatre seating'.

**5** **a** This is an **interpretive** question. It requires you to match the words 'ancient Greek' in the question with 'amphitheatre' in the playbill and 'true' in the question with 'authentic' in the playbill. Answer **b** is incorrect because 'Agnel's' is simply the name of the college and not relevant here. Answer **c** is incorrect because 'available' is not a relevant word here.

**6** Answers may include the following ideas: The noose is positioned directly in line with the quote, so that the viewer's eye is drawn from the noose on the left to the quote on the right and a connection is made. The noose suggests the capital punishment of a 'criminal', which is the key word in the quote.
This is an **interpretive** question. It requires you to look carefully at features of the text and make links between them. Both suggested answers relate to the fact that the heroine, Antigone, is the key link between the noose and the quote.

**7** Suggested answers: The effect of contrasting fonts in the playbill is to highlight individual details and to make the information clearly visible and understandable. The effect of contrasting fonts in the playbill is to attract the viewer's eye and spark their interest—this is particularly true of the title font.
This is an **interpretive** question. It requires you to consider effects of textual features.

**8** Punctuating a quote using both italics and speech marks is technically incorrect. Here, however, the composer has used double punctuation to ensure that the quote stands out from the literal information in the rest of the playbill.
This is an **interpretive** question. It requires you to draw on your knowledge of punctuation.

**9** **c** This is an **interpretive** question. It requires you to link the phrase 'good view' with the adjective 'raised' in the context of seating, and to understand that a 'raised' position indicates a 'good view'. Answer **a** is incorrect because, while an 'authentic' amphitheatre-style seating configuration would provide everyone with a good view, the word 'authentic' is not used in this context in the playbill. Answer **b** is incorrect because 'seating' itself doesn't indicate a good view.

**10** **b** This is an **interpretive** question. The most effective answer process is elimination. Answer **a** is incorrect because 'criminal' is not a 'visual' feature of the playbill as specified in the question. Answer **c** is incorrect because the dress does not create a sense of doom. After eliminating Answers **a** and **c**, you could return to Answer **b** to check that the three items all create a sense of doom, which they do.

**11** Suggested answers: There is an implied link between the play's title (called an eponymous title, meaning that it is also the name of the main character), the figure on the left of the playbill and the quote. The dress, the quote and the embellishment on the noose are white, and white symbolises purity and/or holiness.
This is an **applied** question requiring you to infer meaning from the playbill. You could have expanded on your ideas from Question 6 to show that the heroine, Antigone, is the 'pure and holy criminal' in the play. We link all of these elements with the heroine, because it is implied that she wears the dress and will be hanged by the noose.

# ANSWERS

CHECK YOUR ANSWERS

This leads us to the conclusion that the quote is about her, making her the 'pure and holy criminal'.

**12** **b** This is an **applied** question requiring you to make an informed judgement about a choice the composer has made. It makes sense that, if the play is a Greek tragedy thousands of years old (as explained in the notes on the playbill and the question itself), the story is already well known, and there is little need to state that the heroine will die. Answer **a** is incorrect because 'spoiling the shock' of Antigone's hanging has already happened in the playbill, thanks to the images. Answer **c** is incorrect because, while the first part of the answer is correct, it does not make sense to state that 'nobody cares what happens'—the fact that this ancient play is still being staged suggests that people do care what happens.

## PERSUASIVE TEXT
## Spelling Work
page 64

**1** college, authentic, performance, bazaar, prior, tiered, troupe, ensemble, criminal, online

**2** **a** prior **b** seating **c** promoting **d** troupe **e** online **f** tiered

**3** Sample answers:
- **b** ten, ate, ace, ant, tic, hen, hat, tan, ten, tin; nice, hate, then, than, tent, thin, thine, attic, Haiti
- **c** top, pet, put, pot, toe, rep, per, rot, rut, ute, out; true, rope, pert, poet, pour, pore, port, pout, pouter
- **d** pan, pen, per, for, far, map, car, man, men, nap, can; mane, pram, pane, form, former, prance, perform

**4** **a** promoting **b** college **c** holly **d** tiered **e** troupe **f** bizarre **g** ensemble

## PERSUASIVE TEXT
## Vocabulary Work
page 65

**1** **a** promoting **b** pure **c** criminal

**2** **a** True **b** False **c** False **d** True

**3** Crossed-out words: **a** performance **b** college **c** authentic **d** seating **e** holy **f** pure **g** performance

**4** Sample answers:
- **a** giving cues or instructions to
- **b** combination of overlapping materials; a patchwork
- **c** bush with waxy green leaves and red berries
- **d** lacking energy or wakefulness
- **e** hairpiece used to disguise baldness
- **f** very unusual or strange
- **g** bring together in a group

**5** Set 1: **a** climax—peak **b** alludes—refers **c** symbolise—represent
Set 2: **a** vectors—sightlines **b** attention—focus **c** mystery—enigma

## PERSUASIVE TEXT
## Grammar Work
page 66

**1** Sample answers:
- **a** *Antigone*, a **play** in the tradition of ancient Greek tragedy, is being advertised.
- **b** The chapel at St Agnel's College is the **venue** for the show.
- **c** March 17, 18, 19 and 20 in 2015 are the **show dates**.
- **d** The **show time** each night is 8 pm.
- **e** Patrons can buy **tickets** online or at the door prior to the show.
- **f** Antigone is the eponymous **heroine** because she gives her name to the play.

**2** pro/mo/ting, en/sem/ble, au/then/tic, crim/in/al, am/phi/thea/tre, per/for/mance

**3** **a** no **b** no **c** yes **d** yes **e** yes **f** yes

**4** Circled words: **a** amphibian **b** prior **c** authentic **d** minimal **e** steered
Correct words: **a** amphitheatre **b** buyer **c** athletic **d** criminal **e** tiered **f** droop

## PERSUASIVE TEXT
## Punctuation Work
page 67

**1** **a** yes **b** no **c** no **d** yes **e** no

**2** *Antigone* by Sophocles is a play in a key theatrical tradition: Greek tragedy. This masterpiece features the following classical tragedy conventions: a family of nobles, a heroine, a chorus and a plot that unfolds over one or two days. The blind prophet Tiresias is a character who appears in this and other Greek tragedies. Many people leave a performance like this one in tears: it can be a moving experience.

**3**
- **a** Jackson got what he'd worked so hard for: a recording contract.
- **b** In this instance: it's vital that: you do not stir the mixture.
- **c** Take it easy you've just had: surgery.
- **d** I'm telling you for the last time leave it alone.
- **e** When you go to the shop, please buy: bread, cheese and cat food.

# ANSWERS

CHECK YOUR ANSWERS

PERSUASIVE TEXT
## Writing Work
page 68

1 Sample answers: a tagline that entices or intrigues viewers; special ticket offers or prices; logos of sponsors; a venue image

2 Sample answers: **a** parts or aspects of something
**b** person who composes a play
**c** person in charge of staging a play
**d** commentators or reviewers **e** add to or match

3 Suggested answer: Balance has been created in the layout by the positioning of the dress all down the left side of the playbill and lines of information about the show on the opposite side. Balance is also created by vectors along which the viewer's eye is drawn. The flames, the dress and the noose have all been placed in such a way as to create these vectors, which lead the viewer's eye up to the title of the play.

4 Suggested answer: The most effective visual feature in the playbill is the noose. The impact of this image is strong, as it carries serious connotations. The artist has made an interesting choice in depicting the noose in a cartoon-like style, which lightens the seriousness. Nevertheless, it is a striking and rather shocking image—particularly because it is placed directly above the white dress—and it grabs the viewer's interest.

5 Suggested answer: The visual feature of the white dress complements the quote in the *Antigone* playbill. The whiteness and simplicity of the dress, which the viewer assumes is worn by the heroine, suggest that she is 'pure and holy', which is the descriptive phrase in the quote. Together, these two complementary elements provide the viewer with enough information about the main character in the play to ignite interest in attending the play.

6 Suggested answers:
**a** One visual feature that could improve the playbill is a series of headshots of the main cast members.
**b** One written feature that could improve the playbill is a brief endorsement of the play.

7 Sample answer: The composer of the text 'Antigone' has chosen to symbolise **the purity and innocence of the heroine** in the text through the visual elements of **the white dress and the separate hangman's noose.** Contrast has been created in the playbill by **the use of different fonts and colours.** One effect of this contrast is **a suggestion of the dual themes of innocence/guilt and good/evil; particularly due to the opposing white and black elements.** The banner at the top attracts the viewer's eye because **it is very large with an unusual 'A' and in a font that is reminiscent of Ancient Greece, befitting an advertisement for a Greek tragedy.** Vectors also lead the eye up to the banner. These are created by **the flames, smoke, dress and noose.** The most important informative words on the playbill are **the show dates and starting time.** The quote 'I will be a pure and holy criminal' is significant because **it is spoken by the heroine, Antigone, and sums up her role.** The position of the quote is important because **it is at the top and also adjacent to the noose, which complements the quote.**
The persuasive impact of this playbill is subtle yet effective. It is persuasive because **the various visual and textual elements have been selectively and sparingly used, leaving plenty of questions and mystery for potential audience members.**

## UNIT 8: OPEN LETTER

PERSUASIVE TEXT
## Comprehension Work
page 73

1 **a** This is a **literal** question. We read in the top left-hand corner of the letter *(line 2)* that the group behind the letter is Why Smoking Kills but only one person can actually compose the letter. This is the person who has signed it: Jeffrey Pufflet, the Chief Media Liaison of Why Smoking Kills *(line XX)*. For the same reason, Answer **c** is incorrect. Answer **b** is incorrect because Ms Morg is the recipient of the letter.

2 Sample answer: The composer finds it exciting that one of the NDSHS findings in 2013 was that 'the number of 12- to 17-year-olds who had never smoked was very high, at 95 per cent'.
This is a **literal** question. In the text, we read the question's key word ('exciting') in a slightly altered form: 'excitingly' *(line 37)*. This is the key to answering the question, as it precedes the answer.

3 Sample answer: Why Smoking Kills advocates freedom of expression.
This is a **literal** question. We read the answer explicitly towards the end of the text: 'Why Smoking Kills staunchly advocates freedom of expression' *(line 42)*.

4 **c** This is an **interpretive** question. The best way to answer it is through elimination. We see evidence of Answer **c** in the sentence in question *(line 23)*. Answer **a** is incorrect because there is not enough close repetition of 'oh' sounds to justify calling it

assonance or claiming that 'a moaning sound' is suggested. Answer **b** is incorrect because, while sibilance is present and is sometimes used in texts to create a hissing sound, 'an evil image of a snake' is not necessarily created, nor would it be an appropriate image in this context.

**5** **b** This is an **interpretive** question. To answer it, you need to find and read the full sentence beginning 'You will note …' *(line 30)* and test the function of that sentence against the three answer options. While Answer **a** is almost correct, Answer **b** is more correct. The TAP Act is not exactly 'defined' in this sentence but rather explained, simplified or 'interpreted' for the reader. Answer **c** is incorrect because the sentence does not 'contradict a section of the TAP Act'.

**6** Suggested answer: Why Smoking Kills is 'also reaching out to other Australian arts councils on this matter' because Screen V is not the only organisation that can make an impact regarding the on-screen smoking issue. Similar bodies that help filmmakers get funding should be approached, too.
This **interpretive** question requires you to connect 'Screen V' with 'Australian arts councils' *(line 41)* and realise that all such organisations are appropriate targets of such a letter.

**7** Suggested answer: The composer may have chosen a formal letter structure to raise this issue because it is a serious issue that deserves this format. Were the letter structured informally, such as a social media post, it may not have the impact that a formal letter is likely to have. Also, we read in the letter that it is intended for use in both formal and social media settings anyway.
This is an **interpretive** question that asks you to recognise the importance of the issue of on-screen smoking and to see that the formal letter structure helps to convey this importance to readers.

**8** **c** This is an **interpretive** question. To answer it, you need to understand the meanings of the three answer options; find each answer option in the text; test each option against the question (that is, whether it explains the 'complacency among regulatory bodies'); and finally, ensure that the chosen option is an abstract noun. Answer **a** is incorrect because 'resurgence' is the issue itself, not the 'reason' for the issue. Answer **b** is incorrect because 'screens' is a common noun, not an abstract noun, and it cannot be a 'reason' for a problem.

**9** **a** This is an **interpretive** question. We read in the text where the composer insists that Screen V and similar bodies 'regulate the content of short films and web series eligible for State and Federal funding' *(lines 24–25)*. You also need to note the phrase 'independent filmmakers' in the second last paragraph *(lines 42–43)* and link that with Screen V. Answer **b** is incorrect because we read in the text that bodies like Screen V must 'comply' with legislation *(line 24)*, not 'create' it. Answer **c** is incorrect because, while screen organisations like Screen V might unwittingly 'promote tobacco products', this is not their role.

**10** Sample answer: The composer refers to the findings of the 2013 National Drug Strategy Household Survey (NDSHS) and cites the relevant statistics as evidence for this decline.
This is an **interpretive** question that requires you to note the word 'evidence' in the question and then find the evidence in the text. It makes sense to use statistics from a nationwide survey as evidence.

**11** Suggested answer: The 'Executive Content Advisor', Philippa Morg, is an appropriate recipient of this letter because she is in charge of overseeing all content chosen for film projects that receive funding through Screen V. This means that Ms Morg has considerable influence over what is shown in many independent films, including actors smoking.
This **applied** question must be answered by combining a knowledge of the words in Ms Morg's title *(line 8)* with references in the letter to Screen V's influential role in filmmaking.

**12** **c** This is an **applied** question that requires you to draw a conclusion based on information in the text. We read in the letter (in paraphrased form) that 'smoking's image is not as glamorous now as it was in the past' and can infer from the information about the TAP Act that it 'is the responsibility of film bodies like Screen V to comply with the TAP Act's restrictions'. As such, Answers **a** and **b** as individual answers are incorrect because they are both correct.

PERSUASIVE TEXT
## Spelling Work
page 74

**1** **a** eligible **b** associated **c** government **d** identifying **e** behalf **f** staunchly

**2** **a** hasten **b** recent **c** manufacturer **d** advisor **e** associated **f** excitingly

**3** **a** taxpayer **b** tobacco **c** subject **d** filmmakers **e** utilised **f** dangerous **g** eligible **h** behalf **i** explanation

4 Crossed-out words: **a** eligibleness **b** executar **c** utilisationer **d** manufracture

5 **a** eligible, executive, staunchly
**b** centre, complacency, utilised
**c** behalf, excitingly, identifying

6 **a** associated, complacency **b** utilised, eligible

## PERSUASIVE TEXT Vocabulary Work

page 75

1 Incorrect words: **a** half **b** organiser **c** used **d** legible **e** centre **f** complacency

2 **a** advertiser, advertisement, advertised
**b** advocate, advocacy, advocated

3 **a** executive, execute, executor
**b** advisor, advised, advisory
**c** excitingly, excite, excitedly

4 **a** True **b** False **c** True **d** False **e** True

5 Set 1: **a** conjures—generates
**b** big budget—expensive
**c** responsible—obligated **d** appeals—pleads
Set 2: **a** standpoint—position
**b** recipient—addressee
**c** colloquial—informal **d** plain—obvious

## PERSUASIVE TEXT Grammar Work

page 76

1 years, bodies, series, councils, tobacco, step, decline

2 smoking, funding, writing

3 Possible abstract noun: threat, risks, glamour
Always an abstract noun: consideration, health, misconception, parenthood, belief, opinion

4 **a** collective **b** collective **c** proper **d** abstract **e** abstract

5 **a** common (teenagers), gerund (smoking)
**b** gerund (viewing), abstract (pastime), common (town). Note: In this sentence, 'movie' is not a separate common noun, as it is part of a gerund phrase.
**c** collective (audience), common (kids and snacks), compound (pocket money)

## PERSUASIVE TEXT Punctuation Work

page 77

1 **a** image **b** *u* **c** group, stance

2 Sample answer: This is not an example of apostrophe use because it does not match any of the apostrophe's functions. Rather, quotation marks are used to express an idea or misconception.

3 **a** error **b** possession **c** possession **d** error **e** error

4 Circled words:
**a** raise's **b** doctors **c** filmmaker's, dont, star's

5 A smoking advertisement, according to the TAP Act, is defined as a moving picture that 'gives publicity to, promotes or intends to promote smoking'. If this is the case, how can we continue to allow filmmaking bodies like Screen V to plaster images of smokers all over Australian and international screens as though it's no big deal? The government doesn't seem to think that smoking on-screen is its problem, but if laws like the TAP Act aren't being adhered to, they'd better start thinking about doing something.

## PERSUASIVE TEXT Writing Work

page 78

Suggested and sample answer:

1 **a** place of discussion and/or argument
**b** structure or style
**c** voicing or sharing
**d** literally *weblog*—a series of personal reflections shared on the internet
**e** recipient; the person to whom the letter is addressed
**f** group protest in written form

2 These features are used by open letter writers because they all help to make a text persuasive, which is the main purpose of an open letter.

3 Other elements that can be included in an open letter to make it more persuasive include graphics (such as technical diagrams and pie charts), frequent emotive language and emotive appeals, commands and other forceful statements and a list of well-known supporters.

4 **a** The composer is trying to persuade readers to understand three main things: first, that on-screen smoking is a dangerous phenomenon because it subtly promotes tobacco products; second, that on-screen smoking (and other activities depicted in movies) influences the behaviour of young people; and third, that on-screen smoking has 'lost some of its glamour' but it is still a 'major threat to public health'.
**b** The composer is trying to persuade the specific recipient of the letter (Philippa Morg) to do two

things: first, to comply with 'the restrictions of the TAP Act'; second, to respond in a public forum with an explanation of Screen V's stance on the issue of on-screen smoking and how they intend to address it.

5 **b** Feature(s) to add or change: A shortened form of the letter rearranged into bullet points. Purpose: To make main points of the letter faster and easier to digest.

**d** Feature(s) to add or change: Hyperlinks to anti-smoking Facebook groups and other appropriate anti-smoking groups and websites. Purpose: To encourage readers to stay interested in and learn more about the issue.

6 Correct order: **b**, **a**, **c**, **e**, **d**

## UNIT 9: JOURNAL

NARRATIVE TEXT
### Comprehension Work

page 83

1 Wilson, Bowers, Oates
This is a **literal** question. You simply need to find the three surnames in the text. Since Scott, the team leader, has written this account about himself and his team, and these are the only surnames mentioned, they must be members of Scott's team.

2 Titus Oates
This is a **literal** question requiring you to make a simple connection. At the end of the entry dated 'Friday, March 16 or Saturday 17', which is about Oates, we read that this man 'went out into the blizzard' and didn't return *(line 37)*.

3 **a** This is a **literal** question. The keys to answering this correctly are to locate the date of the entry ('January 18', *line 22*)) and to note the only reference in that entry to an item found inside the tent. This is the written record that mentions the Norwegians having stayed there *(line 24)*. Answer **b** is incorrect because the text says that the Norwegians had already left the tent when Scott and his team arrived. Answer **c** is incorrect because Scott's team brought the Union Jack with them to the tent.

4 **c** This is an **interpretive** question, requiring both a knowledge of personification and an ability to eliminate two incorrect options. Here, the wind is personified by being referred to as a potential friend. Answer **a** is incorrect because chilling something is not necessarily a human ability. Answer **b** is incorrect because personification does not apply to either 'God' or 'place'. God is already a persona and 'awful' does not personify the place.

5 **c** This is an **interpretive** question. The key to answering this question is connecting the phrase 'of course' with the word 'main'. It makes the most sense that Scott and his men are weakening when a lack of food is the 'main' factor. Answer **a** is incorrect because money is not mentioned and seems to have no connection to the lack of supplies. Answer **b** is incorrect because, while the men were losing hope and this would have contributed to their 'getting weaker', it is not the factor leading to their weakness.

6 Scott means that, while they reached their destination, they did not win the race. They were beaten there by the Norwegians.
This is an **interpretive** question. As the Hint advises, this question is best answered with the help of the introduction, in which we read that 'his [Scott's] team made it, but … a Norwegian team had beaten them there by a month' *(line 4)*. The question may also be answered without referring to the introduction. We read that Scott's team suffered 'disappointment' on arriving at the Pole *(line 13)*, and while they were consoled by the fact that it was 'something to have got [there]', they were forced to say 'good-bye to most of the day-dreams' of success that they once had *(lines 27–28)*. These three pieces of information appear in two different entries.

7 'Whirling drift' means a severe snowstorm or blizzard.
This is an **interpretive** question. First, you need to find and read the entry dated March 29. It would also be useful to skim back through the other entries to find references to the weather conditions that give clues to what 'whirling drift' could mean. Having an existing knowledge of the word 'snowdrift' (a large amount of deep snow) and combining this knowledge with the description of the snow 'whirling in a continuous gale' at the beginning of the entry *(line 43)* would also help you answer this question.

8 Answers may include variations of these statements: 'He has borne intense suffering for weeks without complaint'; 'To the very last [he] was able and willing to discuss outside subjects'; 'He did not—would not—give up hope till the very end'; 'He went out into the blizzard'.
This is an **interpretive** question. It requires you to give three specific reasons that justify Scott's

statement about Oates's bravery. All of these reasons can be found in close proximity to the statement in the text *(lines 32–37)*. Full or partial quotes are acceptable; so is paraphrasing.

**9** **b** This is an **interpretive** question. It can be answered by using a combination of existing knowledge of the phrase 'in our tracks' and the word 'path'. It can also be answered through a process of elimination. Answer **a** is incorrect because we read nothing about railway tracks in the text and there is clearly no railway metaphor being used. Answer **c** is incorrect because, while it is likely that the men wore snowshoes and snowshoes can create tracks in the snow, they cannot be referred to as tracks.

**10** **a** This is an **interpretive** question that first requires you to note the word 'best' in the question. Secondly, it requires that a connection be made between the team's 'last chance' and the lack of food and fuel. Third, while the word *days* is missing (remember that a journal is often grammatically incorrect or loose), the phrase 'only one or two of food left' implies that there is only enough food for one or two days, which best explains why this was the men's 'last chance'. Double-checking by a process of elimination shows that Answers **b** and **c** are both incorrect because they do not explain why the next day would be the team's 'last chance'.

**11** Scott's team carried a Union Jack (British flag) to plant at the Pole once they reached it.
This is an **applied** question that requires you to make connections between the flag, the nationality of Scott's team, the practice of adventurers or explorers planting their nation's flag at a destination (particularly when they have raced other nations there) and the description under January 18 of the flag being placed on a makeshift pole *(lines 25–26)*. It would also have been helpful to scan back through the introduction to the text and the text itself to answer this question.

**12** **c** This is an **applied** question, the key to which is the adjective 'natural'. We read shortly after the key statement 'have decided it shall be natural' that the men are prepared to die in the blizzard and not take their own lives (which would be *unnatural)*. Making this connection is the simplest way to find the answer. Answer **a** is incorrect because 'marching' cannot be described as 'natural' or unnatural. Answer **b** is incorrect because, as they neared starvation, Scott and his men would not have cared whether any available food was 'natural'.

NARRATIVE TEXT
## Spelling Work
page 84

**1** temperature, tragedy, monotony, borne, whirling, headwind, depot, circumstances, disappointment

**2** **a** effects **b** apiece **c** priority **d** tragedy

**3** **a** continuously **b** prioritise **c** appointment **d** affects

**4** **a** here **b** been **c** scene **d** bear **e** passed **f** through

**5** time / thyme, witch / which, daze / days, course / coarse, dye / die, find / fined

NARRATIVE TEXT
## Vocabulary Work
page 85

**1** **a** continual **b** continuous **c** continuously **d** continually

**2** **a** unbroken **b** uninterrupted **c** frequent **d** single **e** incessant **f** ongoing

**3** Sample answers:
**a** gear, equipment, supplies and/or personal belongings
**b** supply stop, base or place of safety
**c** British flag
**d** right until the end (usually the point of death)

**4** **a** very **b** wonder **c** reward **d** desperate **e** face **f** solid

**5** **a** borne **b** effects **c** descending **d** piece **e** consistent **f** priority **g** monotone

NARRATIVE TEXT
## Grammar Work
page 86

**1** **a** we've **b** there's **c** that's **d** we're **e** he's **f** didn't **g** wouldn't **h** I'm **i** haven't **j** we'll

**2** **a** I'd **b** what'd **c** she'd **d** that'll

**3** **a** couldn't **b** could not

**4** **a** temperature **b** west-southwest **c** southwest **d** Robert

**5** **a** as soon as possible **b** estimated time of arrival **c** do it yourself **d** very important person

**6** The abbreviations may be used in any order and do not need to be expanded. The sentence can be of any length. Sample answer: The celebrity plumber was meant to be a VIP at the DIY convention, but while he was trying to get there ASAP, his ETA wasn't looking promising.

NARRATIVE TEXT

## Punctuation Work

page 87

**1** **b** It indicates a compound word.

**2** **a** They separate a series of related details.

**3** to-morrow, good-bye, day-dreams

NARRATIVE TEXT

## Writing Work

page 88

**1** **a** Now **b** I think **c** Since **d** of course

**2** **b** they have been descending again, he thinks
**c** the wind may be their friend to-morrow
**d** he wonders if they can do it
**e** they can testify to his bravery
**f** he does not think he can write more

**3** Sample answer: Figurative language is limited in journal writing because there is a greater focus on the literal. The writer is usually not aiming to entertain others but to record personal experiences and reflections.

**4** Sample answers: 'Great God! This is an awful place'; 'I wonder if we can do it'; 'He was a brave soul.'

**5** Sample answers:
**a** to organise and execute an important event
**b** to track progress in a fitness regime and engage in self-motivation
**c** plot summaries; publication details; evaluation of writing style
**d** to collect and keep ideas and resources for various creative uses
**e** to document family history and/or build a collective family record or memory
**f** sketches, diagrams and photographs; botanical and biological jargon

**6** planner, log, record, diary, scrapbook, chronicle, portfolio

**7** Suggested answers: memoir, register, write-up, account, ledger, annals, almanac, daybook, organiser, weblog (blog), videolog (vlog), album

# UNIT 10: ALLEGORY

NARRATIVE TEXT

## Comprehension Work

page 93

**1** 'jewels and precious metals'
This is a **literal** question. The answer is contained in the same line as the key word from the question. You simply need to spot it (in a slightly different form, 'abounding', *line 37*). You may have quoted or paraphrased this answer.

**2** 'for being such a humbug'
This is a **literal** question. We read this accusation from the Scarecrow in the same line as his judgement that the Wizard 'ought to be ashamed' *(line 7)*. It is clear that the two things go together. You may have quoted or paraphrased this answer.

**3** **c** This is a **literal** question. The keys to finding the answer are to locate the earliest reference to 'the Emerald City', where the Wizard explains why he gave it that name *(line 30)*, and to note the word 'as', which indicates that the reason for its name will follow. Answer **a** is incorrect because nowhere in the text is the city said to be made of emeralds. Answer **b** is incorrect because, while the Wizard says there are jewels in the land, this reference is not made early enough to be an explanation.

**4** **a** This is an **interpretive** question. It requires you to do two things: read over a large section of the excerpt to find the correct order and match the word 'impersonator' with 'imitate' *(line 14)*, which is what an impersonator does. Answer **b** is incorrect because 'balloonist' and 'impersonator' are in the wrong order. Answer **c** is incorrect because 'Wizard' and 'balloonist' are in the wrong order.

**5** **a** This is an **interpretive** question. To answer it, you need to understand that, while clouds are mentioned in the balloon story, they have nothing to do with the balloon floating away. Answers **b** and **c** are incorrect because they both mention factors that are involved in the balloon incident leading to the Wizard's arrival in the land of Oz: that is, twisted balloon ropes which prevent the proper use of the balloon and a current of air on which the balloon is carried. *(lines 21–22)*

**6** Suggested answer: Because this scene centres on the Wizard and reveals how he came to be in this situation, it works best when narrated by him in his own words (direct speech).

# ANSWERS

This is an **interpretive** question. It requires you to understand some of the main purposes of direct speech in narratives and to give an answer that is based on this understanding.

7 Suggested answer: Like the citizens of the Emerald City, Dorothy has been given green glasses ('spectacles') to wear.
This is an **interpretive** question. While it asks for your opinion, there is one main likely answer. We read that the citizens all wear these glasses and think that the City is really green *(line 36)*. It makes sense, then, that Dorothy thinks the same thing for the same reason.

8 Suggested answer: The alliteration (a 'w' sound) emphasises pairs of directly contrasting 'w' words, which are all key words in the excerpt. The most obvious pairs are 'Witch' and 'Wizard', 'Wonderful' and 'Wicked'.
This is an **interpretive** question. It requires a knowledge of the language technique of alliteration, which is the repetition of consonant sounds at the beginnings of words near each other in a line. Commenting on the effect of this technique requires you to have an opinion.

9 **b** This is an **interpretive** question. It requires you to notice that in the Wizard's line 'who, seeing me come from the clouds' *(line 26)*, the word 'who' refers to the citizens and 'seeing me come from the clouds' explains why they might be afraid. Answer **a** is incorrect because, whether or not the citizens were 'strange' is irrelevant. Answer **c** is incorrect because when he arrived, Oz was not yet a Wizard (in reality, he was only ever pretending to be one).

10 **b** This is an **interpretive** question. It requires you to note that Dorothy's house is mentioned in close proximity to the Witch of the East *(line 46)*, and to understand that the Witch's death due to the house would have eliminated the Wizard's 'deadly fear' of her. You may also have used a process of elimination. Answer **a** is incorrect because the Witch of the West (not the East) is the one who has been melted. Answer **c** is incorrect because the good Witch of the North is not said to have had any part in the death of the Witch of the East.

11 The best answers from the text include: He is a fraud ('humbug'); He manipulated the citizens; He exploited the citizens; He has no magical powers; He does not keep his promises.
This is an **applied** question that requires you to scan back through the whole text and find three reasons for Dorothy's opinion. An acceptable answer is: He conspired to kill the Witch of the West. This is not the best answer: although she was a significant threat to the people of the land, it is never 'good' to conspire to kill someone—no matter how evil they are.

12 **c** This is an **applied** question that requires you to draw conclusions based on directly quoted facts about Oz in the text and the question, to find the best answer and to eliminate incorrect or irrelevant answers. Answer **a** is incorrect because any ventriloquist might be able to imitate something or someone but it takes training and mastery to be able to 'imitate any kind of a bird or beast'. Answer **b** is incorrect because, while he 'mewed like a kitten', this does not necessarily mean that Oz can 'imitate any kind of a bird or beast'.

## NARRATIVE TEXT
## Spelling Work

page 94

1 **a** scarecrow **b** imitate **c** ought **d** jewels **e** midst

2 **a** jewels **b** imitate **c** abounding **d** fortunately

3 The following words should be circled in the passsage: baloon, twirsted, coulldn't, aggain, whent, clowds, curent, stuck, caried, knight, threw, mourning, floting, stranged, beutiful

4 Sample answers:
imitate: tat, tie, ate, eat; mite, team, item, meat, mate, mitt
emerald: lad, ram, dam, red, mar; dame, dream, meld, lame, deem, dare
spectacles: cat, let, set, tap, lap; salt, seep, pets, tape, slate, tales, spate

5 tough

6 Sample answers: draw, ward over, rove; keep, peek; ears, sear; north, thorn

## NARRATIVE TEXT
## Vocabulary Work

page 95

1 **a** pretender **b** lenses **c** citizens **d** countless

2 **a** wow! **b** a person **c** so similarly to **d** because

3 **a** sorrowfully **b** willingly **c** gradually **d** certainly **e** sorrowfully **f** fortunately

4 Note: There is only one correct answer for each word stem, but the new words given by students will vary.

**b** Word stem: bound; New word: boundary, bounded
**c** Word stem: spect; New word: spectator, inspection
**d** Word stem: grad; New word: graduate, grade
**e** Word stem: will; New word: willed, willful

NARRATIVE TEXT
## Grammar Work
page 96

1. sorrowfully, well, willingly, fortunately, surely, gradually, certainly
2. **a** Incorrect **b** Incorrect **c** Correct
3. **a** Dorothy skipped gleefully through the gates of the Emerald City.
   **b** 'The Witch melted in a flash!' Tin Man exclaimed excitedly.
4. **a** Dorothy's dog Toto was barking loudly and excitedly.
   **b** Dorothy breathlessly explained how her house had arrived in Oz so fast.

NARRATIVE TEXT
## Punctuation Work
page 97

1. **a** Incorrect **b** Correct **c** Incorrect **d** Correct
2. Dorothy took off her old leather shoes and tried on the silver ones, which fitted her as well as if they had been made for her. Finally, she picked up her basket. 'Come along, Toto,' she said. 'We will go to the Emerald City and ask the Wizard of Oz how to get back to Kansas again.' She closed the door, locked it, and put the key in her pocket.
3. Quotation marks are also called inverted commas because they look like commas in an inverted (upside-down) position (, ').
4. with, witch, Supper, boq

NARRATIVE TEXT
## Writing Work
page 99

1. **a** e **b** d **c** c **d** b **e** a
2. Answers should be similar to the following: An allegory is a complete text that contains symbols.
3. Answers may include: to avoid getting the media and/or politicians off-side; because parents were likely to read the story to their children and understand its deeper messages; to avoid having to commit to one side of the political debate. Students may also have other ideas.
4. Sample answers:
   **a** Meaning 1: the land of Oz
   Meaning 2: The United States of America
   **b** Meaning 1: emerald-coloured and/or lush and fertile
   Meaning 2: related to money and material things
   **c** Meaning 1: show with acrobats and animals
   Meaning 2: politics and/or the media
5. Question: What is that? Effect: makes us ask along with Dorothy; opens the way for a symbol to be used

   Question: But isn't everything green here? Effect: shows that Dorothy and her friends have been tricked

# UNIT 11: SATIRICAL SCRIPT

INFORMATIVE TEXT
## Comprehension Work
page 103

1. The style of décor in Lady Darlingcot's parlour is Victorian (that is, in the style associated with the era of Queen Victoria).
   This is a **literal** question. You need to read the stage directions to find it *(line 2)*. You could also have added 'fashionable' to your answer but because this is a vague adjective, 'Victorian' is the main answer.
2. **c** This is a **literal** question requiring you to look for a reference in the text and to use a process of elimination. Answer **c** offers the only option that matches the phrase 'what happened to' *(line 23)*. Answer **a** is incorrect because being Lady Darlingcot's muse isn't something that 'happened' to the milkman. Answer **b** is incorrect because it is something the milkman did.
3. According to Lady Darlingcot, Lady Idleford's coffee is similar to death because both are 'dark and bittersweet'.
   This is a **literal** question requiring you to look for a reference in the text *(line 18)*.
4. **a** This is an **interpretive** question requiring you to make judgement about the purpose of the capitalisation of the first line: 'DARLING!' *(line 4)*. Answer **b** is incorrect because, at this point, we don't know enough about the character to make this evaluation. Answer **c** is incorrect because it is not a specific answer and fails to name what the emphasis is placed on. Avoid saying that *emphasis* is the purpose or effect of a composer's use of a technique. It is never an adequate answer.
5. **a** This is an **interpretive** question requiring you to link the words 'palette' and 'charming' *(line 20)*.

While Lady Idleford uses the words 'charming' and 'striking' to describe the 'bloody' painting *(line 20)*, she specifically calls the palette (or colour scheme, as the Hint tells you) 'charming', making Answers **b** and **c** incorrect.

**6** Lady Darlingcot is 'suddenly inspired' because she remembers last night's 'superb sunset', which reminded her of blood.
This **interpretive** question requires you to link a stage direction with a portion of dialogue *(line 12)*.

**7** When Lady Darlingcot asks Lady Idleford to paint a picture with her, what she really has in mind is to use Lady Idleford's blood as paint.
This is an **interpretive** question requiring you to understand that the audience assumes Lady Idleford will have the same fate as the milkman *(lines 22–23)*.

**8** By the end of the skit, we know that Lady Darlingcot has killed at least three people: the milkman, Harold and Lady Idelford's mother. Lady Idleford would be the fourth, but she is still alive at the end.
This is an **interpretive** question that asks you to add up the victims and realise that Lady Idleford is not one just yet.

**9** **b** 'Idle' means inactive. Lady Idleford's name suggests that she is not active and does not perform any useful work. This **interpretive** question requires you to link aspects of Lady Idleford's personality with a part of her name. Answer **a** is incorrect because while 'idle' and 'idol' are homophones, idols have nothing to do with this question. Answer **c** is incorrect because, among other reasons, we don't know what car Lady Idleford drives, if in fact she drives at all.

**10** **b** This **interpretive** question is best answered using elimination. We can assume, based on other actions of Lady Darlingcot, that she smashed it in a rage and/or during the attack on her husband. Answer **a** is incorrect because this action is not part of the stage directions when the frame is mentioned *(line 36)*. Answer **c** is unlikely, as a 'clue' like that wouldn't help investigators to pin Harold's murder on his wife.

**11** **c** This is an **applied** question that asks you to piece together aspects of the text and the Hint and use this information to draw a conclusion about the text's purpose. As the Hint states, 'a text that satirises something mocks it, often to make a point'. This is the case with Answer **c.** The writer is hyperbolising upper-class people and situations to make fun of them. Answer **a** is incorrect because milkmen aren't mocked in the text. Answer **b** is incorrect because, while they're done in a macabre way, paintings aren't mocked in the text.

**12** Suggested answer: It seems that Lady Darlingcot has become a murderer as a kind of hobby. Like painting, it gives her something to do. Of course, this is ridiculous and unrealistic. But this is a satirical, farcical script. Upper-class women like Lady Darlingcot, especially in times past, were usually housebound and often became incredibly bored. The composer has taken this scenario to an extreme conclusion, suggesting that Lady Darlingcot has become so bored and frustrated that she is literally ready to kill someone.
This is an **applied** question asking you to draw conclusions and apply your knowledge to the text.

INFORMATIVE TEXT
## Spelling Work
page 104

**1** One-syllable words: muse
Two-syllable words: pa–lette, par–lour, pa–tience, ro–bust
Three-syllable words: bi–tter–sweet, cam–em–bert, o–ver–dressed, sim–i–le
Four-syllable words: boi–ster–ous–ly, ex–cep–tion–al, men–ac–ing–ly, pre–sum–ab–ly, pur–pose–ful–ly, what–so–e–ver

**2** **a** simile **b** palette **c** muse **d** exceptional

**3** **a** purposeful **b** exceptionally **c** patient **d** menace

**4** wielding, camembert, they'd, unearthed, basement, whatsoever, certainly, these, peaceful, ordeal

**5** **a** simile **b** muse **c** parlour **d** robust **e** camembert **f** patience

INFORMATIVE TEXT
## Vocabulary Work
page 105

**1** **a** with precision and attentiveness
**b** in a state of great excitement
**c** in an unfriendly or hostile manner

**2** The following should be crossed out:
**a** opening the door **b** sharpening teaspoons
**c** associating sunset colours with blood

**3** **a** purposefully **b** bittersweet **c** whatsoever **d** overdressed **e** patience

**4** Sample answers:
**b** 'Darling!': most beloved one
**c** 'Sublime!': utterly wonderful; extremely good or beautiful

d 'charming': attractive and delightful
e 'Oh, you!': term of endearment but implies that the person is silly

5 a I'm all thumbs
b I'm afraid
c You have no idea

INFORMATIVE TEXT
## Grammar Work
page 106

1 a annoy b envy c tire
d straighten e wrong

2 a creatively b admiringly or admirably
c sleepily d markedly
e deceptively or deceivingly

3 a menacingly, menace b presumably, presume

4 a menacingly, menace
b boisterously, boisterousness
c presumably presumption
d purposefully, purpose

5 Possible answers include: usually, normally, often, frequently, sometimes, occasionally, never, rarely, seldom, ever. Six adverbs of frequency are required.

INFORMATIVE TEXT
## Punctuation Work
page 107

1 a emphasis b stage directions
c part of speech example d partial word
e term from another language
f title of a text or work

2 Sample answers:
a By emphasising '*sleeping*', Lady Darlingcot changes the ordinary term 'fishing' to a euphemism meaning dead, which also carries the implication that the person was murdered.
b The italics denote that '*he*', that is, the milkman, was her muse, as opposed to anyone or anything else.
c This refers to Lady Darlingcot literally using Lady Idleford to paint a picture, as she did with the milkman. The italicised '*we*' distinguishes Lady Idleford from the milkman.

3 Lady Darlingcot took great pride in her Victorian parlour which, despite being small, was very fashionable. The reclusive woman didn't often receive callers, so it was always quite an occasion when she did. She ensured that the larder was fully stocked with the essentials: camembert, smoked herrings, crispbread and, of course, arsenic. At the Darlingcots', an afternoon's entertaining could reach a marvellously murderous conclusion by six o'clock.

4 a understatement b enthusiasm
c amusement d ignorance

INFORMATIVE TEXT
## Writing Work
page 108

1 Suggested answers:
a Example: 'Simile. *(A beat)* Tea?' Function: Among other functions, including creating humour, this beat shows that Lady Darlingcot can't be bothered explaining herself to the dimwitted Lady Idleford. She moves the conversation on quickly.
b Example: 'Ooh that tickles! *(Pause)* Hm, a little to the left.' Function: Humour from a string of unexpected and unlikely responses to being stabbed with a sharpened spoon. The pauses in Lady Idleford's dialogue connect these responses, and also permit the actors to add actions and facial expressions that create even more humour.

2 Sample answers:
a **Ooh** that tickles! **My**, what a striking painting! **Gracious**, how unladylike!
b **So**, where is Harold? **Oh** I'm all thumbs … **Hm**, a little to the left.

3 Suggested answers:
a Example: 'You don't understand, do you?' Tone: Bluntness that borders on pity.
b Example: 'DARLING!' Tone: Exuberance.
c Example: 'Cot. Lady Darlingcot.' Tone: Coldness.
d Example: 'quite ... robust.' Tone: Mysterious and a little sinister.

4 Sample answer: While some aspects of the text 'Lady Darlingcot', including the line 'The weather continues charming', have been borrowed from *The Importance of Being Earnest* by Oscar Wilde, the script is not a direct copy, mockery or parody of that play. It is a satire because the writer is exploring Victorian (or Victorianesque) upper-class society and behaviour in an unbelievable and farcical way.

5 Suggested answers: The absurd action of sharpening a spoon and the equally absurd reaction of Lady Idleford (see the annotations on the text); crazy props, including 'a voodoo doll full of pins and blood-spattered kitchen gloves'; Lady Idleford's highly exaggerated greetings and exclamations; the whole bizarre scenario.

# ANSWERS

## UNIT 12: SHORT STORY

NARRATIVE TEXT
### Comprehension Work
page 115

**1** The giant spitball probably contains diseases, according to Simon.
This is a **literal** question. We read the real and imagined ingredients in the spitball, which are 'paper, glue, spit and who knows what diseases' *(lines 10–11)*.

**2** Simon does not bother looking too hard for the house key because he 'can visualise it on top of the fridge'.
This is a **literal** question. It does not require a direct quote: you could also paraphrase the relevant section, for example because he remembers leaving it on top of the fridge *(line 23)*. An optional addition to this answer is a note about Simon taking his lunch from the fridge at the same time as he left the key on top.

**3** The main features of the night at 9:06 pm are that it is very dark and very cold. Your expression of this may vary. You may also quote the story in your answer.
This is a **literal** question. It requires you to find basic facts reported by the narrator. First, you need to find the correct time in the story ('six past nine', *line 75*) and match that with its digital equivalent in the question ('9:06 pm'). Then you need to note two main features of the night at that time, which are the darkness ('the night is at its inkiest', *line 74*) and the cold ('it is beyond freezing', *line 74*).

**4** **c** This is an **interpretive** question. It requires you to understand that the end of the following sentence is explained by its beginning: 'A skin-crawling growl suddenly comes from the azaleas, and I stop breathing.' *(line 81)*. The conjunction 'and' is the main clue to understanding this connection. Answer **a** is incorrect because if Simon stops breathing, he cannot 'inhale deeply'. Answer **b** is incorrect because it comes too long after Simon stops breathing to be an explanation.

**5** **a** This is an **interpretive** question. To answer it, you need to find two facts from different places in the text and pair them up in one answer option. When the first car comes by, Simon tells us that he knows the manner in which his father drives over the speed bump near their house *(lines 49–50)*. When his father's car arrives, he says he recognises the sound of the engine *(line 87)*. You can also use the process of elimination to answer this question. Answer **b** is incorrect because, while the speed bump is one half of a correct answer, the headlights are irrelevant. The car has already been identified by Simon before he sees the headlights. Answer **c** is incorrect because, as explained above, the headlights are not relevant and Simon can't see or hear the car's suspension, which is part of its underside.

**6** The language technique used in the phrase 'really intelligent insults' is sarcasm.
This is an **interpretive** question. We can see from the dialogue at the beginning that their insults are not intelligent ones. We also read that Simon has very little regard for the Watson twins based on his tone so it is quite likely that he is being sarcastic when he calls their insults 'intelligent'.

**7** The writer has used the present tense to tell the story in order to create tension and to heighten the narrator's sense of fear and his anxiety about what might have happened to his father.
This is an **interpretive** question that asks for your opinion. It requires you to notice that the text is written with lots of emotion-based descriptions, interior monologue and truncated sentences, all of which contribute to the tension.

**8** We assume that 'Thankyouthankyouthankyou' is directed towards God because Simon pleads, 'Please God, don't let Dad be dead' a little earlier in the story.
This is an **interpretive** question. It requires you to pair up 'please' in 'Please God, don't let Dad be dead' *(line 80)* and 'thank you' in the emotional stammering of Simon when his father arrives home.

**9** **a** This is an **interpretive** question. The combined details about Simon attending school and having a History project suggest that he is a school student. As we read the story, this information is complemented by Simon's use of language and the fact that he is old enough to be home alone. Answers **b** and **c** are both incorrect because they could apply to anyone of any age.

**10** **c** This is an **interpretive** question. It requires you to recognise the link between Dad's question and Simon's explanation. Answer **a** is incorrect because we can reasonably assume from the wording of Dad's question and the brief explanation that follows ('He's a pacifist', *line 34*) that he is not in favour of his son reading books on the subject of war. Answer **b** is incorrect for two main reasons: first, Dad is a student himself, so clearly he is not opposed to books; second, Dad specifies that his problem is not with books in general, but 'books

about war' *(line 33)*. This also points us to Answer **c** being correct, because this option states that war is the issue.

**11** The capital letters signify that getting inside the house in the first sentence is related to the mention of irony in the second. By signposting the connection between these two elements, the capital letters show us that it is ironic that Simon's mother is so safety-conscious, she has *unsafely* locked her own son out of the house. This is an **applied** question that requires you to make a connection and possess some basic prior knowledge about irony.

**12** **b** This is an **applied** question. We need to recall Simon's argument last night with his dad, where he 'really yelled' *(line 58)* and lost his temper. Prior to this, he had become frustrated and angry with his dad also. We can reasonably assume that, because of Simon's dad's warning about his temper, Simon's remorse about yelling and his huge relief that his dad is home safe, his behaviour will be different (even for a little while) when he next speaks with his dad. Also, the conjunction 'but' in the relevant section gives a strong sense that Simon is in a similar situation to before but is learning to control his temper. Answer **a** is incorrect because Simon and his dad have already been talking and no mention is made of being quiet in case the neighbours are listening. Answer **c** is incorrect because of syntax. If the intended meaning was that Simon 'unconsciously' raises his voice, the line from the story would read 'I don't consciously raise my voice' (that is, it just happens and is beyond his control).

NARRATIVE TEXT
## Spelling Work
page 116

**1** **a** stargazing **b** inkiest **c** casually **d** azaleas **e** defensively **f** pacifist

**2** **a** allegations **b** naturally **c** necessary **d** embossed **e** dissent

**3** **a** visualise **b** headlong **c** painstaking **d** verandah

**4** Adjectives: inky, inked; dissolved, soluble, solvable; defensive; casual
Nouns: ink; dissolution, solution, solvent ; defence, defensiveness; casualness

**5** stargazing / painstaking / headlong / dissolve / azaleas / verandah / constellations / defensively

NARRATIVE TEXT
## Vocabulary Work
page 117

**1** **a** True **b** False **c** False **d** True

**2** Possible answers:
**a** depths, hollows **b** careful, prudent
**c** irritated, frustrated **d** vista, location
**e** patio, porch **f** old, antique
**g** blackest, darkest **h** head-first
**i** imagine, envision **j** kindly, tenderly

**3** **a** painstaking **b** bump **c** visualise **d** open **e** engrossed **f** cold

**4** **a** painstaking **b** engrossed **c** dissolve **d** casually

Possible new synonyms:
**a** meticulous, rigorous **b** absorbed, engaged
**c** vanish, dissipate **d** mildly, lightly
**e** moodily, crossly

**5** **a** bide **b** uncontrollable **c** imminently

NARRATIVE TEXT
## Grammar Work
page 118

**1** toasty, autumn, afternoon, blue, bloody, final, front, ancient, tattered, combined, street, any

**2** **a** An eternity later, I re-checked my watch. It was six minutes past seven.
**b** I felt like crying; couldn't help it.
**c** I will test myself on some of my favourite constellations, and before long, my mind will wander …
**d** Dad will laugh again and put his hands on my shoulders. (Note: a second 'will' (before 'put') is optional.)

**3** yammering, DOOF, splats, hee hee hee, ugh, roars

NARRATIVE TEXT
## Punctuation Work
page 119

**1** **a** incomplete idea
**b** echoes natural thought patterns
**c** echoes natural thought patterns **d** tension

**2** Sample answers:
**a** Shows Simon's disdain for the swing seat (enhanced by the hyperbole used).
**b** Shows that Simon is trying to reassure himself. This line is repeated numerous times in the story.
**c** Uses understatement to suggest that Simon lost his temper badly.

**d** Stops the action abruptly and makes the reader wait along with the narrator.

3 Jordan and Jett, the evil twins next door, think it's so hilarious to call me names and use me for target practice every afternoon as I walk home from school. You could say that passing the Watsons' house isn't the best part of my day. It's really getting beyond a joke, but Dad always says, 'Just laugh right back at them.'

NARRATIVE TEXT

## Writing Work

page 120

1 Orientation: We meet the twins, Simon comes home from school, we learn about his family and house.
Resolution: Simon's dad arrives home and they go inside.
Twist: Simon's dad asks again, 'What project?'

2 Answers may include: begins *in medias res,* one main character and setting, less description, combined plot points (for example, climax and resolution). Students may give different and/or additional answers to these.

3 Discussion ideas may include: different attitude and tone of voice for narrator, greater danger/fear factor in this situation, different action. Students may give different and/or additional answers to thesec

4 The features should be in the following order: **d**, **e**, **f**, **a**, **h**, **g**, **b**, **c**.

5 There are many possible answers to this question. Students must describe an effect appropriate to the use of each example in the context of the short story 'I told you'.
Sample answers:
**a** 'Awesome!': Sounds like a teenager and conveys the narrator's optimism.
**b** 'would've': Like most contractions, this imitates natural speech.
**c** 'broken': Hints at the family's lack of money.
**d** 'toasty': Sounds safe and comforting; contrasts with the coming cold and darkness.
**e** 'carefully': Emphasises that Mum is safety-conscious; adds to the irony.
**f** 'headlong': Adds detail and a touch of comedy to the action.
**g** 'Why is it so cold?': Emphasises how cold and frightened Simon feels.
**h** 'What's all this mess?': Shows misunderstanding; acts as a trigger for Simon's outburst.

# SAMPLE TEST PAPER 1

SAMPLE TESTS

## Part A Reading and comprehension

page 128

1 its versatility
2 build a PC (personal computer)
3 MWave, Umart and JW Computers
4 haul; carry a heavy load
5 The capitals suggest that the narrator is starting to panic.
6 'Relief floods through me.'
7 a doorbell sound and laying the welcome mat
8 'trusted team'
9 contraction

SAMPLE TESTS

## Part B Language conventions

page 129

1 Suggested answer: We read that 'NUC is what your IT friend means by *bare bone kit*'. By giving this explanation, the writer is revealing that the target reader probably doesn't have this knowledge. We also read 'But don't get bored yet'. This suggests that the reader is unlikely to be thrilled by the idea of a 'semi-finished PC'. Both examples indicate that the target reader of this review has a basic to intermediate knowledge of computers.

2 '*Building*' is italicised for emphasis. The word is emphasised to show that it has a different meaning here from its meaning in Scene 001. The Scene 001 meaning is literal (about constructing a house), while the Scene 003 meaning is figurative (about realising a dream).

3 The first ellipsis suggests that many more things could be named in the list about Alyssa's desire to explore the world. The second ellipsis suggests that Alyssa has nothing useful with her (such as her phone or passport) to get her out of trouble.

SAMPLE TESTS

## Part C Comparing texts

page 129

Suggested answers:

1 Text 1 and Text 3 are both presenting a product. While Text 1 is an informative review, it is still

partly persuasive, as it promotes a product. The purpose of both texts is to present a product or company to a general audience. Text 3, however, is highly persuasive and aims to sell something, while Text 1 does not necessarily do this.

2 Text 2 and Text 3 both feature short, concise endings. The difference is that Text 2's ending gives a resolution to the story, while Text 3 ends persuasively with a slogan ('Be moved …') and the company's name ('Move Me Homes').

3 **a** Text 1: Short paragraphs each address a topic (introducing the product, detailing its features, information about the target market and a summary).
Text 2: The structure is based on the division of action and new lines are also started according to dialogue.
Text 3: Each voiceover (VO) line, which addresses one idea, is given its own row in the table.
**b** Answers will vary, but in your answer you must give a specific reason why you think the structure is effective based on its function in the text. Sample answer: The structure of Text 1 is the most effective because it is a series of information 'bites'. This structure is user-friendly for readers with a basic to intermediate computer knowledge who wish to learn about the NUC.

SAMPLE TESTS
### Part D Themes and meaning page 130

1 Sample answer: Text 2 suggests at least three messages. One message is that we should be careful when in a new or foreign place, especially when we are alone. We read about Alyssa's mistakes in this regard, such as not knowing any words in the local language, not being prepared for her walk by taking her phone and ID; also not taking in her surroundings and noticing landmarks so she could return safely. Another message the composer presents is that it's okay to have travel aspirations and a sense of adventure. A third message is that we should not leave loved ones on a bad note. In the story, we read that Alyssa regrets having an argument with her father before she left the country. We assume that her father felt bad about it too. Further, if things had ended badly for Alyssa, this would have placed a terrible emotional burden on her father.

## SAMPLE TEST PAPER 2

SAMPLE TESTS
### Part A Reading and comprehension page 134

1 abundance or massive amount of something

2 Like a wasp, it stings, but it lives in the sea.

3 It can be found in estuaries.

4 UR is the PM's personal assistant or aide and, as we read in the stage directions, a 'voice of reason'.

5 He makes a pun/joke using UR's name.

6 APEC and OPEC

7 because we are living in a throwaway culture

8 material that is likely to be popular on the internet and receive lots of attention and 'hits'

9 An answer is given. This prevents it from being a rhetorical question (one that doesn't require or have an answer).

SAMPLE TESTS
### Part B Language conventions page 135

1 **a** alliteration. Example of its use: 'Savage serpents'
**b** assonance. Example of its use: 'Suspect insects'

2 Suggested answer: Two ways in which rhythm and pace are created in the script are through punctuation, including the use of ellipses and semicolons to slow down the dialogue, and stage directions such as *'(Beat)'*, *'(Quickly)'* and *'(Trails off)'*, which create and control speed.

3 Answers will vary based on personal opinion but in your answer you must give a specific reason for signing or not signing the petition. For example: No, because the speaker did not give enough evidence to suggest that the legislation would solve the problems of animal cruelty and abandonment.

SAMPLE TESTS
### Part C Comparing texts page 135

Suggested answers:

1 Text 1: to warn people about certain dangerous creatures and help them to avoid being hurt
Text 2: to satirise (make fun of) politicians and politics

2 **a** One common purpose of Text 1 and Text 3 is to create awareness about animals.

b One purpose that applies only to Text 3 is to encourage listeners to sign a petition about domestic pet ownership.

3 a The type of person most likely to read Text 1 is someone interested in wildlife and/or the outdoors. The reader may also be new to Australia and interested in (perhaps also afraid of) the country's dangerous creatures.

b Suggested answer: Texts 2 and 3 are likely to attract people who are interested in society and its laws, concerned about important issues or causes and willing to do something about problems in their community or country. These people are educated and generally knowledgeable about the world around them.

## SAMPLE TESTS
## Part D Themes and meaning

page 136

1 Suggested answer: Two issues that are raised in Text 1 include the importance of being informed about dangerous wildlife for the sake of both interest and personal safety, and the fact that misconceptions and an unnecessary level of fear can be associated with certain creatures. The first issue underpins the entire report and is also specifically addressed in the final section, entitled 'Staying safe'. The second issue is raised in the section 'Suspect insects', where we read that honey bees 'have claimed more lives than any spider' and 'tales of [the Sydney funnel-web's] aggression are exaggerated.'

# NOTES